SECRET CONVERSIONS TO JUDAISM
IN EARLY MODERN EUROPE

BRILL'S STUDIES IN INTELLECTUAL HISTORY

SECRET CONVERSIONS TO JUDAISM IN EARLY MODERN EUROPE

EDITED BY

MARTIN MULSOW AND RICHARD H. POPKIN

TUTA SUB AEGIDE PALLAS
· 1 6 8 3 ·

BRILL
LEIDEN · BOSTON
2004

Illustration on the cover: Second title page for Seder Berachot, a collection of prayers and blessings of the Spanish Jews. Amsterdam, Holland, 1687. The illustrations include: blowing the Shofar, circumcision, take the meal, blessing of new moon, Havdalah and sowing.

This book is printed on acid-free paper.

Library of Congress Cataloging-in-Publication Data

Secret conversions to Judaism in early modern Europe / edited by Martin Mulsow and Richard H. Popkin.
    p. cm. — (Brill's studies in intellectual history ; v. 122)
    Includes bibliographical references and index.
    ISBN 90-04-12883-2
    1. Jewish converts from Christianity—Europe—History—17th century. 2. Jewish converts from Christianity—Europe—History—18th century. 3. Conversion—Judaism—History—17th century. 4. Conversion—Judaism—History—18th century. I. Mulsow, Martin. II. Popkin, Richard Henry, 1923- III. Series.

BM729.P7S43 2003
296.7'14'094—dc22

BM
729
.P7
S43
2004

2003061021

ISSN   0920-8607
ISBN   90 04 12883 2

PRINTED IN THE NETHERLANDS

CONTENTS

INTRODUCTION

Martin Mulsow and Richard H. Popkin

There are conversions throughout history that raise a lot of questions. This is especially the case where conversions to Judaism are concerned for they go against all historic probability: someone, who in medieval or early modern times lost his Christian faith and joined the often persecuted and ghettoized minority of Jews, gave up his career, position, his financial and social safeguard, as well as bonds to family and community. Before the Age of Enlightenment, a convert from Christianity to Judaism would have also run the risk of being arrested and severely punished, even possibly by death. Thus, secrecy was a crucial aspect of conversions from Christianity to Judaism.

It was not always certain whether a non-Jew, in our cases a Christian, could gain admission to the Jewish community. Two diverging opinions existed: according to one, Jewish origin was a mandatory precondition; the other, more liberal, interpretation considered conversions as legitimate.[1] But those communities that accepted converts were extremely rare and Christians who wanted to convert were often forced to engage in a prolonged search until they found a Jewish community willing to accept them.

Nevertheless, we know that these conversions did occur. For the most part, the motivations that led people to convert from Judaism to Christianity were of a different order from those that led people to convert from Christianity to Judaism. In the first case, Jews generally converted to Christianity for social, economic, or political reasons. In the case of conversions to Judaism, however, it was usually powerful intellectual and personal reasons that motivated the convert to leave the dominant Christian world for the insecurity of the

---

[1] See in general, David Max Eichhorn (ed.), *Conversion to Judaism. A History and Analysis* (New York, 1965); Joseph R. Rosenbloom, *Conversion to Judaism: From the Biblical Period to the Present* (Cincinatti, 1978); Walter Homolka, Walter Jacob and Esther Seidel (eds.), *Not by birth alone. Conversion to Judaism* (London – Washington, 1997). On the legal aspects of the issue, see Walter Jacob und Moshe Zemer, *Conversion to Judaism in Jewish Law: Essays and Responsa* (Tel Aviv – Pittsburgh, 1994).

Jewish community. There are, of course, exceptions to this due to personal idiosyncrasies or personal situations.

What kind of convictions could have had such a strong and personal effect as to make the decision to convert to Judaism possible? It is in asking such questions that the individual cases of conversions become crucial tests for the history of ideas. As these conversions do not follow the normal patterns of intellectual history, they provoke a non-linear and non-uniform reading of intellectual currents such as Cartesianism, Hermetism, or Millenarianism.

Never before has the phenomenon of early modern secret conversions to Judaism as a whole been made the subject for inquiry; there has never been an effort made to collect cases and documents, such as the ones presented here, in order to produce a typology or history of motives. We find some individual accounts of these converts in older literature. For example, the Hamburg Hebraist Johann Christoph Wolf mentioned a few cases in the second volume of his *Bibliotheca Hebraea* of 1721.[2] There were also occasional efforts to go beyond the single, exemplifying tale of the Christian who converted to Judaism, to surveying a number of cases. One such attempt was made by Christoph Helwig (Helvicus), who introduced an *Elenchus Judaeorum de adventu messiae* in two Giessen disputations (1609). Scattered references can also be found in the writings of authors such as Johann Jakob Schudt and others.[3]

Obviously, these cases are small in number. Because of their secret nature, the actual number of conversions was probably higher. If the concealment succeeded, no one came to know the fate of the convert. On the other hand, one should not overestimate the actual number of conversions either. Even the smallest bits of information— e.g. if a convert was sighted in Africa, as in the case of Father Clemens[4]—landed directly in the scholarly compendia of those who dealt with questions concerning Judaism.

---

[2] Johann Christoph Wolf, *Bibliotheca Hebraea*, vol. II (Hamburg, 1721), 1108–1110.
[3] Johann Jakob Schudt, *Jüdische Merkwürdigkeiten* (Frankfurt, 1714–1717), Tom. I, lib. 4, 272; Tom. II, lib. 6, cap. 19, 159f.; Tom. IV, Continuatio I, 201. See also Martin Difenbach, *Judaeus conversus [. . .] der am Hochgericht gestorben* (Frankfurt, 1709); Christoph Helwig, *Elenchus Judaeorum de adventu messiae*, (Giessen, 1609); Andreas Eisenmenger, *Entdecktes Judenthum* (Frankfurt, 1700), vol. 2, 997 and 1023; Thomas Crenius, *Animadversiones philologicae et historicae* (Rotterdam, 1695), Part VIII, cap. 3, § 7, 217.
[4] See Wolf (footnote 2), 1109: "P. Clemens, Panormitanus Siculus, & antea magni

In the following, we will outline most of the known cases of conversion from Christianity to Judaism from the sixteenth to the early eighteenth century. At the same time, and will try to place them—albeit tentatively—within a larger framework or context.

1. *Contexts of Anti-Trinitarianism and Protestantism*

In the late sixteenth and early seventeenth century, one finds a number of conversions to Judaism that are evidently linked to Eastern Europe and possibly to anti-Trinitarian Protestants living there in exile. Thus, Helwig tells us of a shoemaker from Friedberg who had gone to Poland as a Jew.[5] And around 1600, we find in Transylvania a certain Simon Pecs (Péchi) (ca. 1567–1639) and his group, who after having been anti-Trinitarian turned to Judaism.[6] Pecs was the successor of Andreas Eössi, the founder of the Sabbatarian sect.[7] This particular form of Sabbatarianism sprang out of Matthias Vehe-Glirius's anti-Trinitarianism. It favored the Old Testament to the New and denied the latter's divine inspiration. In the Ottoman Empire of Sultan Suleiman the Magnificent, Jews were often more respected than Christians. Thus in Transylvania, then under Ottoman control, conversion to Judaism was an attractive choice. That was exactly what Pecs did, and apparently about twenty thousand peasants with him. This changed with the accession of Count Racocki II to the throne, who demanded that his subjects revert to Christianity; if they did not do so within one year, they faced the death penalty.[8]

---

nominis Theologus inter suos, Nubiae in Africa ut Judaeus sub *Mualem Mosis* nomine conspectus est a P. Theod. Krump, ceu ipse refert in Palm-Baum p. 275 sqq. Conf. Schud. Continuat. I. Memorab. p. 203." Wolf refers to: Theodor Krump, *Hoher und fruchtbarer Palm-Baum des heiligen Evangelii* (Augsburg, 1710).

[5] See Ch. Helwig: *Elenchus* (footnote 3), IV, membrum XI of the Giessen disputations, 270. See also Wolf (footnote 2), 1109: "Anonymus, Sutor Fridbergensis, a Judaeis seductus, relicta familia in Poloniam abiit, & ibi se circumcidi curavit."

[6] See Esther Seidel, "Out of the Ghetto and into the Open Society: Conversion from the Renaissance to the Twentieth Century", in: *Not by birth alone* (footnote 1), 36–54, here 41f. Robert Dán, *Az erdélyi szombatosok és Péchi Simon* (Budapest, 1987).

[7] On the Sabbatarians, see S. Kohn, *Die Sabbatarier in Siebenbürgen. Ihre Geschichte, Literatur und Dogmatic* (Budapest, Leipzig, 1894); L.M. Pákozdy, *Der siebenbürgische Sabbatismus* (Stuttgart, Berlin, 1973); Daniel Liechty, *Sabbatarianism in the Sixteenth Century* (Berrien Springs, Michigan, 1993).

[8] Many people from Transsylvania, however, remained crypto-judaic. This became

Anti-Trinitarians were occasionally reproached for being "Judaizers," because they, like the Jews, rejected the Christian doctrine of the Trinity.[9] There was also a connection between anti-Trinitarians and Islam—one need only think of the well-known case of the Heidelberg anti-Trinitarian Adam Neuser, who after being exiled in Hungary finally ended up in Islamic Constantinople.[10]

The Marburg schoolmaster Conrad Viëtor, who in 1614 became the Jew Moses Pardo, withdrew from Christian Europe like Neuser, and lived in the tolerant environment of the Padishah in Saloniki. Viëtor, too, had anti-Trinitarian motives: he could not come to terms with, as he puts it, "the monstrous and fraudulent [. . .] mystery of Trinity."[11] Equally complex is the case of Nicolas Antoine.[12] Antoine was born a Catholic in Lorraine in 1602. He became a Calvinist in 1623 and began studying theology in Sedan. In the course of his studies, which also led him to criticize the doctrine of Trinity, he developed contacts with the Jewish community of Metz, and eventually moved spiritually closer to Judaism. Initially, he tried to convert in Venice. A similar pattern existed already in 1575, when a nobleman from Lyon, convinced of the priority of Judaism, took his sons to Venice to convert.[13] But the Jewish community of Venice rejected Antoine's request. They proposed that he live his life as a

---

clear in 1868, when Transsylvania became part of Hungary and was allowed liberty of religion. Then thousands of crypto-Jews confessed their Judaism.

[9] See Robert Dán, "'Judaizare': a Career of a Term", in: idem and A. Pirnát (eds.), *Antitrinitarianism in the Second Half of the 16th Century* (Budapest, 1982), 25–34.

[10] For literature on Neuser, see Christopher J. Burchill, "Adam Neuser", in: idem (ed.), *The Heidelberg Antitrinitarians*, Bibliotheca Dissidentium 11 (Baden-Baden – Bouxwiller, 1989), 107–159.

[11] Johann Jakob Schudt, *Compendium historiae Judaicae* (Frankfurt, 1700), 494ff.; Wolf (footnote 2) vol. I, p. 886; Wolfgang Philipp, "Spätbarock und frühe Aufklärung. Das Zeitalter des Philosemitismus", in: Karl Heinrich Rengstorf and Siegfried von Kortzfleisch (eds.), *Kirche und Synagoge* (München 1988), Vol. 2, 71–73.

[12] See Bernard Lescaze, "La confession de foi de Nicolas Antoine (1632)", in: *Bulletin de la Société d'Histoire et d'Archéologie de Genève*, 14 (1970), 277–323; Elisabeth Labrousse, "Vie et mort de Nicolas Antoine", in: *Etudes théologiques et religieuses*, 52 (1977), 421–433. Labrousse says (p. 426): "Enfin, une sensibilité réformée diffuse, particulièrement accentuée dans la controverse anti-romaine dont un converti du catholicisme, comme Antoine, dut être particulièrement abreuvé, comporte un théocentrisme insistant et formente une horreur vigilante pour l'"idolatrie" et la "superstition". En un sens, les motifs memes qui ont éloigné Antoine du catholicisme ont pu assez aisément finir par l'écarter du Christianisme lui-meme."

[13] Rosenbloom (footnote 1), 82; Cecil Roth, "Immanuel Abobab's Proselytization of the Marranos", in: *Jewish Quarterly Review*, 23 (1932–33), 137.

crypto-Jew, a marrano. That is what he did, and in 1630 he formally took a post as a Calvinist minister in the vicinity of Geneva. But, by 1632, Antoine was no longer capable of maintaining his dissimulation and confessed his Jewish beliefs openly. This led to his execution in Geneva in April 1632.

This case—along with that of Servetus—was made famous by Bayle and La Roche as an example of Calvinist intolerance.[14] It is probably for this reason that it is one of the few more thoroughly researched examples of conversion to Judaism.

Another case is that of the widow Catharina Weigel (Zaluszowska) from Krakow. In 1539, she declared: "God has neither wife nor son, nor does He need them. For sons are needed by those who die, but God is eternal, and since He was not born, it is impossible that He should die. It is we whom He considers His sons, and His sons are all who walk in His paths."[15] She was burned at the stake at the market place of Krakow. In this case, it is the role of Islamic Ottoman territories as potential places of exile that has been stressed rather than anti-Trinitarianism: "At any rate," one reads, "this sad incident provoked speculation that all over Poland there were Christians who were intending to convert to Judaism. It was rumoured that these converts were being taken to Lithuania after being circumcised, in order to escape from there to Turkey. Detailed investigations into the alleged conversion activity amongst Jews produced no proof, and in 1540 King Sigismund gave a guarantee to the Lithuanian Jews that he would not give credence to any such accusations in the future, unless they were founded on substantial evidence."[16] The history of conversions to Judaism is full of rumors and reports of collective fears—fears of conspiracy and of secession of larger groups from Christianity.

---

[14] Pierre Bayle: *Dictionnaire historique et critique*, 2. (Ed. Rotterdam 1702), Art. 'Antoine'; Michel de la Roche: "Historical account of the life and trial of Nicolas Anthoine", in: *Memoires of Literature* III,3 (1713), 17–28, and idem in Bibliothèque anglaise, tome II (Amsterdam 1717), 237–270. See Margaret D. Thomas, "Michel de la Roche: a Huguenot critic of Calvin", in: *Studies on Voltaire and the Eighteenth Century*, 238 (1985), 97–195, esp. 160–163.

[15] See Seidel (footnote 6), 40.

[16] Seidel (footnote 6), 41. On inclinations to Judaism in Poland, see Zdzislaw Pietrzyk: "Judaizers in Poland in the Second Half of the Sixteenth Century", in: *The Jews in Old Poland 1000–1795*, ed. Antony Polonsky, Jakub Basista and Andrzej Link-Lenczowski (London – New York, 1993), 23–35.

2. *Reversions and Conversions in Spain*

Another context is offered by the special situation found in Spain. Since 1391, when many Jews were forcibly converted, and from 1492 when the remaining Jews were either banished or converted, there existed a culture of marranos in Spain.[17] These marranos often tried to revert to their original religion, Judaism. The Inquisition was given the charge of finding out who was actually a genuine Christian and who was a secret Jew. Many of these marranos, in order to escape the Inquisition, fled from Spain and settled, as Jews, in Jewish communities in cities such as Amsterdam.[18] One example is Diego Pires, who came from a Portuguese marrano family. He converted to Judaism during the 1520s and changed his name to Salomon Molcho (Molkho, Molco).[19] He joined the kabbalists of Saloniki and was so successful making prophecies that he gained the protection of Pope Clemens II, who then sent him to the Regensburg Imperial Diet in 1532. Molcho joined with David Reubini who claimed to be from a large Jewish African tribe that would protect Europe. They both lived in the Vatican for a while and were later executed by Charles V. Another example is Diego da Assumpcao, a Franciscan monk, who intended to flee Portugal in order to live freely as a Jew.[20] Finally, there was Francisco Maldonado da Silva, a surgeon of Portuguese marrano origin from Peru, who called himself Elias Nazarenus. Nazarenus, with six other marranos, was executed for his Jewish convictions in 1639.[21] Allegedly, there was even a crypto-Judaic conspiracy in Lima in 1634. In Mexico, from 1642 on, numerous autos-da-fés occurred. The biggest of them took place in April

---

[17] See Cecil Roth, *A History of the Marranos* (New York, 1974).
[18] See for cases like this Yosef Kaplan, *From Christianirty to Judaism. The Story of Isaac Orobio de Castro* (Oxford, 1989).
[19] See Wolf, *Bibliotheca Hebraea*, vol. I (Hamburg, 1715), 1076. See the collection of sources by Aaron Z. Aescoly-Weintraub, *hat- Tenû'ôt ham-mesî.hiyyôt be-Yi'srâ'êl* (Jerusalem, 1956); the classical account is: Heinrich Graetz, *Geschichte der Juden von der Verbannung der Juden aus Spanien und Portugal (1494) bis zur dauernden Ansiedelung der Marranen in Holland (1618)*, Reprint der Ausg. letzter Hand, 4., durchges. Aufl., Leipzig 1907 (Berlin: Arani-Verl., 1998).
[20] See David Max Eichhorn, "From Expulsion to Liberation (1492–1789)", in idem (ed.), *Conversion to Judaism* (footnote 1), 96–135, here 112f.; Esther Seidel (footnote 6), 38.
[21] Eichhorn (footnote 20), 113f.

1649, when 109 "Judaizers" were executed.[22] This indicates that fears of conspiracy and secession prevailed here, too.

One must examine the accounts of Spanish converts to Judaism both in light of their marrano context and also independently from it: For example, in the case of Tomas Treminnode Sobrimente[23] or that of Lope de Vera y Alacrón, originally from a Christian family.[24] Lope de Vera was thrown into jail in 1639, called himself Judah, and was burnt at the stake in 1644. Another interesting case was Lorenzo Escudero's, who around 1650 became the Jew Abraham Israel.[25] Somewhat mysterious was also the fate of Father Mena. Mena was a Jesuit theologian in Salamanca, who had persuaded a woman, whose confession he was hearing, into marrying him by alleging a revelation of God's will for this marriage. The Inquisition imprisoned him, but he was later freed by Jesuits who claimed he had died; Mena escaped to Genoa on a mule and there he became a Jew.[26] The possibility for Iberian refugees to practice their faith existed not only in Genoa, but also in other Italian-Jewish communities.[27]

[22] Seidel (footnote 6), 39.
[23] See Miguel de Barrios, *Triumpho del Govierno popular* (Amsterdam 1683), 42.
[24] See Kaplan, *From Christianity to Judaism. The Story of Isaac Orobio de Castro* (footnote 18), 336f. Eichhorn (footnote 20), 114f.
[25] See Miguel de Barrios, *Relacion de los Poetas*, 59; I.S. Révah, *Spinoza et Juan de Prado* (Den Haag, 1959), p. 31.
[26] Wolf (footnote 2), 1109: "P. Mena, Jesuita Salamantiansis, celebris inter suos concionator, ob concubinatum Inquisitioni subiectus, dolo autem suorum liberatus & profugus, tandemque ad Judaeos dilapsus inter eos legis Doctorem egit. Vide Ernstii Confect-Tafel Part. III. c. 23. p. 403sq. ex libro Christenthum der Jesuiten." Wolf refers to: Jacob Daniel Ernst, *Der Neu-zugerichteten Historischen Confect-Tafel Zweyter und Dritter Auffsatz*, s. l. ["bei Johann Ludwig Richter"] 1698, pp. 406–412: "Der Jesuitische Grund-Heuchler". In Genoa, "woselbst er den Orden fahren ließ, nahm ein ander Weib und zugete Kinder/endlich warff er die Christliche Religion gar von sich hinweg/ward ein Rabbi/und erkläreten den Jüden öffentlich das Gesetzt Mosis/die Kinder/so er in Hispanien gezeuget/wurden zu Salamanca in das Jesuiter-Collegium genommen." The Mena that is mentioned may be a certain Gasparo Mena, of whom De Backer/Sommervolgel, *Bibliographie de la Compagnie de Jesus*, Vol. 5 (Brüssel – Paris 1894), 881, list a handwritten commentary on the Psalms which exists in the library of Salamanca.
[27] See the volume *L'identità dissimulata: Guidaizzanti Iberici nell' Europa Cristiana dell' Età Moderna*, ed. Pier Cesare Ioly Zorattini (Firenze 2000), especially the contributions by Benjamin Ravid: "Venice, Rome, and the Reversion of New Christians to Judaism: A Study in Ragione di Stato", 151–194, and by Pier Cesare Ioly Zorattini, "Derekh Teshuvah: la Via del Ritorno", 195–248.

The case of the Sicilian theologian Clemens, who—under the Spanish crown—retreated to Africa to become a Jew, still remains be examined.[28]

In the category of Iberian Judaism also fits the case presented by Arthur Williamson in this volume. George Buchanan, a Scottish humanist who lived in exile, worked at the Collège de Guyenne in the 1540s, where many Portuguese conversos (and presumably also marranos) lived. The charge of crypto-Judaism, which Buchanan faced in 1550, may, as Williamson speculates, be a result of his supposed participation in a Seder meal in the company of marranos.

There also seems to have been conversions that were not particularly traumatic or dramatic but which involved business convenience. One striking example is that of Antonio Lopes Suasso, the son of New Christian parents who had fled from Spain to Belgium via France to avoid persecution. His parents arranged for the various male children to take up occupations such as doctor, lawyer, Catholic theologian, businessman and so on. Antonio became a very successful merchant in Antwerp in the early seventeenth century. He decided to move his business to the Dutch Republic because of problems in the shipping channels in Belgium. He visited Amsterdam to see what opportunities were there and met one of the richest Jews there, Abraham de Pinto. This led to his arranging to marry de Pinto's daughter and to his joining the Amsterdam synagogue. There is no evidence that there was any theological or religious issue involved, only new commercial opportunities. He quickly became the Secretary Treasurer of the Amsterdam synagogue and was the one who wrote up Spinoza's excommunication in 1656. A few years later, when the Jewish congregation began fundraising to build a new synagogue, he quickly dropped out rather than pay any funds to them. Apparently, he did not join any other group and after his death his son, Baron Francisco Lopes Suasso, had him buried in the Jewish cemetery at Ouderkerk. There may be quite a few other cases like this regarding people who moved to Amsterdam, London, or Hamburg for commercial reasons.[29]

---

[28] See footnote 4.
[29] See Daniel Swetschinski, *Reluctant Cosmopolitans: The Portuguese Jews of Seventeenth-Century Amsterdam* (London: Littman Library, 2000).

3. *Failed Christianization: Reversions of German Jews*

In her contribution, Elisheva Carlebach focuses on the reversions of Jews from the German territories who had previously converted to Christianity.[30] These reversions are particularly interesting for their migrations: many went to Amsterdam. Amsterdam was not only a center for reversions of Iberian Sephardic marranos, but also for Ashkenazim, namely the Jews of Germany and Poland. According to Carlebach, the "Sephardic model" proves insufficient to explain the apparently similar phenomenon of reversions among German Jews. Upon their arrival, ex-Jews coming from Protestant Germany did not have to be newly introduced into Jewish communal life. They faced mainly psychological struggles and a form of repentance for having converted in the first place. But there were also motivations. "Rather than the experience of the Sephardic community, the call of the open society sounded in Amsterdam must have served as the primary attraction for the German Jewish returnees."

Amsterdam was, no doubt, a special place for converts to Judaism. It was already well known that the Jews of Holland accepted and even circumcised converts from Christianity. In 1686, a man from Nikolsberg in Moravia arrived in Amsterdam, converted, and changed his name to Moses ben Abraham Avinu Haas.[31] He married a daughter of a rabbi, learned Hebrew and Yiddish, and started printing books in these two languages. From 1692 on, he traveled through Europe and opened print shops, not only in Halle, but also in Berlin, Dessau, and Frankfurt/Oder. Another person, a Catholic monk, changed his name to Israel ben Abraham Avinu, or Yisrael Ger— also in Amsterdam.[32] Like Abraham ben Jacob, a German who in 1695 made the illustrations for the Haggadah of Amsterdam,[33] he also became active in the printing business.

---

[30] For the conversions of Jews to Christianity, see Elisheva Carlebach, *Divided Souls. Converts from Judaism in Germany, 1500–1750* (New Haven – London, 2001).

[31] Wolf (footnote 2), 1109: "Moses ben Abraham, ex Christiano Judaeus factus Amstelodami, hinc autem Halam delatus officinam typographicum instruxit, eam vero mandato Regio an. 1714. amisit, postquam varios libros a se editos calumniis in Christianorum sacra conspurcasset, id quod imprimis factum est in libro precum Judaicarum, quam sub tit. [. . .] recudi curavit. Postea fuga se proripuit."

[32] See Seidel (footnote 6), 43; Eichhorn (footnote 20), 121f.

[33] See Rosenbloom (footnote 1), 82; Cecil Roth, "New Notes on Pre-Emancipation Jewish Artists", in: *Hebrew Union College Annual*, 17 (1942–43), 501.

Carlebach emphazises how reversions could turn into openly anti-Christian polemics.[34] This was peculiar to Amsterdam. At the same time, Amsterdam became a sort of a religious testing ground, since numerous sects and religious confessions coexisted. Carlebach quotes from a poem by Andrew Marvell, which says:

> Hence Amsterdam—Turk, Christian, Pagan, Jew
> Staple of sects and mint of schism grew:
> That bank of conscience where not one so strange
> Opinion but finds credit and exchange.

This poem about the pluralism of sects can be complemented by the following verses, which appear on a handwritten copy of a pamphlet that promotes an eclectic and indifferent view of religion.

> Born was I in Rome,
> Awakened then in Basle,
> Wedded in Wittenberg.
> In the first they venerated the Pope,
> In the second Calvin,
> In the third Luther.
> I died in Amsterdam.
> Where many faiths prevail,
> Which let me loose then myne.[35]

This poem illustrates that the "Amsterdam experience" could go beyond mere conversion to Judaism and lead to indifference, deism, or even atheism.

---

[34] On the anti-Christian polemics among the Jews of Amsterdam, see Richard H. Popkin, "Jewish Anti-Christian Arguments as a Source of Irreligion from the Seventeenth to the Early Nineteenth Century", in: Michael Hunter und David Wootton (eds.), *Atheism from the Reformation to the Enlightenment* (Oxford, 1992), 159–181; David Kaplan, *From Christianity to Judaism. The Story of Isaac Orobio de Castro* (footnote 18); Martin Mulsow, *Moderne aus dem Untergrund. Radikale Frühaufklärung in Deutschland 1680–1720* (Hamburg, 2002), 41–84.

[35] These are handwritten verses on the last sheet of the copy of the ‚Ineptus religiosus‘, Ms. fö II 43, Helsingin Yliopisto Kirjasto: "Zu Rom bin ich geboren,/ Zu Basel jung erwecket,/ Zu Wittenberg getrauet,/ Dort ward der Pabst verehrt,/ Hier Luther, Dort Calvin./ Ich starb in Amsterdam./ Wo so viel Glauben sein,/ Daß ich vom Glauben kam." On the Ineptus religiosus, see Mulsow (footnote 33), 355–408.

4. *Polish, Lithuanian and Russian Contexts*

From the early eighteenth century we know about a certain Estko, who came to Amsterdam from Minsk.[36] His wife had developed an inclination towards Judaism through her private reading of the Bible. She celebrated the Sabbath with her Jewish moneylender and eventually both left for Amsterdam. Estko followed them and converted to Judaism as well. A Jewish tax collector, Baruch Leibov, together with other Jews, was expelled from Russia to Poland in 1727. He continued to visit Russia for business purposes. At one point, he met the retired Russian Naval officer Alexander Voznitzin in Moscow. Voznitzin had immersed himself in the study of the Bible. Leibov taught him Hebrew and travelled with him to the Polish border, where Voznitzin was circumcised and converted to Judaism. Upon his own wife's denunciations, Voznitzin was arrested in 1738 and burned at the stake.[37] Similar to the case of Catharina Weigel from Krakow and Nicolas Antoine, here, too, biblical studies preceded contact with Judaism. The circumstances are slightly different in the case of the Lithuanian Count Valentin Potocki, who, on his peregrinatio academica, befriended the Polish student Zaremba. Both men made the acquaintance of a Jew in a tavern, who then taught them Hebrew. Later, they converted to Judaism; Potocki became Abraham ben Abraham in Amsterdam, and Zaremba, who hesitated for a long time, arrived in Amsterdam much later with his wife and his son and converted as well. Homesickness drove Potocki back to Lithuania, where he managed to live under his Jewish identity in the vicinity of Vilna, until he was denounced and burned at the stake in 1749.[38]

---

[36] Marcin Matuszewicz, *Diarius zycia mego*, vol. 1:1714–1757, ed. Bohdan Królikowski und Zofia Zielinska (Warzawa, 1986), 385f. This source is cited by Waldemar Kowalski, "From the 'Land of Diverse Sects' to National Religion: Converts to Catholicism and Reformed Franciscans in Early Modern Poland", in: *Church History*, 70 (2001), 482–526.

[37] See Eichhorn (footnote 20), 126–128.

[38] See Eichhorn (footnote 20), 128–131; Valentin Karpinowitz, *The story of the Vilnian righteous proselyte count Valentin Potocki* (Tel Aviv, 1990) (Jiddisch); AVRAHAM BEN AVRAHAM, by Rabbi Selig Schachnowitz. Adapted by Yehoshua Leiman, and Illustrated by Bat-Sheva Frankel (New York, 1977).

5. *Philosemitic Hebraists*

The notorious case of the Hebraist Johann Stephan Rittangel (1606–1652), which invoked keen interest and discussion around 1700, indicates how philosemitism played a role with some Hebraists. It never became clear whether Rittangel was originally a Jew before making his appearance as a Christian scholar, or if he indeed had lived a decade with Caraite Jews in Constantinople without accepting their faith.[39] Rittangel personifies the attempt to bridge the gap between Judaism and Christianity through a Trinitarian interpretation of the Kabbalah. Similar are the rapprochements to Judaism by millenarians such as Petrus Serrarius or Oliger Paulli.[40] John Dury's reflections, discussed by Richard H. Popkin in this volume, whether it is possible to be a true Christian and a faithful follower of the Law of Moses at the same time, belong in this context. Dury, however, did not push it to the extremes as several Quakers did, about which Popkin tells us. One of them, Samuel Fisher, participated in the Jewish ritual in synagogues and lived inside Jewish communities.

Whether the conversions of the brothers Charles Marie and Louis Conpiagne de Veil must also be seen in the same context, needs yet to be investigated. The brothers acted around 1680 as Hebraists in England, publishing commentaries of the Psalms and the Song of Solomon before converting to Judaism.[41] Already during the Cromwell era there existed pro-Jewish tendencies, and some English Protestants are likewise known to have converted to Judaism.[42]

---

[39] See Pierre Bayle: *Dictionnaire historique et critique* (Rotterdam, 1697), Art. 'Rittangel'; P.T. van Rooden and J.W. Wesselius, "J.S. Rittangel in Amsterdam", in: *Nederlandisg Archief voor Kerkgeschiedenis*, 65 (1985), 131–152; E.G.E. van der Wall, "Johann Stephan Rittangel's Stay in the Dutch Republic (1641–1642)", in: J. van den Berg and E.G.E. van der Wall (eds.), *Jewish-Christian Relations in the Seventeenth Century. Studies and Documents* (Dordrecht, 1988), 119–134. See also the contribution of Elisheva Carlebach in this volume.

[40] On Paulli, see Julius Schoeps, *Philosemitismus im Barock* (Tübingen, 1952); on Serrarius, see Ernestine Van der Wall, *De mystieke chiliast Petrus Serrarius (1600–1669) en zijn wereld* (Leiden, 1987).

[41] For the situation in England see e.g. Matt Goldish, "Jews, Christians and Conversos: Rabbi Solomon Aialon's Struggles in the Portuguese Community in London", in: *Journal of Jewish Studies*, 45 (1994), 227–257.

[42] See David Katz, *Sabbath and Sectarianism in Seventeenth Century England* (Leiden, 1987).

6. *Contexts of Millenarianism and the Kabbalah*

There are other cases where the complex world of messianism, millenarianism and the Kabbalah prompted conversions to Judaism in
the late seventeenth century, which are difficult to separate from the
cases of scholarly philosemites.[43] The difference is that the former
had a greater influence even on ordinary people. We find the somewhat bizarre mixtures of Jewish and Christian imagery that crop up
in the very private forms of adopting these ideas. Already the above-
mentioned convert Salomon Molcho at the beginning of the sixteenth century was a messianist. During the late seventeenth century
we know about the case of Benedictus Sperling in Altona, who in
1680 turned Jewish and became Israel Benedeti.[44] In letters he wrote
to his mother, we find the Apocalypse as well as the Prophecy of
Daniel, and Luther appearing as an angel (a motif of the Reformer
Johannes Bugenhagen),[45] and then the same motif being used further on Calvin, so that the two Protestant confessions appear as
wings of one great eagle marking Judaism; kabbalistically Sperling
calls up the *Chokma*.

The case of the Augsburgian Johann Peter Späth has become well
known. He turned to Judaism under the name of Moses Germanus
in Amsterdam in 1696, after many conversions and reversions.[46]
Allison Coudert's contribution takes a look at Späth's decision to
become Jewish. Späth's unpublished letters to Franciscus Mercurius
van Helmont reveal how Späth, in his search for religious truth, was
inspired by Helmont's and Knorr von Rosenroth's revival of Lurianic
Kabbalah.[47] He eventually turned his back on this kabbalistic millenarianism and, by digesting biblical criticism and anti-platonic arguments, he converted to Judaism. A certain Polish Johannes de Clerc,
who likewise became a Jew under the name of Daniel Abraham, is

---

[43] See in general H.J. Schoeps (footnote 40).

[44] Staatsarchiv Hamburg, *Akten des Geistlichen Ministeriums*, Tom. VII. CCXLIV.
1529 und CCXLVIII. 1567, of the year 1682. See Gerald Strauss, "A Seventeenth
Century Conversion to Judaism: Two letters from Benedictus Sperling to his Mother",
in: *Jewish Social Studies*, 36 (1974), esp. 170.

[45] See Johannes Bugenhagen's exegetical commentaries.

[46] See the account in Schoeps (footnote 40), *Kirche und Synagoge* (footnote 11), Vol.
2, 70f.

[47] On this milieu see Allison Coudert, *The Impact of the Kabbalah in the Seventeenth
Century. The Life and Thought of Francis Mercury van Helmont (1614–1698)* (Leiden, 1999).

also known to have lived in Späth's Amsterdam.[48] The fact that even more Christians were coming to Amsterdam because of their fascination with Judaism, is made clear by an account of Uriel da Costa.[49] One assumes that some of them were driven to Amsterdam by their dissatisfaction with confessional disputes among Christians, as well as a repugnance to idolatrous practices in Christian ritual. The biblical scholar Hermann von der Hardt of Helmstedt reports in 1703, that "recently" three Calvinists converted to Judaism: "The break with Christianity and the adoption of Judaism obviously is not as rare as it seems, since he [von der Hardt] himself knows that only recently three Reformed theologians were circumcised—one of them, however, died soon afterwards as a consequence of the pain inflicted by circumcision."[50]

Kabbalistic Judaism plays a major role in the conversion of Lord George Gordon, the Scottish politician, whom Martha Keith Schuchard examines in this volume. Apparently, Gordon converted under the influence of the Sabbatian kabbalist and freemason Samuel Jacob Falk. But Schuchard also shows that Gordon continues an ancient philosemitic Scottish tradition, in which radical patriots identified themselves with Jews. Gordon died in 1793 in prison in London.

7. Contexts of Skepticism and Deism

It is so far uncertain whether skepticism and deism around 1700 also form part of the context of conversions to Judaism. The use of

---

[48] Wolf (footnote 2), 1109: "De Clerc, (Joh.) Borussus, Sacrificulus quondam prope Vilnam a Judaeis Danielis Abrahamidae nomine vocatus. Vid. idem Schudtius l. c. pag. 204."

[49] Uriel da Costa, "Exemplar Humanae Vitae", in: Carl Gebhardt (ed.), *Die Schriften des Uriel da Costa* (Amsterdam – Heidelberg – London, 1922), 111: "Inter haec accidit adhuc aliud novum: Nam forte fortuna sermonem habui cum duobus hominibus, qui ex Londino in hanc civitatem venerant, Italo uno, altero vero Hispano, qui Christiani cum essent, nec ex Judaeis originem ducerent, inopiam indicantes, consilium a me postularunt super ineunda eum Judaeis societate, & transeundo in religionem illorum."

[50] This is reported by Gottlieb Stolle in the journal of his journey through Northern Germany and the Netherlands. Extracts are given by Günter E. Guhrauer, "Beiträge zur Kenntnis des 17. und 18. Jahrhunderts aus den handschriftlichen Aufzeichnungen Gottlieb Stolles", in: *Allgemeine Zeitschrift für Geschichte*, 7 (1847), 385–436 and 481–531; here 403: "Der Abfall vom Christen- zum Judenthume [. . .] sei so gar seltsam nicht, denn er [von der Hardt] wisse selbst, daß vor wenig Jahren

"Judeo-Christian" and Islamic traditions were part of the eighteenth-century discussions of religion (see the very popular *Memoirs of the Turkish Spy* by **. This book came out in many languages and editions.)[51] On the other hand, anti-Jewish tendencies were prevalent among many of the deists and freethinkers, since the intellectual reevaluation of religion posited the "moral" New Testament against the Old Testament.

Already the earliest deist case shows a connection with Judaism. Martin Seidel, in his work "Origo et fundamenta religionis Christianae," which appeared around 1680 and circulated among the above mentioned judaizing anti-Trinitarians and Sabbatarians, developed his Natural Theology without recourse to any revelation, in the wider context of the discussions of the Heidelberg anti-Trinitarianism.[52] In the course of the seventeenth century, the situation became more explosive as a result of Cartesianism and skepticism.

Skeptical tendencies also affected conversions. The case of d'Antan, which Martin Mulsow discusses in this volume, proves this connection. D'Antan was a young Frenchman, who, at the beginning of the eighteenth century, experienced a skeptical crisis, which led him to embrace Judaism in Amsterdam. Here, the kabbalist-hermeticist context is present but not dominant. Instead, a possible link to clandestine skepticism—as manifested in such handwritten treatises of the time as the "Ars nihil credendi"[53]—cannot be ruled out. According to d'Antan, God is, in a very abstract sense, the infinite sphere of which no concrete knowledge, in the sense of Christian revelation, is possible to us. The non-Trinitarian God of the Judaic religion

---

auch drei Theologi reformati sich beschneiden lassen, davon aber der eine, weil er den Schmerz der Beschneidung nicht verwinden können, bald gestorben." I am currently preparing an edition of the whole of Stolle's journal.

[51] [Giovanni Paolo Marana,] *L'Espion dans les cours des princes chrétiens, ou lettres et mémoires d'un envoyé secret de la porte dans les cours de l'Europe: avec une dissertation curieuse de leur Forces Politique et Religion*. The book had many sequels. On the discussions of "monotheistic" traditions of Judaism and Islam, see Justin Champion, *The Pillars of Priestcraft Shaken. The Church of England and its Enemies 1660–1730* (Cambridge, 1992).

[52] See Robert Dán, "Martin Seidel's 'Origo et fundamenta religionis christianae' and Simon Péchi", in: Lech Szczucki (ed.), *Socinianism and its Role in the Culture of the XVIth to XVIIIs Centuries* (Warzawa – Lodz, 1983), 53–57; Winfried Schröder, "Martin Seidels 'Origo et fundamenta religionis christianae'", in: Martin Mulsow (ed.), *Spätrenaissance in Deutschland 1570–1650* (forthcoming).

[53] See Alain Mothu, "La beatitude des Chrétiens et son double clandestin", in: Anthony McKenna and idem (eds.), *La Philosophie clandestine à l'Age classique* (Oxford, 1997), 79–117.

resembles that of a natural religion. To d'Antan seems to apply what Hermann von der Hardt told us about Späth's conversion: "Since he could not find any agreement among those he had talked to, and since everybody believed in something, which contradicted the belief of the other, he came to the following conclusion: omnia esse incerta, nisi hoc: unum scilicet esse Deum; to satisfy his conscience, he converted to Judaism, which promoted this very idea from the beginning and has preserved it ever since."[54] The desire to find a last grounding in the oldest monotheistic religion, Judaism, springs out of a fundamental doubt concerning revealed religion.

*   *   *

The historical "improbability" of conversions to Judaism makes them historiographically interesting. Since they form an exception to the rule, both the rule they break and the reason why becomes apparent. It is therefore useful to examine the exemplary cases—reconstructed from sources and typified—in their own historical contexts as far as this is possible. Conversions from Christianity to Judaism highlight the issues of intellectual conviction and personal identity that were the usual motivations for the converts. Similarly, individual examples of these cases disclose a dense net of intellectual and social correlations. As the collection of pardon tales, for instance, allows us to gain deep insight into the fantasy and needs of ordinary people,[55] one should, as far as sources admit, write a microhistory of the circulation of documents related to conversion, of the transmittal of convictions, and of the results of the decisions taken. It does not seem a coincidence to me that Carlo Ginzburg's studies concerning popular mentality should arise from Italian research on sixteenth-century radical Protestantism. There, too, one would find strong convictions and personal adoptions of intellectual cur-

---

[54] Again quoted from Stolle: Reisejournal (footnote 50): "Weil er nun unter diesen und andern, so er gesprochen, keine Einigkeit in Meinungen angetroffen, sondern ein Jeder immer etwas gehabt, das des Andern Meinung contrair gewest, habe er endlich geschlossen: omnia esse incerta, nisi hoc: unum scilicet esse Deum, und sei zu Befriedigung seines Gewissens zu den Juden übergegangen, als welche diese Wahrheit vom Anfange gehabt, und bisher erhalten."

[55] See Natalie Zemon Davis, *Fiction in the Archives. Pardon Tales and their Tellers in Sixteenth-Century France* (Stanford, 1987).

rents that would provoke a miller like Menocchio to stand up for his ideas, even when faced with the Inquisition. Much the same can be said of conversions to Judaism.

How do such "hard" conversions, that went against all convenience, then differ from "light" conversions of conformity? "Light" conversions here mean not only those which gave way to social pressure but also those that took place in a political milieu, such as the conversion to Christianity of Jewish high officials of early modern courts. Theological polemics of the time blamed them for politicizing religion, or for "religio prudentum," and thus leading to religious indifference and a political orientation of religion.[56]

In contrast to that, conversions to Judaism, in most cases, seem to indicate notably steadfast convictions and by no means indifference. Yet might not both forms of conversion lead to the same outcome? Namely, at that moment when Judaism was chosen on grounds of religious authenticity and simplicity (against Trinitarianism)? At the moment when religious minimalism, concerns about irenic matters, fundamental articles of the doctrine, and deism ended up in a similar habitude as did the indifferentism of opportunistic "politicians" and their private religion? Such a moment was reached in 1700, and it remains to be examined whether cases the likes of d'Antan or Späth offer evidence that would point out in this direction.

---

[56] See e.g. Johannes Müller, *Atheismus devictus* (Hamburg, 1672), 459; for the 'politician' as an indifferentist see e.g. Christoph Peller, *Politicus sceleratus, impugnatus: Id est Compendium politices novum* (Nürnberg, 1665); see in general Wilhelm Kühlmann, *Gelehrtenrepublik und Fürstenstaat. Entwicklung und Kritik des deutschen Späthumanismus in der Literatur des Barockzeitalters* (Tübingen, 1982); Wolfgang Weber, *Prudentia gubernatoria* (Tübingen, 1992); Mulsow, *Moderne aus dem Untergrund* (footnote 34), chapter VIII.

GEORGE BUCHANAN, CRYPTO-JUDAISM, AND THE CRITIQUE OF EUROPEAN EMPIRE

Arthur Williamson

Few students can ever have broken with their professor more completely than did George Buchanan (1506–1582) with John Mair, (1467?–1550). Mair, often Latinized as Major, was one of the most eminent late medieval scholastics. Buchanan was one of the most regarded humanists and neo-Latin poets. Mair's nominalism and concilliarism underwrote a thorough-going clerical world. Buchanan's uncompromising anti-clericalism and almost anti-scriptural approach to political thought led to a Circeronian civic culture and, eventually, to a quasi-republicanism. Mair felt a positively blood-thirsty obsession to extirpate heresy. Buchanan embraced Calvinism, developed perhaps the most radical defense of political revolution to appear in the sixteenth century, and became thereby the leading apologist for the political (and religious) upheavals in Scotland of 1560 and 1567.

Now all of this is familiar enough to anyone even remotely acquainted with Scottish history or, more generally, with the history of the Reformation. But it has never been recognized that Buchanan's break with Mair involved two additional issues no less important than those we have already noticed: first, the European conquest of the New World and second, the Jews. On both of these matters the two clashed at least as violently and as tellingly as about anything else. These clashes will reveal new dimensions to the cultural textures of early modern Europe and to Christian-Jewish relations during the period.

A. *John Mair: Philosophical Racism and Theological Anti-Semitism*

Conservative sensibilities in Scotland today have ensured that Mair now enjoys an astoundingly good reputation. Hugh Trevor-Roper and Alexander Brodie have variously stressed his "modernity" and the ways in which his thought might appear to anticipate the

Enlightenment. John Durkan has agreed that Mair's cutting-edge work made him an "up-to-the-moment logician." J.H. Burns and others have insisted that he is a political theorist of moment. He is especially celebrated currently for his *Historia Maioris Britanniæ* (1521), a work first applauded by K.D. Kendrick nearly forty years ago for abandoning a great many medieval mythologies and perceiving social cause in a more naturalistic fashion—a celebration that has picked up tempo since the 1970s. This rather warm and fuzzy view of Mair has been qualified by Scottish historians only occasionally through notice of his militant intolerance. But Scottish historians have yet to recognize him as an apologist for the Spanish conquest of the New World, indeed as an apologist quite specifically for the dispossession of the barbarian. In 1519 Mair published a commentary on the second of Peter Lombard's *Sentences*; and, as Anthony Pagden has indicated, while discussing the legitimacy of Christian rule over the pagans Mair made an extraordinary statement.

> These people [the inhabitants of the Antilles] live like beasts on either side of the equator; and beneath the poles there are wild men as Ptolemy says in his *Tetrabiblos* [2.2]. And this has now been demonstrated by experience, wherefore the first person to conquer them, justly rules over them because they are by nature slaves. As the philosopher [Aristotle] says in the third and fourth chapter of the first book of the *Politics*, it is clear that some men are by nature slaves, others by nature free; and in some men it is determined that there is such a thing [i.e. a disposition to slavery] and that they should benefit from it. And it is just that one man should be a slave and another free, and it is fitting that one man should rule and another obey, for the quality of leadership is also inherent in the natural master. On this account the Philosopher says in the first chapter of the aforementioned book that this is the reason why the Greeks should be masters over the barbarians because, by nature, the barbarians and slaves are the same thing.[1]

Pagden has described how the Spanish monarchy seized on Mair's remarks. For here was a justification of the vast conquests in the New World which derived entirely from nature—a justification un-

[1] Cited and translated by A. Pagden, *The Fall of Natural Man: The American Indian and the Origins of Comparative Ethnology* (Cambridge, 1986), pp. 38–9; cf. A.H. Williamson, "Scots, Indians, and Empire: the Scottish Politics of Civilization, 1519–1609," in *Past and Present*, 150 (1996), pp. 46–83.

troubled by any complicated claims for papal or imperial lordship and right. Here too nature worked to the distinct disadvantage of the inhabitants of the Americas. Mair proved useful to the royal confessor and strident imperialist, Juan Ginés de Sepúlveda, while he was quite the reverse to the Indians' great defender, Bartolomé de Las Casas.

If Mair promoted the new imperialism, he also supported still other aspects of Spanish policy. The launching of Columbus's first voyage coincided with the expulsion of the Jews from Spain and, with strong Spanish encouragement, from the whole of Iberia by 1498—events which were closely associated for many Spaniards. Judaism appeared to compromise the integrity of the realm, and that integrity was seen as prerequisite to Spain's higher purposes. Mair is unlikely to have shared the Spanish view of the Catholic kingdom's messianic mission and destiny. But his highly traditional hostility to usury (together with his repressive orthodoxy) led him to concur with the fierce anti-Judaism so characteristic in Spain and Portugal. Partially on this basis, he enthusiastically endorsed in his *Historia* the 1290 expulsion of the Jews from England and his terms are truly blood-curdling.

> And since a great complaint was raised, and justly raised, about the Jews, that, through their usurious and fraudulent dealing, they drained poor people of all they possessed, he drove out of the kingdom all Hebrews—who are wont to make their profit out of Christians, much as mice will do out of a find of clean wheat . . . Hence it is plain that kings in their kingdoms, and in each aristocratic polity its leading men, would do well to drive from their midst those obstinate Hebrews, if they would escape the necessity of imposing heavy taxes. . . . God is provoked by their sin of usury, no less than by their obstinate observance of the ceremonial parts of the Mosaic law, which in these respects is obsolete. Now, for any sins that meet not with their due punishment from the magistrate, and by which the divine goodness is provoked, God sends his scourge upon the state. . . . I praise, therefore, the expulsion from the kingdom of the Jews, for, by the introduction of the undesirable conditions of which I have spoken, they place a stumbling-block in the way of many who are weak in the faith . . .

The great defender of the Spanish conquests in the Americas (and the enslavement of their inhabitants) was also a strenuous defender of Jewish expulsion. Although Mair made his remarks in reference to England, they quite explicitly bore a universal application, and it hard to see how he could have done other than applaud the 1492

Iberian diaspora. Moreover and perhaps still more telling, Mair seems to have accepted the blood libel: that is, the medieval accusation that Jews murdered Christian children at Passover for ritual purposes. Thus he duly recounted the story of the Jews' crucifixion of "little" Hugh of Lincoln (1255) and of their subsequent condign punishment. Mair may have dispensed with a number medieval mythologies, he may have scoffed at popular prophecy and astrology, he may have urged a greater Britain and therefore in the traditional sense an imperial Britain. But Mair also perpetuated medieval fantasies, not ones about some distant mythical past, but ones which bore immediate and frightful consequences within his own lifetime. At the same moment, Mair's assessment of the social activities of the Jews, like his evaluation of the Americans, was at once naturalistic and devastating.[2]

Mair's anti-Judaism assumed immediate and personal application in 1514 when he served as a member of the commission at the University of Paris that condemned Johannes Reuchlin and Jewish studies for Christians. Reuchlin's self-defense, the *Augenspiegel*, was denounced as "false, temerarious, scandalous, erroneous, offensive to pious ears, contumelious, and blasphemous to the Church." The commission made its reasons for this torrent of denunciation quite explicit: the *Augenspiegel* defended the Talmud and was "manifestly favorable to the Jews." Traditionally, the Reuchlin affair—a controversy that rocked the early sixteenth-century intellectual world— has been seen as a dispute between scholasticism and humanism, the issue of Jewish learning being only incidental. But James Overfield, Heiko Oberman, and others have shown unassailably just the reverse. Anti-Judaism not only lies at the heart of the matter, it is the whole of the matter. Thus, at Paris the condemnation holds forth at length about Judaism and Reuchlin's supposed attitude towards it, but never once mentions his connection with humanism.[3] For Mair and his

---

[2] A.H. Williamson, "George Buchanan, Civic Virtue, and Commerce: Europan Imperialism and its Sixteenth-Century Critics," in *Scottish Historical Review*, 75 (1996), pp. 20–37.

[3] J.H. Overfield, *Humanism and Scholasticism in Late Medieval Germany* (Princeton, 1984), pp. 263–4; H.A. Oberman, *The Roots of Anti-Semitism in the Age of Renaissance and Reformation*, trans. by J.I. Porter (Philadelphia, 1984); B.P. Copenhaver and C.B. Schmitt, *Renaissance Philosophy* (Oxford, 1992), p. 97; C.G. Nauert, Jr., *Humanism and the Culture of Renaissance Europe* (Cambridge, 1995), pp. 139–40.

colleagues there was not an argument about learning and texts but an argument about religion and ethnicity.

Overseas conquest, philosophical racism, theological anti-Judaism, all featured signally in late medieval and early modern Iberia, a world to which Mair spoke with compelling cogency. It would be a world with which George Buchanan broke decisively.

B. *George Buchanan and the Portuguese* Conversos

If the Reuchlin affair did not involve a controversy about scholasticism and humanism, the dispute between Buchanan and Mair certainly went beyond controversy about scholasticism and humanism. When Buchanan blasts not only Mair's "trifles," but also his "lies"—deemed fully worthy the proverbial Cretan mendacity of antiquity—it is hard not to think that he intended contemporary mythologies like the blood libel.[4] Buchanan's own history, *Rerum Scoticarum Historia* (1582), contrasts strikingly with Mair's *Historia*. Unlike Mair he never mentions the Edwardian or the Iberian expulsions. The blood libel never surfaces and clearly runs counter to the entire tenor of his thought. For Buchanan the Jews just do not seem to be an issue.

---

[4] In Joannem solo cognomento Majorem,
    ut ipse in fronte libri sui scripsit.

Cum scateat nugis solo cognomine Major,
    Nec sit in immenso pagina sana libro:
Non mirum titulis quod se veracibns ornat:
    Nec semper mendax fingere Creta solet.

    [To John Major, only by surname,
as he himself has written in the frontispiece
        of his own book.
Since he blathers in trifles, Major by surname alone,
    And since there is not one sane page in the whole of his big book,
No wonder that he advertises himself with title insurance.
    Even in Crete they tell the truth every now and then.]
The phrase "Major by surname only" appears on the title page of a number of Mair's books and seems to have been a kind of signature. The "book" to which Buchanan refers is probably the corpus of Mair's work. The Cretan reputation for lying derives from the claim that the gods originated there in a cave on Mt. Ida and was a classical commonplace. Buchanan, *Omnia opera* (Edinburgh, 1715), ii, p. 78; *Omnia opera* (Leiden, 1725), ii, p. 373; P.J. McGinnis and A.H. Williamson (eds.), *George Buchanan The Political Poetry* (Edinburgh, 1998), 70/4, (forthcoming).

Yet in one way the Jews came to matter profoundly to Buchanan. In the early 1540s Buchanan took up a teaching position at a Latin school near Bordeaux, the Collège de Guyenne. Headed and largely staffed by Portuguese *conversos*, the school was regarded locally and especially by the local, reactionary archbishop, Charles de Grammont, as a hotbed of heterodoxy. The sixteenth-century *collèges* had subversive reputations just about everywhere in France, and to a considerable extent the suspicions about Guyenne were well-founded. The sudden forced conversion of Portugal's Jewish community in 1497—it required only one cup of water—effectively guaranteed that, unlike in Spain, hidden Judaism (marranism) and residual Judaism would persist in many areas. The principal, André de Gouvea, hailed from Beja, long a center for marranism, and his family most likely had come to France in the wake of the 1506 pogroms. Probably we will never know his true religious convictions, but, whether or not he actually was a marrano, he did obtain from Henri II the charter that secured the Portuguese New Christian community and effectively founds French Sephardic Jewry. The scholars that de Gouvea attracted to Guyenne embraced a wide range of opinion. Some of the New Christian faculty like João de Costa and Diogo de Teive probably were (or became) sincere converts. Others were variously radical. Antonio de Gouvea was strongly anti-clerical, initially favorable to reform, but may have ended his days with his thinking "tinged with scepticism." Another professor, Jean Gelida, found himself in difficulty because his wife did not sufficiently conceal her Judaism. Within this community, layered as it was with public pretense and private profession, George Buchanan, by then a notoriously anti-clerical refugee from both Scotland and England, found a home with striking ease and visible comfort. He much later recalled that he subsequently joined a group of them who set out to reestablish the University at Coimbra in part because, with them, he would be "among family and friends" (*inter propinquos et familiares*).

Initially the migration to the new Arts College at the revitalized University of Coimbra seemed enormously promising. Here were royal professorships modeled on those recently established in France and at a university now under the crown's protection and thereby largely free from clerical interference. Events utterly dashed these expectations. André de Gouvea's unexpected death in 1548 left the college open to orthodoxy, Jesuit conspiracy, and the newly empowered Portuguese Inquisition. In the summer of 1550 Buchanan and two of his colleagues were arrested and taken to Lisbon to face a range of religious charges.

Among these charges the most interesting in the context we have been examining is that of Judaizing. Buchanan was specifically accused of "fleeing Scotland [in 1539] because he was a heretic and a Jew, who said that he might partake of the Passover lamb; and five others, who were with him [then] in this heresy, were all burned alive." Buchanan was indeed jailed in 1539, and at least five others in Scotland were burned for heresy at that time. Buchanan's subsequent flight from prosecution was highly fortuitous and possibly aided by no less a figure than King James V himself. The Judaizing charge seems considerably more problematic. It originated with Portuguese academics in 1548 and found support from Simon Simson, a Scottish professor of theology at the Sorbonne, and apparently from another Scot, John Stewart, a regent at the Parisian College of Sainte Barbe—an institution with which Buchanan had earlier been associated.

Buchanan responded by dismissing the "fable" of the paschal lamb which, he claimed, was the first he had ever heard of such a thing (*fabula illa agni paschalis . . . de qua hodie primum aidivi*). "Of Judaism I have never thought . . . there are no Jews in Scotland." The Inquisitors certainly knew that Buchanan was an Old Christian, and they almost certainly knew that, as Buchanan claimed, there had never been a Jewish community in Scotland. They chose not to pursue the matter, and it does not figure it his subsequent punishment or in his lucky release (possibly at João III's intervention) in 1552.

So far as we know, Judaism never thereafter posed a problem for Buchanan. But the tradition persisted nevertheless and enjoyed an extraordinarily long history. Buchanan's contemporary, James Laing, another doctor at the Sorbonne, claimed that Buchanan's "Ebionite" madness went so far as to urge James V in Lent "to eat the paschal lamb if you wish to achieve salvation." According to Laing, no less a figure than Buchanan's professor John Mair was summoned and commented, "Whoever says, Most Christian King, that you should eat the paschal lamb, he would wish you to become a Jew and live as the Jews do." Somewhat later a Scottish priest, David Chambers, also promoted the tradition in a work eventually published by the Parisian Oratorians. Thereafter Buchanan's Jewish "scandal" became standard stuff for Catholic polemic—turning up in all sorts of continental annals and even in the history of the University of Paris. The story eventually found its way into no less than Pierre Bayle's dictionary.[5]

Buchanan's long-lived reputation may simply be an indication of his importance for the reformed cause and of the problem this extremely popular writer posed for the Counter-Reformation. And yet, in context, the Inquisition—however cynical in its objective of seizing the college, however hostile its attitude toward a lay intelligentsia—may have sensed something real. The Inquisition had assumed power in 1547 in the wake of powerful anti-Jewish currents. The clerics sought Jews, and they may have actually found them. Like Beja, Coimbra was a major center for marranism.[6] Possibly for some in the Guyenne party that circumstance may have held appeal, but it could be exceedingly and increasingly dangerous as events proved.

Buchanan undoubtedly inhabited a highly ambivalent, unmistakably crypto-Jewish world first at Guyenne and then at Coimbra. Buchanan's Latin play, *Baptistes, sive calumnia tragédia*, written in the early 1540s to be performed by the students at Guyenne, speaks to just such a world. The play dramatizes the story of John the Baptist and is normally seen as a discussion of political tyranny. That is how Buchanan sought its exculpation before the inquisitors—the tyrannical Herod like Henry VIII, the martyred John the Baptist like Thomas More. Buchanan again stressed its anti-tyrannical message, though also noting its religious significance, in his dedication of the play to the young James VI in 1577 (after all, James' religion was thought to be secure). But the drama, although profoundly political, concerns a great deal more than a "speculum" for classically conceived tyranny. It is also about prophecy, reform, and ultimately—

[5] Nauert, *Humanism and the Culture of the Renaissance Europe*, p. 171; Jerome Friedman, "New Christian Religious Alternatives," in R.B. Waddington and A.H. Williamson (eds.), *The Expulsion of the Jews: 1492 and After* (New York, 1994), pp. 19–40; Y.H. Yerushalmi, "Prolegomena," to Alexandre Herculano, *A History of the Origin and Establishment of the Inquisition in Portugal*, trans. by J.C. Branner (New York, 1972); Théophile Malvezin, *Histoire des Juifs à Bordeaux* (Bordeaux, 1875/1976), pp. 88–145; Henry Léon, *Histoire des Juifs de Bayonne* (Paris, 1893), pp. 16–26; I.D. McFarlane, *Buchanan* (London, 1981), pp. 29–30, 34, 80–1, 95–8; A.H. Williamson, "British Israel and Roman Britain: The Jews and Scottish Models of Polity from George Buchanan to Samuel Rutherford," in R.H. Popkin et al. (eds.), *Jewish Christians and Christian Jews in Early Modern Europe* (Dordrecht/Boston, 1994), pp. 97–117.

[6] J.I. Israel, *European Jewry in the Age of Mercantilism, 1550–1750* (Oxford, 1989), p. xiv.

as some modern critics have observed—it concerns judging language and appearances.

That the play should reflect favorably upon the experience of a prophet, a subject otherwise altogether missing from Buchanan's political writings, is itself significant. But the truly striking feature is the way it treats the nation of the Jews. The Jewish priesthood is by no means composed of cardboard villains—and still less of proto-Christians. The young rabbi Gamaliel insists against the older, repressive rabbi Malchus that the Baptist must be given a chance to prove his insight, which, if wrong, needs be confronted at least initially with reason rather than authority and repression. Pride, violence, and arrogance, he comments in a voice not unlike Buchanan's 1539 poem in support of Thomas Cromwell, "was not this regimen which raised high our fore-fathers." The Jewish community, represented by the chorus, seems still more favorable to the Baptist. Yet even Malchus is not altogether unambivalent. He defends clerical authority by the absolutist (for Buchanan, tyrannical) argument: "the man in authority . . . must be his own law; if he sins, God is there to witness and punish him for his crime." He is obsessed with tradition, seeks "concordia" within society, is utterly distrustful of the "plebs", and is fully prepared to calumniate the prophet to King Herod by insisting that religious reform will mean political revolution. But Malchus *does* know that things are deeply wrong in Israel and that some of the things the prophet says have merit. The flashpoint of course is the authority of the clergy and their immunity from judgement: "I burst with anger. Am I to listen to this in silence?" Now all of this is in context quite remarkable. The profoundly anti-Judaic attitudes virtually everywhere in late medieval and early modern Europe made it almost inevitable that reformers would compare the persecuting Catholic hierarchy to the pharisaical priesthood and that they would see themselves as the successors to the early Christians. As the Jews persecuted the original Christians, so too did the medieval church now persecute the reformers of the sixteenth century—latter-day Jews persecuting latter-day Christians. This trope would reach Scotland in a powerful way at least by the 1550s. But not a trace of this sort of thing is to be found in Buchanan. The Jews are simply ourselves.

Baptistes enters upon wide-ranging matters of central importance to the sixteenth century: tyranny, reform, prophecy. Yet at its heart lies something else, the question of authenticity. Nearly every scene features some comment on people misrepresenting themselves through language or other forms of disguise. Malchus claims that John "has beguiled the simple folk with the appearance of stern sanctity." "I have seen men parading an austere sanctity in dress, so that they readily fostered the belief that they were moderate and simple in mind." Gamaliel laments that "However much we may flatter ourselves, be proclaimed as blessed, or be considered god-like, holy, chaste, and dutiful by the common folk, none of us is free from the greatest vices." "We have long ago transformed the sense of virtue because we shine with no virtue; but in our arrogance we deceive the ignorant crowd with shining claims to it." The chorus agrees: "An assumed modesty cloaks the shameless; the cover of piety conceals the impious." "Feigned devotion cloaks the cruelty of tyrants, the fringed robe wicked manners. Naked virtue hides herself in thin rages in the shade of a rustic hut." John's new baptism itself raises questions about the real and the apparent in the most direct and even painful ways. How can we be sure of anything? Buchanan clearly indicates that real understanding can only occur in a more open society where claims and counter-claims might be freely and seriously considered without recourse to blinkered authority. Precisely such mindless authoritarianism in the church, Buchanan later claimed to the Inquisition, had led him to take heretical opinions seriously. Buchanan's play therefore might easily be seen as calling for a fair hearing for the latter-day prophets, the reformers—before the dangers of clerically-induced government repression. But Buchanan, from early on was deeply hostile to all forms of prophecy (whether apocalyptic, Galfridian, or astrological), surely has more in mind than simply the emerging movement for reform. Seen from the crypto-Jewish context in which it was written, as inevitably it must be, the play speaks before anything else to the disguised community of the *conversos*. Fair play for reformers really meant openness and security for the people at the Guyenne school. Buchanan's concern with ambiguous and hidden meaning articulated a central concern of the community he had firmly embraced.

The initial trigger for the Lisbon prosecutions appears to have been a disgruntled Guyenne alumnus, one João Pinheiro. In addition to the talking of Buchanan's Judaizing in Scotland, Pinheiro spoke of a meal at Advent in Bordeaux in which meat was eaten, at which the monastic orders and the Church generally were criticized, and at which the human origins of fasting, Advent, and Lent were discussed. Is it possible that Pinheiro happened upon a seder or at least a celebration of half remembered family traditions? If so, Buchanan may well be one of the first post-medieval Scottish intellectuals to participate in such an event.[7]

C. *After the Debacle: The Critique of Empire and Commerce*

Buchanan and his colleagues were lucky to survive the Inquisition. The Arts College and their community did not survive. Although the University continued to possess a nominal independence until the departure of its rector, Diogo de Murça, in 1554, power had shifted decisively, and education at the university (and in Portugal generally) fell into the hands of the Jesuits where it would remain for the next three hundred years. Buchanan's anger at this experience is difficult to overstate, and we can easily understand how, reputedly, he declined an offer from Dom João to stay on—in what was an increasingly authoritarian and clerical environment. Instead, he immediately departed for France, and for the rest of his life struggled against the global Iberian empires, against the Hapsburgs, and against the universal order they sought to create. In France he devoted his talents to promoting the Valois dynasty against its rival, imagining the French realm as leading a great counter-empire that protected the liberties of Europe. Sometime after 1560 he returned to his native Scotland which he sought to visualize as an autonomous aristocratic semi-republic that realized the classical civic ideal and thereby achieved the full possibilities of human potential.

Buchanan's appointment at Coimbra had involved more than simply teaching Greek to the sons of the Portuguese elite. A royal professor, he was expected to celebrate the realm, its monarch, its truly vast empire. And so he did in stately Latin verse that continued to thrill the Lisbon court long after his entire corpus was officially banned in 1581. But even while in Portugal Buchanan indicated that royal power could never be absolute. The crown for Buchanan protected patriotic culture against clerical subversion, thereby allowing space for public life, for the intellect, for morality. His *converso*

---

[7] P. Sharratt and P.G. Walsh (eds.), *George Buchanan Tragedies* (Edinburgh, 1983), pp. 135, 151–2, 136, 139, 140, 141. Discussed by Williamson, "British Israel," pp. 101–5.

compatriots typically found it difficult ever to imagine their community independent of monarchical protection, even in the most ghastly moments of persecution and pogrom. Buchanan's departure from Portugal encompassed as well a deepening departure from the sensibility of his shattered community.

The new global empires, Buchanan now insisted, subverted human capacity because they precluded the citizen and politics where value and self were realized through public discourse and were self-imposed. Clericalism and commerce underwrote this new imperialism. In words that anticipated by more than two decades the famous essay "Of Cannibals" written by his sometime student Michel de Montaigne, Buchanan claimed that Portuguese Brazil corrupted the local inhabitants and that the settlers—clergy-led "degredados" (transported prisoners)—behaved more barbarically than even the most primitive aborigine. Cannibalism itself, the ultimate mark of barbarism for early modern Europeans, paled before the grotesque practices of the "sodomite" Europeans whose behavior, Buchanan intimated, had led to nothing less than the syphilis pandemic.[8]

Commerce proved nearly as troubling. Its inherent instability prevented its practitioners from having the autonomy required by the Ciceronian ideal. If the Iberian empires looked powerful, they were in fact sleazy and highly vulnerable mercantile enterprises that had nothing noble or grand about them. In Latin verses that must driven the courts at Lisbon and Madrid apoplectic, Buchanan declared that when storm or war shuts down the pepper stall, then "the great king of many names" will need to "take out a loan or starve." Buchanan's poems doubtless contributed materially to João III's subsequent and most unwelcome sobriquet, "the grocer king."

It is in this context that Buchanan betrayed his only recorded instance of anti-Judaism. Although Inquisition procedures prevented Buchanan from knowing who his accusers were, he believed with some reason that a junior colleague, one Belchior Beleago (or Beliagoa), had been the the clerics' agent (the "quadruplator"—an informer who in antiquity would receive a quarter of the penalty). Beleago had therefore in the fullest sense "sold out" the university, and once out of jail and out of Portugal Buchanan launched into a series of

---

[8] See A.H. Williamson, "Unnatural Empire: George Buchanan, Anti-Imperialism, and the Sixteenth-Century Syphilis Pandemic," in J.E. Force and D.S. Katz (eds.), *Everything Connects: In Conversation with Richard H. Popkin* (Leiden, 1998), forthcoming.

furious poems against his former colleague. Today the Beleago cycle will strike its readers as thoroughly nasty, exuberantly vulgar, scurrilously witty; they are normally sanitized in English translation. Unfortunately, several of them are also poisonously anti-Judaic. Buchanan's claims are straight-forward: Beleago is not a professor interesting in learning or capable of it, but a cut-rate huckster who will sell anything (and especially his senior professor, Buchanan himself). If Beleago had his way—and if Laverna, the goddess protecting thieves and imposters, would allow it—he would control the water supply and the sewers as well. Pay privies, perhaps? The Inquisition may have charged Buchanan with Judaizing, but Buchanan inverts the charge, for it is really Beleago who is Jewish. Beleago betrays himself as being such by his "raging passion for money" (*lucri tam furiosus amor*). In fact, as a Portuguese, Beleago was actually far more vulnerable to the characteristic Iberian accusation of having "impure" or "unclean" Jewish blood. Buchanan intimates that Beleago tried to secure certification of his blood from the Inquisition, something commonly done at the time.

> Jewish, Beleago, that's what you say you're not, And you wish to prove that by great testimonies ("testis," a pun on "testes"); You're wrong, the matter is not proved (as I think you know) by testimonies ("testes") but by the prick.

Yet the point of the remaining seven poems in the cycle, only two of which reference the anti-Jewish aspersion, is the demeaning ethos of commerce.[9]

Buchanan's commercial anti-Judaism differs profoundly from Mair's theological anti-Judaism. But, even so, its significance can be overdrawn. Within the stultifying, truly McCarthyite world of sixteenth-century Iberia—obsessed as its was with blood and race, hysterically concerned to deny (or hide) the stain of Jewish ancestry—Buchanan's anti-Jewish postures are rather commonplace than notably bloodthirsty. They were probably most striking to contemporaries for being

---

[9]   In Beleagonem
    Judæum, Beleago, quod negas te,
    Et vis testibus id probare magnis:
    Erras, testibus ista non probatur
    Res, (ut scis, puto) mentula probatur.
See McGinnis and Williamson, *George Buchanan The Political Poetry*, "Introduction: Poetry and Politics," 2/1 and the Beleago Cycle 1–8/1 (forthcoming).

nearly entirely secular. Moreover, the anti-Judaism in the poems, though certainly real, appears to serve the larger anti-mercantile purpose. At the heart of the matter for Buchanan is large-scale trade and the commercial enterprise itself rather than any Jewish rapacity. There is no plea for the good trader being squeezed out by sharp practices. For all the hostility expressed in these poems to the "solus arbiter" and to "monoplium," we do not find the slightest hint of economic liberalism or any vindication of the virtues of free trade. Trade itself appears unworthy, demeaning, contemptible. It is relevant to Buchanan's political order only because it threatens to subvert that order. For Buchanan the civic and the commercial simply did not mix. The new, grotesquely distended world empires derived from the latter and for that reason were incompatible to the former. The expansion of Europe was a massive tragedy: it corrupted the New World while subverting the Old.

D. *Conclusion: From Crypto-Judaism to Philo-Semitism*

Buchanan had no difficulty becoming a part of an unmistakably crypto-Jewish community on what had promised to be a permanent basis. Arguably, it comprised one the happier moments in his long life. Its complex textures undoubtedly shaped his writing, from his *Baptistes* to his attitudes towards toward the indigenous population of Brazil. If after 1552 Buchanan proved capable of making anti-Jewish comments, his mentality, informed by humanism and ultimately Calvinism, remained drastically removed from that of his professor, John Mair, and it pointed to better things.

Nevertheless, Buchanan's call for openness and his easy interaction with crypto-Judaism is still very far removed from modern toleration. It would be the next generation of Calvinist English-speakers, like Thomas Brightman and John Napier of Merchiston, who, beginning in the 1590s, looked the Jews *as Jews* to play a vital role in realizing human destiny. These people and their radical successors eventually opened the way for the 1655 Jewish readmission. All of them thought in deeply apocalyptic terms—categories quite uncongenial to George Buchanan. They mark the transition from the Renaissance to the Baroque, from Cicero to Tacitus, from crypto-Judaism to philo-Semitism.

CAN ONE BE A TRUE CHRISTIAN AND A FAITHFUL FOLLOWER OF THE LAW OF MOSES? THE ANSWER OF JOHN DURY

Richard H. Popkin

When Martin Mulsow and I started planning this volume on Christian converts to Judaism in early modern times, I thought that a document I had copied from the Hartlib papers would fit with the theme. On careful reexamination of the document, which is reproduced below, it is obvious that it only deals with the problem of whether practicing Jews can be true and believing Christians at the same time and does not touch on whether practicing Christians can be true and believing Jews at the same time. The role that John Dury played in the seventeenth-century attempt to bring all the churches together might well have extended to bringing Jews into Christianity and Christians into Judaism.

Dury was early convinced of the imminent Second Coming of Jesus in the 1650s, and entered into the millenarian fervor of the Puritan Revolution in 1641 and 42. He was a Scot who had been raised and trained in Leiden and had been a pastor in Germany. He came to London in 1641 and there worked with Samuel Hartlib and Jan Amos Comenius to put forth a blueprint for the Reformation of the English-speaking world.[1] The three of them proposed large-scale reforms in agriculture, economy, and especially in education. They were going to transform education in England from pre-school to graduate school, so it would lead to spiritual and complete knowledge. A crown jewel of the original proposals was a project put forth by Dury, published by Hartlib, for a college of Jewish Studies (called Oriental Studies in the original). This was proposed in a pamphlet entitled *Englands Thankfulnesse, or An Humble Remembrance presented to the Committee for Religion in the High Court of Parliament with Thanksgiving for*

---

[1] See Charles Webster, *The Great Instauration*, (London, 1975), 48–51; Charles Webster (ed.), *Samuel Hartlib and the Advancement of Learning* (Cambridge, 1970), 26–46; Hugh Trevor-Roper, "Three Foreigners: The Philosophy of the Puritan Revolution," in Religion, *The Reformation and Social Change* (London, 1967), 262–274.

that happy Pacification betweene the two Kingdomes. By a faithful well-wisher to this Church and Nation. Wherein are sumarily discovered a naïve and most subtile Plot of the Pope and his conclave against Protestancy. Their true method and policy how to undermine the same. The best and principal meanes of re-establishing the Palatin House and preserving all Evangelical Churches. As like-wise three special Instruments of the publique good in the ways of Religion Learning and the Preparatives for the conversion of the Jewes.[2] The purpose of the college would be to make Christians more knowledgeable about Judaism and make the Jews find Christianity less offensive.[3] The college was to be based in London, to have had three professors, Menasseh ben Israel, a rabbi from Amsterdam; Adam Boreel, the leader of the Dutch Collegiants; and a Professor Johann Stephan Rittangel, who taught Hebrew in Amsterdam and edited the important kabbalistic text, *Safir Yesira*.[4] The Hartlib papers indicate that Menasseh was ready to accept the post even though he did not live in England and had not yet arrived there. Dury had to convince Hartlib of Boreel's bona fides and described him as an important Hebraist and philo-semite. Rittangel turned out to be a bone of contention. Nobody could tell what religion he had started with and what he believed in the present. He was fighting with everybody. It was rumored that he had been a Jew, who had become a Catholic, who had become a Lutheran, who had become all sorts of things. He dressed like an Eastern European rabbi and had spent twenty years in Turkey with Jews and Caraites. Pierre Bayle tells us that, in the attempt to discover whether Rittangel had been born a Jew, questioners approached Mrs. Rittangel and asked her whether her husband had been circumcised. She refused to answer, so the mystery remains.[5]

The flaw in the project was not the personnel but rather the financing. Dury had modestly proposed that Parliament expend a

---

[2] For more detail about it, see, Richard H. Popkin, "The First College for Jewish Studies", *Revue des études juives*, Vol. 143, July–December 1984.

[3] See Popkin, "The First College for Jewish Studies," in: *Revue des études juives*, Vol. 143. July–December, 1984, 353.

[4] Dury knew all three from his years in The Netherlands. He was especially involved with Menasseh and Boreel. Rittangel is a curious character who proved too difficult to manage for the project.

[5] See Pierre Bayle's article, "Rittangel," in his *Dictionnaire historique et critique*. Written over fifty years after the college plan, in which he still wonders whether Rittangel was a Jew who became a Christian or a Christian who became a Jew or went through a series of conversions in different directions.

thousand pounds per annum for the college; a huge sum at the time and a huge sum for a college with three faculty members. The funding was approved by the Westminster assembly and by Parliament but as Dury explained, the money vanished into projects to pacify Ireland and so the college never got its official financing.[6]

The outline of the college project indicates that what the college would do was provide lectures by the faculty, instruction in oriental languages that would be useful to Jews and Christians, and editions of Jewish works not known to the general Christian world.

Though the college project did not get discussed after 1642, offshoots of it appear to have developed first in the Netherlands and later in England. Adam Boreel personally financed the work of Rabbi Judah Leon Templo in the reconstruction of Solomon's Temple. For four years Templo and Boreel worked on constructing an exact model of Solomon's Temple, which the rabbi said was an exact microcosm of the universe. The model was displayed next to the synagogue in Amsterdam and was one of the featured tourist stops for people who came to the city. So many people wanted to see it that the synagogue had to forbid the rabbi from taking money from viewers on the Sabbath because the noise was interfering with services. Templo put out a small book in Portuguese, Spanish, French, and Dutch, describing his achievement. The Temple project had an ongoing history into the eighteenth century when the rabbi took it to England in the 1670s and there it was apparently taken over by the Freemasons who were exhibiting it throughout the eighteenth century. (The librarian of the Rosenthalia Library told me that the model of the Temple was made something like a Lego construction so it could be taken apart, packed up in a box, and then reconstructed somewhere else).[7]

The Temple project seems to be a Jewish-Christian project, which everyone could enjoy and profit from regardless of their religious beliefs or practices. In the period 1642–46, Templo and Boreel also worked on a project, which seems to be an outgrowth of the Jewish

---

[6] See Popkin, "The First College for Jewish Studies", 361.

[7] On the model of the Temple, see A.K. Offenberg, "Jacob Jehuda Leon (1602–1675) and his Model of the Temple" in: *Jewish-Christian Relations in the Seventeenth Century*, J. Van den Berg and Ernestine G.E. Van der Wall (Dordrecht: Kluwer, 1988), 101–110; On Boreel's investment in Leon's model, see Dury's letter to Boreel, 8 August 1649, Hartlib Papers Sheffield, 1/31/1.

studies project; namely, an addition of the Mishna with vowel points and footnotes. The rabbi provided the vowels and Boreel, the footnotes. The work on this went on in the rabbi's house. Boreel moved into the rabbi's house and learned Portuguese, so he and the rabbi could work together easily. In 1646, they had the completed text.[8] They got some Dutch Millenarians to finance the publication of it and approached Menasseh ben Israel to do the actual printing. At this point, troubles developed. Menasseh was happy to be the printer, but pointed out that no Jew would use the document if Boreel's name was on it and they would only trust the text if it was attributed to a Jewish editor. Menasseh either volunteered himself or accepted being the name on the title page. The work was printed with plans to publish folio editions, Latin editions, Spanish editions, presumably so everyone could know what was in the Mishna, which would let Jews and Christians alike know what the messianic age would involve.[9] As I showed in a study of this, the publication was a financial disaster. They shipped copies all over Europe, to England, to Germany, to Poland, to France, and nobody would buy them. Only a few copies have been located, two in the Netherlands and two in Dublin, so as an educational scheme this did not work out, but the work on the Spanish edition and the Latin edition went on through the century.[10] Rabbi Isaac Abendana was working on the Latin in Cambridge in the 1660s and 70s and was being paid by the page, each page checked by the Regis professor of Hebrew, Ralph Cudworth.[11]

Another outgrowth of the school project may well have been the launching of a new form of the Jewish Indian theory about the ancestry and nature of the occupants of the New World. A Portuguese explorer had personally reported to Rabbi Menasseh ben Israel in

---

[8] See Popkin, "Some Aspects of Jewish-Christian Theological Interchanges in Holland and England 1640–1700", in: *Jewish-Christian Relations*, 7–9. In a letter of Boreel's to Father Marin Mersenne, 3 Sept. 1646, Boreel said he had been working on the Mishna edition since 1639, much of it "aven l'aide d'un Juif que j'ay eu alimente environ cinq ans pour cette affaire", *Correspondance de Mersenne*, Tome XIV (1646), 431.

[9] See Popkin, "Some Aspects of Jewish-Christian Theological Interchanges", in: *Jewish-Christian Relations*, 9.

[10] Ibid., 8–9.

[11] In 1990 the librarian at Cambridge University showed me the manuscript of Abendana's work with chits authorizing payment to Abendana for each tractate that he finished.

1644 that he had come across a group of natives in the Andes Mountains in present day Ecuador, and found them on Friday night conducting a Jewish service. The Portuguese explorer, Antonio Montezinos, was so impressed that he rushed back to Europe to inform Rabbi Menasseh ben Israel that he had located one of the lost tribes of Israel. Menasseh took the explorer before a notary and had him relate his story and then had the account notarized.[12] Word of this spread to England and elsewhere. John Dury asked Menasseh for a copy of the Montezinos report and the Jesuit missionary in Brazil, Antonio de Vieira, came to Amsterdam to discuss the matter with Menasseh. Dury used the material in his preface to a book by Thomas Thorowgood, entitled *Jews in America, or the Probability that the Indians are Jews*, about whether the American Indians were the lost tribes. This book was set forth with a wild millenarian preface by Dury as a fundraiser for a new educational system in the Massachusetts colonies to train the Jewish Indians. Harvard was to be the center of this. Dury included material from Menasseh in his preface, which led the Amsterdam rabbi to write his best known work, *The Hope of Israel*, a careful assessment of the evidence that the Jewish messianic hopes would soon be fulfilled.[13] Menasseh took a minimalist stand on the Jewish Indian matter, holding that the evidence was that a part of the lost tribe may have been contacted, but that other inhabitants of the New World may have other origins and destinies altogether. Menasseh's work was written and published in Spanish. Dury immediately arranged for an English-language edition and a Latin edition appeared followed by French, Dutch, Hebrew, and other languages. The English edition was translated by a gentleman named Moses Wall, a wild millenarian enthusiast, who was a friend of Samuel Hartlib and John Milton. He slanted the text into a conversionist document and wrote a further explanation at the end on why the Jews, on the basis of this, should convert.[14]

---

[12] See Popkin, "The Rise and Fall of the Jewish Indian Theory", in: *Menasseh Ben Israel and His World*, Yosef Kaplan, Henry Méchoulan and Richard H. Popkin (eds.), (Leiden-New York: Brill, 1989), 67.

[13] Ibid., 68.

[14] Idem. See the recent English re-edition of Menasseh Ben Israel's *The Hope of Israel*, Henry Méchoulan and Gérard Nahon (eds.), with an introduction by Méchoulan (Oxford: Oxford University Press, 1987). At the end of this edition there is a note by myself on Moses Wall, showing his role in the millenarian world at the time based on letters of his to Samuel Hartlib, 165–170.

Although Menasseh and Dury did not hold the same view about the material, they seemed to have worked together to use it as a common Jewish-Christian project to bring the Jews back to England. Dury was very involved in the negotiations that led to the English government inviting Menasseh to come to England in 1665 to discuss the terms by which Jews could be readmitted into England.[15] Menasseh, in England, was the only official Jew in the Protectorate. There is plenty of indication that Menasseh's arrival was seen by many as a monumental event in the stream of signs leading to the millennium. Some Swedish diplomats described the wild statements being made in the weeks before Menasseh arrived, and they complain it was impossible to get Oliver Cromwell to concentrate on the fur business. All he would talk about was the coming of the Messiah.[16] Menasseh met with Oliver Cromwell, dined with him, gave him a copy of his one book in Hebrew. He was wined and dined by Lady Ranelagh, the sister of Robert Boyle. The Dutch Collegian leader, Adam Boreel, came to London and had parties for Menasseh. Scholars like Henry More and Ralph Cudworth came to meet him. His stay in England, which lasted about twenty months, was a genuine Jewish-Christian enterprise in which there was no attempt from the leadership in England in Church and State to convert Menasseh. He consulted with people in Oxford and Cambridge. There were only a couple of odd figures, like the Quaker leader, Margaret Fell, who tried to convert him.[17] Otherwise, in effect, a Jew could co-exist in England with the Christians without any problem and they could share ideals. We do not know what Menasseh did about his religious practices. We do know that he went to lots of dinners and nobody mentions him having any particular dietary requirements.[18] He seems to have been able to discuss the similari-

---

[15] On this see David S. Katz, *Philo-Semitism and the Readmission of the Jews to England 1603–1655* (Oxford: Oxford University Press, 1982).

[16] Michael Roberts (ed.), *Swedish Diplomats at Cromwell's Court, 1655–1656: The Missions of Julius Coyet and Christian Bonde*, Camden Fourth Series, vol. 36 (London, 1988).

[17] Margaret Fell, *For Manasseth-Ben-Israel; the Call of the Jews out of Babylon, which is good tidings to the meek, liberty to the captives, and of opening of the prison doors* (London, 1656). A French reform minister in London tried to get Menasseh to debate about the truth of the Christian religion, but he refused.

[18] On Menasseh's social life in England see Cecil Roth's *A Life of Menasseh ben Israel, Rabbi, Printer and Diplomat* (Philadelphia, 1934).

ties and contrasts between Jewish religious beliefs and Christian ones. The only work he published in England, *The Vindication of the Jews*, attempts to answer various charges made against Jews by English people. He does this calmly and often quite forcefully, but there is no sense of polemic. In fact, in this work he offers a sort of compromise between Judaism and Christianity, namely the theory put forth in Isaac La Peyrère's *Recall of the Jews* in which there would be two Messiah's, one for the Gentiles and one for the Jews. The former had come in the first century, the latter would turn up at any moment. This, Menasseh said, would fit with European history, as La Peyrère said, the King of France would join with the Jewish Messiah, help rebuild the Holy Land, bring the Jews back to Palestine, and then rule the world with the Jewish Messiah from Jerusalem.[19] Nobody I have found comments on this aspect of Menasseh's thought and we don't know how well it went down in England, especially with the French political implication in it. We do know that the first person who met Menasseh in England got into a discussion with him whether it would be the next King of England, that is the son of Charles I, or the King of Sweden, or the King of France that would rule with the Messiah and Menasseh was holding out for the third choice.[20]

Menasseh never succeeded in getting official admission of the Jews to England. He himself applied for citizenship and a pension and did not get them. He returned to Holland in 1657 and died very soon thereafter.[21] With his death, there seems to have been less active Jewish-Christian, Christian-Jewish enterprises. However, we know, partly from a statement of Menasseh's, in the *Vindiciae Judaeorum*, that about half the people who attended synagogue services in Amsterdam were not Jewish. Many of the Millenarians in Amsterdam regularly went to the synagogue for services and discussed common interests

---

[19] Menasseh ben Israel, *Vindiciae Judaeorum, or a Letter in Answer to Certain Questions propounded by a Noble and Learned Gentleman, touching the Reproaches cast on the Nation of the Jews, wherein all objections are candidly, and yet fully, cleared* (London, 1656). The noble gentleman concerned is probably Robert Boyle. See also: Popkin, *Isaac La Peyrere (1596–1676): His Life, Work and Influence* (Leiden, 1987), 102–103.

[20] This person was a Welsh royalist Millenarian named Arise Evans. He records the first conversation with Menasseh in his book, *Light for the Jews, or the Means to convert them, in Answer to a Book of theirs, called the Hope of Israel, written and printed by Manasseth Ben-Israel, Chief Agent for the Jews here* (London, 1656–1664).

[21] See David S. Katz, *Philo-Semitism* and Cecil Roth, *Life of Menasseh ben-Israel*.

afterwards.[22] Spinoza's patron, Peter Serrarius, who reports that when strange things appeared in the sky, or a two-headed cow is born, he would rush to the synagogue to discuss these omens, and to do kabbalistic calculations with the rabbis. His picture is that the synagogue was open to him all the time and that he was always welcome.

In 1657, a rabbi from Palestine, Nathan Shapira, appeared in Amsterdam trying to raise funds for the starving Jews of Jerusalem.[23] The Sephardic synagogue refused to do anything for him. He encountered some Dutch Millenarians who took him to Serrarius's house, where they had happy discussions about theology. The rabbi was presented in a pamphlet put out by John Dury, based on a description he got from Serrarius, as a Jew who was just about to become a true and believing Christian.[24] When the Millenarians asked the rabbi if he thought the messiah had already come, he answered "yes, he comes in every generation, but finds mankind too wicked so he does not stay." In Rabbi Shapira's list of messianic figures who have come and gone back, he included several biblical figures as well as Jesus of Nazareth.[25] When he was asked what he thought of the Sermon on the Mount, he said it is the teaching of our wisest rabbis.[26] Serrarius told Dury that he felt the rabbi's Christian spirit from these remarks.[27]

---

[22] John Dury, Peter Serrarius, and several others report going to synagogue services in Amsterdam and many visiting tourists from other countries went to the synagogue as one of the main attractions in the city. The Queen of England, Henrietta-Marie, the wife of Charles I and the daughter of Marie de Medici, attended a service in 1642. Many other visiting dignitaries mention their visits to the synagogue.

[23] On this see Popkin, "Rabbi Nathan Shapira's Visit to Amsterdam in 1657", in: *Dutch Jewish History*, Jozeph Michman (ed.) (Jerusalem: Hebrew University, 1984), 185–205.

[24] Dury's pamphlet, published in 1658, is entitled, *An Information Concerning the Present State of the Jewish Nation in Europe and Judea. Wherein the Footsteps of Providence preparing the way for their Conversion to Christ, and for their Deliverance from Captivity are Discovered*.

[25] See Dury, *An Information*, 17 and Popkin, "Rabbi Nathan Shapira's Visit", 194–195.

[26] See Popkin, "Rabbi Nathan Shapira's Visit", 195.

[27] "For my own part, I confess, I think, I see Christ in his Spirits, and I cannot but love him, and those that are like him . . ." Ibid., 196–197.

The rabbi ate with the Millenarians. He explained to them the sad state of affairs of his brethren in Jerusalem. They then organized a fund-raising appeal in the Netherlands and England for the Jews of Palestine.[28] He went back to Palestine carrying with him a copy of the Gospel According to Matthew, which his Dutch millenarian friends wanted him to get translated into Hebrew. There is no evidence he ever got this done. The next thing we know is that he was charged by Jewish authorities in Palestine with the terrible crime of taking money from Gentiles.[29] He only got cleared of this years later when it was decided that the money from the Millenarians went directly to the Turkish authorities to pay the taxes and not the starving Jews. He seems to have kept in touch with them. However, he is reported to have left the Jewish community and died in Italy for reasons not known.

Some of the Dutch and English Millenarians seemed to have almost fused Judaism and Christianity. Serrarius regularly went to synagogue services and participated in other Jewish activities. We do not know if he started adopting Jewish dietary habits. He became an ardent follower of Sabbatai Zevi and died on his way to meet the new Messiah.[30]

A more remarkable fusion of Judaism and Christianity occurred in the early Quaker movement. The purported first founder of the Quakers, George Fox, in 1652 went around England proclaiming "to be a Jew externally is nothing; to be a Jew internally is everything."[31] Fox and some other early Quakers seem to have taken this to mean that finding the light within themselves was conversion to spiritual Judaism, the same that existed in ancient times before it

---

[28] Ibid., 198. See also *The Life and Death of Mr. Henry Jessey, Late Preacher of the Gospel of Christ in London*, anon., (n.p., 1671), 69–71.

[29] The full story of what happened to Rabbi Shapira when he returned to Palestine and was charged with taking money from Gentiles is told in David S. Katz, "English Charity and Jewish Qualms: The Rescue of the Ashkenazi Community of Seventeenth-Century Jerusalem", in: *Jewish History: Essays in Honour of Chimen Abramsky*, ed. A. Rapoport-Albert and S.J. Zipperstein (London, 1988), 245–266.

[30] See Ernestine G.E. van der Wall, "De Hemelse Tekenen en het Rijk van Christus op Aarde. Chiliasme en Astrologie bij Petrus Serrarius (1600–1669)", in: *Kerkhistorische Studien* (Leyde, 1982), 45–64; Popkin, note on Serrarius in *Spinoza et son cercle*, K.O. Meinsma (ed.) (Paris: J. Vrin), 277–279.

[31] This is a truncated text of Paul's *Romans*.

was dimmed by external Judaism. William Penn explained that, for the Quakers, the Second Coming had already occurred when the spirit of the Quakers emerged in England.[32] One of the early Quakers, Samuel Fisher, exhibited a kind of conversion to Judaism. He went to the Netherlands in early 1657. He was the only one of the early Quakers who knew Hebrew, being an Oxford graduate. He was working on translating two of Margaret Fell's pamphlets, which urged the Jews to become Quakers. Fisher apparently met Spinoza shortly after Spinoza's ex-communication and may have worked together with him on this project. Fisher and Spinoza later independently published their biblical criticisms in which they both developed the same points about the unreliability of the manuscripts of the Bible.[33] Fisher's account appeared ten years earlier than Spinoza's. They both stressed the point that the true meaning of Scripture cannot be marks on parchment, but instead have to be spiritual beliefs or attitudes in the hearts of men.

Fisher describes attending synagogue services and interrupting them as in a Quaker meeting. When he was quieted the members told him he could come home with them after the service and discuss it. Fisher said proudly that he spent three or four hours at a time in their homes.[34] A few months later he left the Netherlands on a journey to convert the pope and the sultan. En route he apparently lived in Jewish communities in Germany and Italy. Letter from Fisher describe him spending weeks in the Jewish community in Livorno and both he and the other people there being happy with his presence. His internal Judaism must have seemed convincing for them to let him stay, since they were not allowed to have outsiders stay in the ghetto. His behavior must have been acceptable to them, so one presumes he adopted enough of external Judaism in terms of

---

[32] William Penn, *Visitation to the Jews*, in: *The Works of William Penn* (London, 1726), Vol. 2, 853.

[33] Popkin, "Samuel Fisher and Spinoza", *Philosophia*, Vol. 15 (1985), 219–236 and "Spinoza's Relations with the Quakers", *Quaker History*, Vol. 70 (1984), 14–28; Christopher Hill, *A Radical Bible Critic*, "The World Turned Upside Down" (London, 1972).

[34] Popkin, "Christian Jews and Jewish Christians in the 17th century", in: *Jewish Christians and Christian Jews*; William I. Hull, *The Rise of Quakerism in Amsterdam* (Philadelphia, 1938); See also, William Caton's letter to Margaret Fell, in the *William Caton Mss.*, London Friends House Library (London), fol. 507.

dress, eating habits, Saturday activities, etc., to get on with his hosts.[35] All of this would indicate that in some serious sense he had become a convert to Judaism.

We don't know much about what happened to him in the next couple of years, when he was supposedly trying to convert the pope and the sultan, ventures which do not seem to have succeeded. He reappears on the historical scene in England in 1659–60 as a rich man. He was accused of taking money from the Jesuits and never explained the source of his wealth. He published an enormous book detailing his Bible criticism called *The Rustik Alarm to the Rabbis*, a work of over 900 pages.[36] At the end of the edition put out by William Penn, Fisher is quoted as saying, "Is the Light in *America* then any more insufficient to lead its Followers to God, then the Light in *Europe, Asia, Africa*, the other three parts of the World. I have ever lookt upon the Light in all men (since I began to look to it in my self) as one and the self-same Light in all where it is," a universalistic view much like that of Spinoza.

It is not known if some other Quakers moved as far toward Judaism as Fisher. David Katz found some indications that in the earliest Jewish settlement in North America, at Newport, Rhode Island, that some of the members are both Jews and Quakers.[37] Since the Quakers were being persecuted by the Congregationalists, they may have found a happier and safer world within the Jewish community.

John Dury did not follow Fisher's path. Dury, at the beginning of the Puritan Revolution, was given official authorization by the Westminster assembly to reunite all the Christian churches of Europe. One of the signatories to his statement is Samuel Fisher, before he had become a Quaker. Dury spent a good deal of time trying to find a unifying creed for the wide variety of Christian churches, but he did not go beyond this to include the Jews. Dury, as indicated

---

[35] London Friends House Library Ms. Portfolio 17, fols. 72–78.

[36] Samuel Fisher, Rusticos ad Academicos, in Exercitationibus Expostulatoriis, Apologeticus quatuor. The Rustick's Alarm to the Rabbies: or, the Country Correcting the University, and Clergy, and (not without good cause) Contesting for the Truth, against the Nursing-Mothers, and their Children (London 1660), in: The Testimony of Truth Exalted (n.p. 1679), 696.

[37] David S. Katz, *Sabbath and Sectarianism in Seventeenth-Century England* (Leiden: Brill, 1988), especially chapter five, "English America: Sabbatarians, Quakers, Freemasons and Jews", 134–177.

above, played a very important role in trying to get the Jews readmitted to England. At the height of the negotiations in England,
Hartlib wrote to Dury for him to submit a statement about readmitting the Jews. This statement, which is one of the prime documents now about the readmission, was sent from Kassel and was
received in January 1656 after the negotiations had collapsed.[38] In
it, Dury gave strong and serious reasons for readmitting the Jews
but made clear they should be treated as a separate and somewhat
unequal group. He proposed adopting some of the stern measures
in effect in Kassel, such as making the Jews attend conversions,
speeches, and sermons, and to be tested on them. He proposed some
economic restrictions on Jewish business activities. Ten years later,
Dury got very excited when Peter Serrarius sent him a copy of Sabbatai Zevi's *Letter to the Amsterdam Synagogue* announcing the beginning
of a messianic age and portraying Sabbatai Zevi on his messianic
throne.[39] In subsequent letters, Dury was trying to figure out what
status Sabbatai Zevi had. Initially, he was willing to accept him as
king of the Jews, that is, a distinct ethnic group within the Ottoman
Empire. Later on, he felt that this was not sufficient, so adopted a
view like Jean de Labadie, that the messiah had been sent to the
Jews instead of the Christians because the Christians had not been
good enough.[40] None of this was accompanied by any effort to get
further involved in Jewish affairs. He apparently never found another
rabbi like Menasseh to associate with.

The document of Dury's that has led to this paper cannot be
dated. It is written in the same script as Dury's document on the
Jewish readmission. It begins with the question as to whether one
can be a true and believing follower of the Law of Moses and a
true and believing Christian. The question could apply equally well
to Jews who converted to Christianity or Christians who converted
to Judaism. Dury just considers the problem in terms of Jews converting to Christianity wanting to keep up their Jewish practices. He
then analyzes the question in terms of what happened in the first

---

[38] John Dury, *A Case of Conscience. Whether it be lawful to admit Jews into a
Christian Commonwealth?* (London, 1656).
[39] Zürich Staatsarchiv Ms. E. II. 457 e, fol. 747.
[40] Ibid., fols. 1167 and 1179–1183. See also Popkin, "The End of the Career of
a Great 17th Century Millenarian: John Dury", in: *Pietismus und Neuzeit*, Vol. 14
(Göttingen: Vandenhoeck & Ruprecht, 1988).

centuries of Christianity and what the Apostles taught on this matter. He found sufficient support for the view that Jews could keep
up their practices while becoming Christians and that this must have
been common in early Christian times. The reverse situation must
have been common. Peter and Paul had discussed whether one had
to become a Jew in order to become a Christian. It was Paul's opinion that the answer was no, and Peter's, that the answer was yes.
One, therefore, presumes that some of the converts to Christianity
in ancient times first became converts to Judaism. Paul himself proclaimed that he always kept up his Jewish practices, so a true and
believing Christian could also be a true follower of the Law of
Moses.

It would be interesting to know what had occasioned Dury's analysis of the subject. There were many quasi-Jewish groups in the
Netherlands and Western Germany. I've never come across a Christian
group of ex-Jews keeping up Judaism. When I saw the title of Dury's
paper, I had hoped it was about people like Moses Germanus, who
had started as a Jesuit in Germany and ended up a Jew in Amsterdam.
Recent research by Yosef Kaplan and Matt Goldish have found cases
of people belonging to both Jewish and Christian communities and
keeping up the practices of both. It would be interesting to find out
the prior history of such people, whether they began as Jews or as
Christians, or possibly both.

The interface between Judaism and Christianity in the mid-seventeenth century produced a wide and dynamic group of religious views
and practices. Most of the study has been on Jews becoming Christians
and Marranos returning to Judaism. Exploring the people outside
these groups who converted to Judaism may throw more light on
the dynamics of the different religious positions of the time.

Appendix

Memorandum on Conversion of the Jews, Undated, 25\4\lA, 1B, 2A, 2B, 3A, 3B, 4A: 4B blank]

[25\4\lA]
1   Quer: Whether the Law of Moses be abrogated or ceased. So as that a Jew remaining obedient to the Law of Moses and believing and obeying Christ cannot in Truth be called a Christian

Answ: We are to Consider of whom the question is Namely of a Jew observing the Law of Moses
2   what of him is required Namely whether he so remaining obedient to the Law of Moses and withall believing in and obeying Christ Can in truth be Called a Christian
Concerning the first we are to note by the by that a Jew cannot observe the whole Law of Moses which Commended somthings to be only don in the temple as the Sacrifises which cannot now be performed the temple being destroyed, also that all the males were [blank] a yeare to appeare at Jerusalem before which now Cannot be performed by many who are led Captiue in fare remote Countryes from Iudea, 21y Ierusalem is in the power of the strangers that they perform those things required by the Law of them at their appearance there[?] Yet som things there are which may not withstanding be by them performed as the Circumcision and abstinence from forbidden meates and the like of these things then is the question whether the observance of them is Consistant with Christianity
If they are not Consistant with Christianity then must it be 1 in their difference of Nature the one forbidding what the other Commandeth or 21y Commanding the performance in that manner as not leauing time or convenience for the performance of the others Commands
which two Contrarietyes are not found in these two Commands Compared together [25\4\1B]
notwithstanding their agreement as before if the Law of moses haue a time limited from God its author beyond which it shall not be obliging then when that time is Com it seaceth[?] or 21y if a profet or one sent from God with particular order to annull the

same appeare his declaration causeth the same to cease + (left margin: + the same also if God in any way declare his will to be such] but without these it remaineth in force

But 1 we find no such limitation from God at his giuinq the Law by the hand of moses nor at any time after neither 21y haue either Christ or any of his apostles declared ought to that effect As for our Sauior Christ liuing and Conversing with the Iewes who then were such greate admirers of moses Law, if he had intended aught Concerning the abolition of the said Law he would probably haue either spoken plaine to that effect or at least haue hinted soinwhat of that unto them, as preparatory, that at the effecting thereof they might not think it strange, as he did of his sufferings to Com. but on the Contrary we find math[ewl 5: 17: 18:29.20 Our sauior Expressing in the[se words?] Think not that I am com to destroy the Law or the profets I am not com to destroy but to fullfill (th[ereforel to observe them and be obedient thereto) for Verily I say unto you till heauen and earth passe one Iot or one tithe shall in no wite passe from the Law till all be fullfilled, whosoever therefore shall breake one of these least Commandments and shall teach men so he shall be Called the least in the kingdom of heauen but whosoever shall doe and teach them the same shall be Called greate in the kingdom of heauen for I say unto you except your righteosnes exceed the righteousnes of the scribes and farizees ye shall in no wise enter into the kingdom of heauen [25\4\2AI]

3   where obserue that by our sauiors words the Iewes or
     som of them thought he had Com to alter the Lawes by putting other in their place which he declareth to be so far from doing that he rather maintaineth and defendeth the Law and the enIunction of obedience thereto but say som he saith he Came to fulfill the Law and profets that is to accomplish by his sufferings and death what the Law and profets had foretould and prefigured of him which being fulfilled the Law was to cease but that his meaning was likewise that hee came actiuely to be obedient to the Law and intended not the abrogation thereof appeareth from the 20 verse where he sayeth whosoeuer shall breake any of these least Commandments and shall teach men so shall be Called least in the kingdom of heauen in which words he giueth not any one at any time leaue to doe the same, but if any object Our sauior intended here

only the duration of the morall but not of the Ceremoniall Commands I answ[erl this distinction is not extent in our sauiors words and therefore no safe Conclusion.

But haue not the Apostles as knowing the will of our sauior declared such a Cessation to be after our saviors <death> to wit som time after when the Iewes by their duration for a time had bin gained to Christianity Let us to that effect examin the apostles writings, and preparatory thereto [word deleted] is to be Considered that at Antioch a question was raised by som Christian of the Iewes and of the sect of the farisees whether it was not necessary that the Christians of the heathen should likewise be Circumcised and obserue the Law of moses which question being brought to Ierusalem [25\4\2B] was by the apostles decided in the negatiue which decision the apostle <Paul was> one who was employed in the message and brought the answer bak still Constantly maintained to the Gentiles to whom he was cheifly sent as himself witnesseth and so Gall[atians] 5.2 preaching unto the Gallatians who were Christians of the Gentiles and among whom this question was rased he saith if you be Circumsized Christ shall profit you nothing, for in that appeared theire zeale more for the Law then for Christ.

And where paul saith to the romans c[hapterl 3.20 none shall be Iustified by the workes of the Lawes he speaketh of the Iewes but his drift is there to declare that even the Iewes by the workes of the Law could not be Iustified without Christ for it was the effect of his death was the ground of saluation to all that were saued yea even of those Iewes who haply before his Coming had but litle or no knowledge of him only were Iealous of the Law and in none of pauls writings or of any of the other apostles doe we find any exhortation to the Iewes upon their Conversion to Christianity to leaue the Iewish rites but the Contrary as hereafter

But lastly let us obserue the apostles practise in this Case and first their decision of the Question at Ierusalem St Iames propounding that which they Concluded on this/[left margin: Act 15:191 that we trouble not them which from among the Gentiles are turned to God but that we write unto them that they abstain etc. for moses hath of ould time in every Citty them that preach him being read in the synagogues every sabbath day [25\4\3A]

5   in which words are to be noted the distinction of those which of
    the Gentiles are turned unto the Lord and of those of the Iewes

turned unto the Lord so that this decision leaueth the Iewes untouched who are tacitly referred to the Law read in in the synagogue every Sabbath day and in the following chapter after this decision on Ierusalem [left margin: Act 16.31 Paul Circumciseth timothy for the Iewes with whom he Conversed at Lystre and Iconium which would haue bin opposite to his <own> doctr[ine] Gall[atians] 5.2 if that his doctrin had likewise reached[?] the Iewes turned Christians and further afterward chap[ter] 21.20 Paul being Com to Ierusalum to Cleare himself of a false report raised of him that he had taught the Iewes turning to christian-ity that they should not circumcize their children nor teach accord-ing to the Customes of the Law and according to the advice of the apostle Iames he purifieth himself according to the Law of moses which he ought not to haue don if as before his doctrine to the Gallatians had likewise related to the Iewes.

But that which will further giue light unto the apostles practise is to observe that for the better effecting their ends they diuided them-selfes in two generall diuisions som taking the Charge of Converting of the Gentiles others of the Iewes cheifly and 21y they diuide them selfes again in severall provinces and Countreyes on going one way others another way. for the first devision we haue pauls word Gall[atians] 2.7 but Contrarywise when they saw that the Gospel of the uncircumcision was Committed unto me as the Gospel of the Circumcision was unto Peter, it is true st peter said acts 15.7 men and bretheren yea kn[ow page curled] [25\4\3B]

6 how that a good while ago God made choice among us that the Gentiles by my mouth should heare the word of the Gospel, but in this speach he relateth to his sermon made to Cornelius unto which God for that time Called him, but the apostle paul relateth th7 to that let or designement which among the apostles was afterwards fallen on peter and paul distinct as further appeareth Gall(atians] 2.8.9 for he that wrought effectually in peter to the apostleship of the Circumcision the same was mighty in me towards the Gentiles and when Iames Cefas amd Iohn who seemed to be pillars per-ceiued the Grace that was giuen unto me they gaue to me and barn-abas the right hand of fellowship that we should goe unto the heathen and they unto the Circumcision [left margin: as the Church str . . . [?] mention quoted by H Hammond in his treatise of chisnno[?]]

and accordingly St paul and St peter, being together at antioch they
erected two Churches of Christians. St peter of the Iewes and st
paull of the Gentiles hauing likewise at the same time each their
distinct bishops, as Euodius and Ignatius it was upon this account
that st paul reprehended st peter at Antioch [left margin: ch[apter?]:
2.12.13.14] that he being a Iewes and apostle of the Iewes and who
taught the Iewes the observance of moses Law, and yet practised
the Contrary also at Rome the ancient writers mention that st peter
and st paul were there and Constituted each their bishop as Linus
the bishop of the Gentiles constituted by st paull and Clemens[?] of
the Iewish Christians by st peter at efesus likewise st Iosenthef?]
apostle and bishop of the Iewes and timotyh of the Gentiles were
[word deleted] at the same time ruling [25\4\4A]

6   but upon what ground or reason both Iewes and Gentile Christians
    <afterwards> united I find not, only from hence[?] I conclude
    that it being practised by the aposteles namely the distinction of
    Iewes and Gentile Christians it was Lawfull then and not by them
    being forbidden to future ages it may be now also lawfull

object But som object that this Lawfullmes was only for a time untill
the Iewish Christians should be Com in and then was the Law of
moses to Cease
   answ: but this reason we find not in scripture neither the limitation of time how long it should be admitted and when it should
Cease neither 21y are all the Iewes yet Com in nor probably so
many as may yet Com in
   Wherefore I conclude upon what I haue before said that the Law
of moses is not yet abrogated or ceased, but that a Iew beleeving
on Christ may remain a Iew[?] and may also in Truth be Called
a Christian and if I Conclude rightly I could wish that this might
be publickly taught and maintayned as a meanes to draw the uncon-
verted Iewes to Christ who remain to sealous for the Law of moses
for probabely this being thus taught it might moue them more seriously to Consider of our sauior who was so far from being an Enemy
to their Law that hee was a Zealous performer and maintainer thereof
and if this be a truth and so necessary a truth how blameworthy
shall we be in suppressing thereof and hereby so much as in us
lyueth hinder their Conversion

"ICH WILL DICH NACH HOLLAND SCHICKEN . . .": AMSTERDAM AND THE REVERSION TO JUDAISM OF GERMAN JEWISH CONVERTS

Elisheva Carlebach

Amsterdam has long been celebrated in Jewish historiography as the model center for the return of Iberian Marranos to full-fledged and open Judaism. A significant body of scholarly work in recent decades analyzes the formal rituals, psychological battles, and educational efforts undertaken by the young community to integrate newcomers out of Catholic Iberia into a living Jewish tradition.[1] The Amsterdam Sephardic community's exemplary role in the rejudaization of marranos, along with its bitter confrontation with non-conformists such as Uriel da Costa and Barukh Spinoza have justifiably formed a major narrative strand in the historiography of early-modern Jewish Amsterdam. The reversion of baptized German Jews to Judaism, and the role of Amsterdam in providing a haven for these returnees, forms a neglected but no less compelling story.

Regretful converts who had been baptized in early-modern German lands and wished to reverse their deed and escape its consequences could not publicize their plights nor reveal their plans, even to their closest associates. In the eyes of both church and state, Catholic or Protestant, baptism effected an indelible change of status. Any attempt

---

Research for this article was supported in part by a grant from the PSC/CUNY Research Award Program (#27). I completed the article in the magnificent surroundings of the Cullman Center for Scholars and Writers at the New York Public Library.
[1] On the re-judaization of former marranos and the ramifications of marranism in Amsterdam, see Yosef Hayim Yerushalmi, *From Spanish Court to Italian Ghetto: Isaac Cardoso: A Study in Seventeenth-century Marranism and Jewish Apologetics* (New York, 1971); idem, "Marranos Returning to Judaism in the Seventeenth Century: Their Jewish Knowledge and Psychological Readiness," (in Hebrew) *Proceedings of the Fifth World Congress of Jewish Studies*, 1969 (Jerusalem, 1972), 2:201–209; Yosef Kaplan, *From Christianity to Judaism: Isaac Orobio de Castro* (Oxford, 1989); Miriam Bodian, *Hebrews of the Portuguese Nation: Conversos and Community in Early Modern Amsterdam* (Bloomington, 1997).

to deny or reverse it constituted a blasphemous transgression for which the punishment, through the late seventeenth century and even later, could still be a terrible death. For many of these regretful converts, Amsterdam emerged as a beacon, a refuge from harrassment for religious boundary crossers. While there are no records for the number of Jews who had converted to Christianity in German lands and then came to Amsterdam to revert, anecdotal and literary evidence, taken in the aggregate, suffices to show that this pattern which began in the mid-seventeenth century, became more significant and endured through the eighteenth century. Amsterdam provided a safety net for those who later regretted an overly hasty decision or received a less than warm welcome from Christians.

Undermining conversion

The earliest report I have found of Amsterdam as a destination for German Jewish converts dates to 1643, when two Jews who converted to Christianity in Cologne, bastion of Dominican zeal, subsequently went to Holland where they reverted to Judaism.[2] Most of the anecdotal data dates from the late seventeenth or the eighteenth centuries. The German institutes founded in the late seventeenth century by Esdras Edzard in Hamburg and in the first decades of the eighteenth by Heinrich Callenberg in Halle devoted exceptional resources, spiritual and material, to the conversion of (mostly German) Jews. Each of their successful conversions was duly noted and hailed as another triumph. German society proferred many inducements to effect Jewish conversion, although once converted, many were disappointed with the cold reception and lingering suspicion of their motives.

A shadow statistic hides behind the record of conversions established by these proselytizing institutes. As the number of converts out of Judaism rose with more Jews seeking to disencumber themselves from the burdens of their Jewishness, the number of conver-

---

[2] Joseph Klersch, *Volkstum und Volksleben in Köln: Ein Beitrag zur historischen Soziologie der Stadt* (Köln, 1965–68) =Beiträge zur kölnischen Geschichte, Sprache, Eigenart; Bd. 43–Bd. 1), 211ff.; Carl Brisch, *Geschichte der Juden in Cöln und Umgebung, aus aeltester Zeit bis auf die Gegenwart* (Muelheim am Rhein, 1879–82; repr. Cologne, 1968), 2:133, ff.

sions back to Judaism rose quietly alongside them. According to
reports of both the converts and their missionaries, a significant number of the converts made their way to Amsterdam to return to
Judaism. One Jew told Heinrich Callenberg that he was wasting his
time dealing with converts from Judaism "as there are currently in
Amsterdam some two hundred Jews who had been baptised, and
have returned to Judaism there."[3] Caspar Joseph Friedenheim, a former Jew who converted c. 1760, complained that the great freedom
to practice their religion that some Christian princes bestowed as a
misguided sign of piety constituted one of main obstacles to the mass
conversion of Jews. He cited as a special example the freedom granted
to Jews by the "Holländern," the Dutch. "Yes, they even boast that
it is permitted to circumcize Christians there and to educate them
to become Jews."[4] "While to be sure it is difficult to understand how
it is even possible for a Christian to become a Jew, and so long as
I was a Jew, I never encountered such a Jew who had descended
from Christians, it is nevertheless well known that many new converts who revert back to their Jewish error seek their freedom in
Amsterdam."[5] To those formerly baptized Jews he addressed a proselytizing tract in the hope of stimulating debate that would lead to
discussion and missionary success.[6] When Christian Salomon Duitsch
was still a Jew contemplating conversion, he recalled that an instance
of reversion to Judaism in Amsterdam temporarily deterred him.
During a prolonged exchange with a Christian fellow traveller from
Switzerland, the Christian urged him to emulate the example of an
earlier convert: "Become like R. Jechiel Hirschlein who was chris-
tened in Zurich in 1746." Duitsch, then still a Jew, replied, "But he

---

[3] Azriel Shohat, *Im hilufei tekuphot: reshit ha-Haskalah be-Yahadut Germanyah* (Jerusalem,
1960), 193 and note 204.

[4] C.J. Friedenheim, *Yehudi me-ba-Hutz: das ist der äusserliche Jud in Ansehung ihres der-
maligen vermeintlichen Gottesdienstes* (Wirzburg, 1785), 120: "Ja, sie rühmen sich so gar,
dass ihnen dort erlaubt sey, die Christen zu beschneiden und Juden aus ihnen zu
bilden."

[5] Friedenheim, *Yehudi me-ba-Hutz*, 120–121: "Ob es mir zwar hart eingeht, wie
es möglich sey, dass ein Christ ein Jude werde, und mir auch so lange ich bin Jude
war, kein solcher Jude, der von Christen abstammte, unter die Augen gekommen
ist; so ist doch das gewiss, dass viele neugetaufte, die sich wieder zu ihrem judi-
schen Irrthume wenden, **alle ihre Freyheit zu Amsterdam suchen.**"

[6] Friedenheim, *Yehudi me-ba-Hutz*, 113: "Ich habe, auch meine lieben Juden, bey
der zu Amsterdam aufgestellten Preisfrage eine kleine Abhandlung eingeschickt, die
ich zum allgemeinen Bessten Herzen will."

is an imposter. He has reverted to Judaism in Amsterdam where I've seen him begging for alms. Now he's dead and buried there."[7] Convert Johann Conrad Leonhard summed up a widespread impression when he noted: "Here in this land, Jews don't dare to convert others; . . . in Holland however, where almost all religions have the highest degree of freedom, there they often dare, although only clandestinely, to accept proselytes."[8]

The jurist Beck cites a responsum from the faculty at Wittenberg, from 1727, concerning Christian Glaubtreu, the former Jew Michael David. This convert apparently travelled to Holland and England after his conversion in 1724, and ultimately reverted to Judaism, returning to Mannheim where he acquired a pair of tefillin, and served in Reinganheim as a Jewish schoolteacher.[9] Schudt reported on a Jew, Conrad Jacob Hang, who was baptised in Frankfurt; he later reverted in Amsterdam.[10]

Very little information remains on which Ashkenazic Jews actively welcomed new or reverting Jews in Amsterdam. It remainss unclear whether Ashkenazic Jews in Amsterdam ever organized sufficiently to care for all the refugees from baptism who sought their aid. When the wife of convert Mordechai Shemaya of Fürth sought refuge with her two small children in Amsterdam after her husband converted in Nuremberg in 1701, the overburdened community in Amsterdam could not offer her the support she needed. Eventually she returned to Fürth with her infant son, leaving her daughter in hiding with a Jewish family in a small village. The converted husband immediately notified the local magistrate who ordered the child "reclaimed" for the Christian father. The father had his son immediately baptized to Christianity, in a pattern repeated many times in cases where one parent converted out of Judaism.[11] Christian Salomon Duitsch recalled

---

[7] Christiaan Salomon Duitsch, *De wonderlyke leidinge Gods: omtrent eenen blinden leidsman der blinden* . . . (Amsterdam, 1768), 69.

[8] Johann Conrad Georg Abraham Gottfried Friedrich Leonhard, *Erweiss, dass die Rabbinen schnurstracks wider das Mosaische Gesez lehren, aus den Kirchen=Gesez=Büchern der heutigen Juden geführt, und mit Erzaehlung seiner eigenen Bekehrungs=Geschichte in einem Gespräch vorgetragen* (Nürnberg, 1781), 146.

[9] Shohat, *Im hilufe tekufot*, 192.

[10] Shohat, *Im hilufe tekufot*, 184–185.

[11] Johannes Friedrich Alexander de le Roi, *Die Evangelische Christenheit und die Juden unter dem Gesichtspunkte der Mission* (Karlsruhe and Leipzig, 1884) 1:406. For further discussion of the practice of removing children from the custody of the non-baptized

that he stayed in the home of Samuel Jacob Hanau in Arnheim sometime before his conversion. The family attempted to dissuade him from leaving the Jewish faith. They appear to have been running an "underground railroad" for educating converts to Judaism, as Duitsch met a woman, Rebecca, in their home "who turned in Amsterdam to the Jewish religion."[12]

The existence of a place where converts to Christianity could revert freely to Judaism encouraged Jews in German lands to invest great effort to prevent catechumens from going through with baptism and to persuade converts to revert to their ancestral faith. While Jewish communities throughout the medieval period would accept those converts who reverted to Judaism of their own will often at the risk of great danger, in the seventeenth and eighteenth centuries there were more reports of active efforts to detain potential converts and prevent conversions.[13] Shortly after Gottfried Selig, then a youth who had recently converted to Christianity, came to visit his Jewish father, his father proposed that the baptism be undone and his life "made good again." The specifics of his proposal: "I will send you to Holland, and as soon as you arrive there I will send six-thousand thaler, which will put you in a position to earn something, and eventually find a good marriage partner."[14] Other reports concerning converts confirm a similar pattern. In 1715, on the verge of his conversion to Christianity in Frankfurt, Leib Alexander, son in law of R. David Grünhut, suddenly ended up in Amsterdam with his plans changed.[15] When convert Johann Zacharias Heilwort, formerly Amsel Isaacs zum Hinter-Hecht of Frankfurt am Main, began fomenting trouble among his former co-religionists in Frankfurt, in 1708, they spirited him to Amsterdam in the hope that he would return to Judaism, although their efforts to change his mind ultimately proved

---

parent, see my *Divided Souls: Converts from Judaism in Germany, 1500–1750* (New Haven and London, 2001), 149–156.

[12] Duitsch, "De wonderlyke", 73.

[13] On efforts to prevent baptisms, see the cases cited in Shohat, *Im hilufei tekufot*, 176–181. Cf. the case of early modern Poland in Edward Fram, "Perception and Reception of Repentant Apostates in Medieval Ashkenaz and Pre-Modern Poland," *AJS Review* 21:2 (1996), 319–339.

[14] Johannes Graf, ed. *Judaeus conversus: christlich-jüdische Konvertitenautobiographien des 18. Jahrhunderts* with Michael Schmidt and Elisabeth Emter (Frankfurt am Main; New York, 1997), 295.

[15] Johann Jakob Schudt, *Jüdischer Merckwürdigkeiten* (Frankfurt and Leipzig, 1714–18), Vol. 4, part 6, chapter 29, par. 8.

unavailing.[16] Eighteenth century chronicler Andreas Würfel recorded the baptism of a "Portuguese" Jew, Levi de Pomis, related to the renowned Italian Jewish physician David de Pomis, who came to Nürnberg from Amsterdam where he converted and took the name Christian de Pomis. He was sent to Altdorf to complete his education in Hebrew and rabbinics. He gave a sermon comparing the paschal lamb of the Old Testament to that of the New, but within a month of its publication in Altdorf, reported Würfel, he had "ridden away on a borrowed horse."[17] If he had come from Amsterdam, he could presumably have returned there. One Christian writer expressed relief that insincere converts had a place to expose their true nature: "Many convert hoping to gain certain advantages, and if these do not materialize, they hasten to Amsterdam." The author bemoaned the many such converts "neither Jew nor Christian," who remained nominally Christian in German lands, betraying the trusting people and the Christian religion.[18]

Some Jews took advantage of the freedom by subverting Christian baptism repeatedly for profit. Isaac Joseph of Paderborn converted to Christianity in Wittenberg, taking the name Christian Leib. He later reverted to Judaism in Amsterdam. He returned to German lands and pretended to be a Jew seeking conversion to Christianity. When his history was uncovered, Paderborn was imprisoned, made to confess his heretical deviation from the church, and forced to reconcile with it in a penitential ceremony. The penitential sermon, (Buss-Predigt) preached at the ceremony by Johann Helwig Engerer on 13 January 1732, chastised him for having abandoned Christianity in Amsterdam after his conversion, and forced him publicly to

---

[16] Schudt, *Jüdischer Merckwürdigkeiten*, Vol. 4, part 6, chapter 29, par. 22. Martinus Difenbach, *Judaeus Conversus* (Frankfurt a.M., 1709), published the baptismal sermon which he preached for Heilwort. Heilwort's father had apparently been converted to Christianity by Difenbach while incarcerated for theft. "Zu Endt findet sich: Die Nachricht wegen der vor 5 Jahren alhier geschehenen Tauffe/Amsel Isaacs zum Hinter-Hecht/hiesigen sesshafften Judens Sohns/nachmahls Johann Zacharias Heylwart genanndt/und der mit ihm seithero vorgefallenen bedencklichen Begebenheit/ Mit Zweyen dahin gehörigen Juden-Predigten/und behörigem vollständigem Register."

[17] Andreä Würfel, *Historische Nachrichten von der Juden-Gemeinde welche ehehin in der Reichstadt Nürnberg angericht gewesen aber Ao 1499 ausgeschaffet worden* (Nürnberg, 1755), 111b. (Page numbers 111–112 are erroneously paginated twice; this is the second set.)

[18] Anon., "Der getaufte Jude: weder Jude noch Christ" (Vienna, 1781). I thank Michael Silber for bringing this treatise to my attention.

renounce his relapse into Judaism.[19] The sermon contains many details of a reversion to Judaism ceremony in Amsterdam, including an account of a counter-baptism. The convert was made to confess the details of the ceremony of reversion to Judaism in Amsterdam:

> You were made to undergo a very severe penitence in Amsterdam for your unfortunate backsliding to Judaism, with bathing, immersion, fasts, lying down on the threshold of the synagogue floor, and lashes with a leather strap. . . . You acknowledged in writing and orally while you were in prison, that for the immersion in the *mikva*, the hair on your head was shaved and your finger and toenails were clipped (which custom may have its origin in Numbers 21:12).[20]
>
> According to your understanding, the rabbi in Amsterdam gave you the *viddui* prayer to say, a prayer which contains acknowledgement of general and specific sins, to say daily. You, however, did not understand it. According to your own confession, you endured the lashing twice daily under the entrance to the synagogue, while others stepped over you, and some spat on you.[21]

Most strikingly, the confessor had the multiple convert admit, "according to his own confession, that the rabbi in the Portuguese

---

[19] Johann Helwig Engerer, "Die verlohrnen Kinder offentlichen Kirchen Buss Eines zu Wittenberg getaufften=aber wieder abgefallenen Juden, namens Christian Leib von Paderborn. So die Heil. Tauffe aufs neue betrügerischer Weise gesucht, Der Christlichen Gemeinde in der Hoch=Fürstl. Brandenburgischen Haupt Stadt Schwabach unter Gottlichen Beystand." 13 Jan., 1732. For the charge that the convert pretended to seek instruction in Christian teaching toward baptism, deceitfully and for pecuniary motive, without acknowledging the earlier baptism, see p. 4. Engerer claimed that this was first such reconciliation in the history of Schwabach, and, he hoped, the last. Engerer also published the work of a "righteous" convert to Christianity, Paul Ernst Christfels, *Geschpräch in dem Reiche der Todten über die Bibel und Talmud, zwischen dem seeligen Herrn Doctor Luther und dem berühmtn jüdischen Ausleger namens Raschi* (Schwabach, 1737).

[20] Engerer, "Die verlohrnen Kinder" 19: "Man hat dir eine weit schwere Busse in Amsterdam bey deinem unglücklichen Ruckfall zum Judenthum mit Baden, Untertauchen, Fasten, Niederlegen unter die Thür=Schwelle der Synagoge mit Peitschen der ledernen Riemen u. als diese Unsere ist, aufgelegt . . . Du hast mir mehr als einmahl mündlich und schrifftlich im Gefängnuss bekannt, es sey dir zu Amsterdam die Mikva, das ist, das Untertauchen des Wassers, alle Tag dreymal aufgelegt, die Haare am Kopff abgeschoren, die Nägel an Händen und Füssen abgeschnitten worden (welcher Gebrauch ans 5.B. Mos. XXI, 12, mag seinen Ursprung haben)."

[21] Engerer, "Die verlohrnen Kinder" 20: "Nach deinem eigenen Geständnuss hat dir der Rabbiner zu Amsterdam eine Vidde oder Viddui, das ist, ein Gebet, sein allgemeines und besonderes Sünden Bekänntnuss in sich hält, vorgelegt, zu beten täglich **das du aber nicht verstanden**. Nach deinem eigenen Bekänntnuss hast du dich täglich zweymal zur Straffe unter die Thür der Juden=Schul legen müssen, dass Andere über dich getretten, über dich theils ausgespeyet."

synagogue asked you before the 'Almemor,' "Have you sinned by denying the Unity, the One God? By taking upon yourself belief in the 'Tole,' the hanged one?" Engerer's sermon took every opportunity to contrast the synagogue's harsh process of reconciliation, to that of the church which demands only inward repentance and removal of all evil and deceitfulness. Although the convert was not deserving of any leniency, the church's requirements for reconciliation would be sweeter than the synagogue's had been.[22]

If it could be confirmed by additional sources, and is not merely a projection of the Christian imagination, this description would constitute a unique and important source for the early eighteenth century. Unfortunately, Engerer's sermon contains references to admissions extracted under duress.[23] The local Prince who took the Jewish deceit as a personal affront ordered the entire ceremony.[24] Because the descriptions may have been obtained using torture, we must cast their veracity into doubt. Although some of the details, including the public nature of such a ceremony, and its occuring in the Portuguese synagogue (these seem to be borrowed from the reconciliation rites of Jewish heretics such as Acosta) are questionable, the existence of some form of ceremonial dechristianization for reverting Jews within the Ashkenazic world is attested in several places.[25]

The Yiddish translation of the moral guidebook *Orhot Tsadikim*, published decades before the Hebrew text as *Sefer Middos*, contains a prescription for the renunciation of baptism, if not a formal cer-

---

[22] This testimony raises many questions. It is unclear whether the convert was originally descended from Ashkenazic or Sephardic stock. The reversion to Judaism recounted here apparently took place within the Sephardic synagogue of Amsterdam, as the testimony refers to a Portuguese rabbi and synagogue. The elaborate penitential ceremonial required of him sounds similar to the one described in the 'autobiography' of Uriel Acosta.

[23] Engerer, "Die verlohrnen Kinder", 19: "mündlich und schrifftlich **im Gefängnuss** bekannt . . ." How this was extracted from him in prison is left to our imagination, and some or all of details may well have been supplied to him by his interrogators.

[24] Engerer, "Die verlohrnen Kinder", 4, recounts that the penitent appeared before the court, "auf Befehl unserer Hohen Landes=Obrigkeit"; the first crime recounted after the obvious theological one was the deceit of "unsere Gnädigste Hohe=Landes Obrigkeit." Engerer mentions that the Prince had given an explicit order for this ceremony: "auf ergangenen ausdrücklichen Hoch Furstlichen=Befehl," 20.

[25] A comprehensive discussion of a medieval testimony to this rite can be found in Yosef Hayim Yerushalmi, "The Inquisition and the Jews of France in the time of Bernard Gui," *Harvard Theological Review*, 63 (1970), 363–68.

emony. "If someone is an apostate and wishes to repent, he must take off his good clothes and wear bad clothes. He should cry and feel sorrow for his sins, and should torment himself all the days of his life and walk humbly among all men. He should admit his sins twice daily, and he should refrain from eating meat and drinking wine. . . . He should not bathe. He should not attend any dance or go to '*Breilaf*'. Only when the Seven Blessings are recited may he listen. He should distance himself from all false religions (*avoda zoros*) and from those that serve them. He should not speak with priests or monks (*komrim un galochim*) about matters of faith. . . . Once he has repented, he should immerse himself and must suffer great torment to counter the great sins: That he denied the Living Eternal God, may He be Blessed, and violated sabbaths and holidays; that he slept with gentile women and ate all manner of food and drink."[26]

Anti-Christian Polemic in Ashkenazic Amsterdam

Amsterdam's publishers began publishing Yiddish refutations of Christianity in the late seventeenth century, and there is ample evidence that they were not all intended for export. *Bukh der Far Zaykhnung*, an anonymous compendium of Biblical verses intended to serve as a handbook to refute Christian polemicists, was published in 1696.[27] The book is addressed to "learned and common folk, even women will be able to read it and enjoy it." The introduction explains that: "All kinds of 'religious' come to dispute and question with Jews, and most of them do not know how to respond. Therefore, I took these consolations out of Torah, Prophets, and Scriptures, so that none should be able to come against them. This little book uses the same prooftexts as the "aven gilyon" [Evangelion]. . . . We show that everything relates to the redemption." The book consists of Biblical prooftexts translated into Yiddish. The verses from the Hebrew Bible demonstrate the superiority of Israel as God's beloved people and His promises never to reject them. Verses from the Christian Bible relate to the humanity of Jesus and his inability to bring true redemption. Isaac Troki's classical anti-Christian polemic *Hizzuk Emunah* was

---

[26] *Sefer Middos* (Isny, 1542), 89b.
[27] *Bukh der far zaykhnung* (Amsterdam, 1696).

translated into Yiddish, and published in Amsterdam in 1717, while Solomon Zvi Aufhausen's *Jüdischer Theriak* was completely re-edited and reprinted in Amsterdam, in 1737. It is clear both from the resources invested into making the book accessible, as well as its format, that it was addressing a live concern. The title page anounced that the book would bring joy to the disputationists and happiness to the polemicists. "For I have seen the misery of my people oppressed in exile, scattered in the villages and suffering persecution, and their spirit weary . . . from the troubles brought on by converts who open their mouths . . . making mountains out of molehills. . . . Most of the people do not know how to reply to the mockery of the scoffers and those who have abandoned God and his Torah. However, for the most part, the apostates do not have good fortune smiling on them, and their path is foolish and not smooth."[28] Did the Yiddish polemics reach their intended audience? One German- Jewish convert to Christianity, Ernst Friedrich Anton Augusti recalled that the text which he called "Buche der Verzeichnisse" along with other similar works were used by his converter, Reinhard, to remind him of his earlier anti-Christian state of mind. He characterized the book as "containing refutation and mockery of the New Testament with sources and prooftexts rendered to make them useful for lay persons, to put into the hands of even the common Jew weapons against the Christian teachings."[29] As Augusti struggled with his Jewish identity during his pre-conversion crisis, this exemplar of a popular Jewish polemic printed in Amsterdam made its way into his hands in German lands.

---

[28] Solomon Zvi Aufhausen, *Tsri ha-yehudim ha-niqra sefer nizzahon*. Yiddish transl. Sussman ben Isaac Roedelsheim (Amsterdam, 1737), intro. This work was first published in Hanau, 1615 as a response to the anti-Jewish book of convert Samuel Friedrich Brenz. It was republished in 1680 by Christian Hebraist Johannes Wülfer.

[29] *Nachrichten von dem Leben, Schicksalen und Bekehrung Friedrich Albrecht Augusti eines vormaligen jüdischen Rabbi* . . . (Gotha, 1783), 62: "welche Einwürfe und Spöttereyen gegen das neue Testament in sich hält Erläuterungen und Zusätze gemacht hatte, um es für einem jeden recht brauchbar zu machen, und auch dem gemeinen Juden Pfeile gegen die Christliche Lehre in die Hände zu geben. Reinhard [his converter] der diese Schrift, **nebst andern Papieren dieser Art**, zu sich nahm, hat sie jederzeit als ein Denkmal seiner vorigen Gesinnungen abgehalten." [My emphasis]

Gentile conversions to Judaism in Amsterdam

Benedictus Sperling was a young man from a Lutheran family of Hamburg who left for Amsterdam where he converted to Judaism. Two fragments of his story survive, letters to his mother from 1682, which allow us a very partial glimpse of his motives and the effects of his deed. Primarily moved by powerful apocalyptic and spiritual yearning, Sperling, now called Israel Benedeti, made it clear that he still loved his family but feared their resentment and retribution. "I beg you, mother, to respond by the next post . . . Please know that I am not the first Christian who has turned Jew. Nor shall I be the last. . . . I have written five letters to my brother, but not one has been answered."[30] Benedeti wrote that he had an additional spur to conversion to Judaism: "I have recently discovered that I am myself descended from the Jewish race, as are my brother and sister who have sprung with me from the same father. . . . My father left a document written in his own hand, as a bequest and declaration to his children, to make known that my father's ancestors in order to save their lives during the ill fortunes of war, became Christians." While nothing else is known about this convert, he left one additional tantalizing trace. He asked that his mail be addressed in care of Rabbi Chaim Lubliner, on the Eulenborg in Amsterdam, a sign that he had been taken into the care of an Ashkenazic rabbi and perhaps belonged to a circle of converts like himself.[31] An eighteenth-century Polish man of noble descent who came to Berlin to find support in his quest to convert to Judaism, hoped to collect his fare in order to proceed to Amsterdam and "formally join the Jewish people through circumcision there."[32] Moses ben Avraham Avinu, a convert to Judaism from Moravia in the late seventeenth century, travelled to Berlin, Dessau, Frankfurt a.d. Oder, and Halle, ultimately settling in Amsterdam, where he worked as a printer. The printing houses themselves became spaces where Jews and converts worked side by side. Employment as a proofreader or typesetter often provided the necessary incentive for the hesitant convert to revert.

---

[30] Gerald Strauss, "A Seventeenth-Century Conversion to Judaism: Two Letters from Benedictus Sperling to his Mother, 1682," *Jewish Social Studies*, 36 (1974), 170.

[31] Strauss, "A Seventeenth-Century Conversion", 170, 171.

[32] Graf, ed. *Judaeus Conversus*, 343, from "Johann Friedrich Heinrich Seligs eigne Lebensbeschreibung."

Amsterdam's reputation as a haven for converts from Christianity grew apace.

The Mahamad of London, for example, refused to sanction conversions to Judaism because it believed that such conversions traduced the terms on which they were admitted into England. Those terms included an agreement not to proselytize. English Christians, particularly women, who wanted to marry English Sephardim in London were told to travel to Amsterdam for their conversion.[33] There, they would find an openly anti-Christian polemical strain unparalleled anywhere in Christian Europe. Sephardic rabbis and laymen wrote scathing polemics against the Christian religion intended for marrano or former-marrano audiences. Preachers within the Sephardic community of Amsterdam often referred to the Christianity left behind by their congregants in terms which stressed its inferiority to Judaism. Saul Levi Morteira, for instance, not only wrote anti-Christian polemics but inserted pointed anti-Christian barbs into his public weekly sermons, even devoting some sermons entirely to refutation of Christian claims against Judaism.[34]

Christian Hebraist Johann Andreas Eisenmenger who stayed in Amsterdam during 1681, engaged in polemical discussions with David Lida, Sephardic rabbi of the Ashkenazic congregation. Eisenmenger was infuriated when Lida cited Horowitz' *Shne luhot ha-berit* to demonstrate that Samael, king of the devils, was the heavenly representative of the Christians. He devoted the only diagram drawings in his immense tomes to the demonstration by Lida and his own refuta-

---

[33] Todd Endelman, *The Jews of Georgian England 1714–1830: Tradition and Change in a Liberal Society* (Phila., 1979), 145.

[34] On Morteira's anti-Christian tract, see Yosef Kaplan, "R. Shaul ha-levi Morteira ve-hibburo *Ta'anot ve-hasagot neged ha-dat ha-nozrit*," *Mehkarim al toledot yahadut Holland* (1975), 1:9–31. As noted by Marc Saperstein, *Jewish Preaching 1200–1800: An Anthology* (New Haven and London, 1989), 270, n. 3, two of the sermons published in Morteira's *Give'at Shaul* (Amsterdam, 1645), on pericopes Va-etchanan and Nizzavim, address Christianity overtly, and the one on Balak also contained anti-Christian polemical passages. The two omitted sermons have recently been printed in the back of a facsimile edition of the Warsaw, 1912 edition, Brooklyn, 1991. See also the anti-Christian barb in Morteira's sermon cited in Saperstein, "Your Voice Like a Ram's Horn": *Themes and Texts in Traditional Jewish Preaching* (Cincinnati, 1996), 31; 111, n. 10, and Saperstein's discussion of Christian history in Mortera, in his "History as Homiletics: The use of Historical Memory in the Sermons of Saul Levi Morteira," in *Jewish History and Jewish Memory*, eds. Carlebach, Efron, and Myers (Hanover and London, 1998), 120–127.

tion of it.[35] Eisenmenger also expressed his dismay upon hearing that three Christians had converted to Judaism in Amsterdam during his stay. He provided only meager details, but it appears that one had come to Amsterdam after becoming convinced of Judaism in Prague.[36] He cited as one of the chief reasons for the difficulty of converting Jews the fact that there is a space within Christendom where Jews accept converts from Christianity and even circumcise them. This occurs only in one place: "als nur in Holland geschiehet."[37] He then quoted Menasseh ben Israel to the effect that every Christian who converted to Judaism strengthened the Jews in their belief that God had not abandoned them. When Eisenmenger complained of a *Yotzer* that Jews recited on Yom Kippur as insulting to Christianity, he singled out Amsterdam as one of the few places in which Jews dared to publish this *Yotzer*.[38] Johannes Müller, mid-seventeenth century Hamburg pastor complained that, "They [the Jews] seduce the Christians. In Holland, there are examples of men who converted from Christianity to Judaism and had themselves circumcised. Helvicus in *Elencho* tells of eight different examples of such seductions which took place in Germany and gives the name of each one. In 1638 a Christian in the Netherlands was led into error through a dispute with a Jew over Isaiah 7 and converted to Judaism."[39] The reference to circumcision indicates that these were not Jews reverting from a conversion to Christianity.

---

[35] Johann Andreas Eisenmenger, *Entdecktes Judenthum* (Königsberg, 1711), 1:843–845. (His citation from *Shne luhot ha-berit*, from fol. 243, col. 4.)

[36] Eisenmenger, *Entdecktes Judenthum*, 2:996: "im Jahr 1681 in welcher Zeit ich mich in Amsterdam auffgehalten/drey solcher gottlosen Bösewichte deselben gewesen/deren einer ein studiosus von Prag war, welchen ohne allen Zweiffel die Juden von gedachtem Prag in seinem Glauben irre gemacht/und zu solcher abscheulichen That verführet haben."

[37] Eisenmenger, *Entdecktes Judenthum*, 2:997.

[38] Eisenmenger, *Entdecktes Judenthum*, 1:137.

[39] Johannes Müller, *Judaismus, oder Judenthumb. Das ist Ausfuhrlicher Bericht von des jüdischen Volckes Unglauben, Blindheit und Verstockung* (Hamburg, 1707), 1387. For another list of Christians who purportedly converted to Judaism in Amsterdam, see Duitsch, *De wonderlyke*, 77–78.

A New Model?

The Sephardic model does not suffice to explain the superficially similar phenomenon of return to Judaism among German Jews. Although the precedent of converso return surely contributed somewhat to the Ashkenzic phenomenon, there are many structural differences. Dutch Calvinists disdained Catholic Papism almost as much as Judaism; the defections of Iberian Jews from Catholicism did not cause them great concern. The same, however, could not be said of German Jews, many of whom had converted to a Protestant denomination. In terms of the Jewish community, the reversion to Judaism of Iberian conversos who had been deprived of Jewish life and lore for generations required an intensive effort to re-acquaint them with Jewish knowledge and communal life in a systematic way. For penitent German-Jewish converts, the sole requirements were psychological. Their need for some form of expiation or penance, of ceremonial reconciliation, was great; but the returning convert had presumably received a full Jewish education early in life.[40]

Even if their formulae for educating returning Jews had been more applicable to the Ashkenzic returnees, the Sephardim were unlikely to have provided their resources or model for other reasons. The Sephardic community disdained the much poorer Ashkenazim, particularly after their numbers grew in the wake of the persecutions of 1648 in Poland.[41] The socio-economic rift between the two communities was very wide. Ashkenazim served as menial servants in the homes of wealthy Sephardim, and expected and received generous amounts of charity from them. They were regarded as such an unpleasant burden that in some cases the Sephardic community paid for the deportation of Ashkenazim. Ashkenazim were not permitted to pray in the Sephardic synagogues; their children could not study in the same schools. In the words of historian Yosef Kaplan,

---

[40] On the autobiographical statements concerning the prior Jewish education of converts in German lands, see my "Converts and their Narratives in Early Modern Germany: The Case of Friedrich Albrecht Christiani," *Leo Baeck Institute Yearbook*, 40 (1995), 70, ff.

[41] On the Ashkenazi community in Amsterdam, David M. Sluys, *Beelden uit het Leven der Hoogduitsch-Joodsche Gemeente te Amsterdam in het Begin der 18de Eeuw* (Amsterdam, 1925); Florike Egmond, "Contours of Identity: Poor Ashkenazim in the Dutch Republic," *Dutch Jewish History*, 3 (1993), 205–225.

"The Spanish and Portuguese community of Amsterdam had formed a stereotype of the *tudescos* [German Jews] and *Polacos* [Polish Jews]. That image identified them with poverty and beggary, moral corruption and degradation, and even deviation from the ways of Judaism and the observance of the Torah."[42] Regarding German Jews as even lowlier than Polish Jews, the Sephardic community would not devote significant resources to the redemption of fallen German Jews. For a more cogent explanation for the attraction of Amsterdam as a center of reversion to Judaism for Ashkenazic Jews we must look to the local framework of relative religious openess, experimentation, and transformation.

Andrew Marvell described Amsterdam in his *Character of Holland*, (1653): "Hence Amsterdam—Turk, Christian, Pagan, Jew/Staple of sects and mint of schism grew:/That bank of conscience where not one so strange/Opinion but finds credit and exchange." Another Englishman likewise saw Amsterdam as the most tolerant of lands, particularly to Jews. In a satirical broadsheet mocking the Presbyterians, a coat of arms appears with four pieces impaled on it. The third represents "ye family of Amsterdam, she beares for her arms, in a field of Toleration, three Jewes heads proper, with as many blew caps on them."[43] The boldest European experiments conducted in crossing confessional boundaries took place in Amsterdam. By the mid-seventeenth century, Amsterdam had become a magnet for individuals of many faiths and denominations who sought new religious destinies with the least harmful consequences.[44] Many of these

---

[42] The discussion in this paragraph is based on material in Yosef Kaplan, "The Portuguese Community in Seventeenth-Century Amsterdam and the Ashkenazi World," *Dutch Jewish History*, 2 (1989), 23–45; at p. 39; J. Michman, "Between Sephardim and Ashkenazim in Seventeenth-Century Amsterdam," in I. Ben-Ami, ed. *The Sephardi and Oriental Jewish Heritage* (Jerusalem, 1982); Y. Kaplan, H. Mechoulan, and Richard Popkin, eds. *Menasseh ben Israel and his World* (Leiden, 1989); Gordon Weiner, "Sephardic philo and anti-Semitism in the Early Modern Era: The Jewish adoption of Christian attitudes," in Richard H. Popkin and Gordon Weiner, eds. *Jewish Christians and Christian Jews from the Renaissance to the Enlightenment* (Dordrecht, 1994), esp. 189; and Yosef Kaplan's illuminating study, "The Self-Definition of the Sephardic Jews of Western Europe and Their Relation to the Alien and the Stranger," in Benjamin R. Gampel, ed. *Crisis and Creativity in the Sephardic World 1391–1648* (New York, 1997), 121–145.

[43] British Museum #702, entitled "Atchievement of Sir John Presbiter." Cited in Alfred Rubens, *A Jewish Iconography* (London, 1954), 36.

[44] See *Wegscheiden der Reformation: Alternatives Denken vom 16–18 Jh.* ed. Günter Vogler (Weimar, 1994) esp. the article of Blok on religious pluralism in the Netherlands. English

individuals tested the boundaries of organized religions by adopting several religions or denominations or advocating the union of "irreconcilable" religions. Johann Rittangel, who had arrived in Amsterdam in 1642, can serve as a prominent example.[45] Some of his near contemporaries assumed that he was born Jewish, then converted to Roman Catholicism, then to Calvinism and finally to Lutheranism.[46] Others maintained that he was Roman Catholic from birth, had later converted to Judaism, after which he turned to Protestantism.[47] A third group opined that he had never been a Jew, but was of Jewish descent. Several other religious trajectories have been posited for Rittangel.[48] Aside from the problem of verification of his actual religious odyssey, Rittangel is significant for the very fact that he could exist, that so many religious boundaries could be crossed with apparent ease, with no dire consequences, and that the world of letters speculated about his metamorphoses with such avid interest. His biography presented a journey through religious confessions that seemed utterly novel. But it was far from unique.

In 1695, Oliger Paulli left his wife and children in Denmark to realize his religious dreams in Amsterdam. There he published some 20,000 pages of his visions, whose central theme was the union of Paul and Maimonides, of Jews and chiliast Christians, into one true faith. While he was eventually ejected from the city in 1701, the numerous refutations devoted to his work prove that he was not dismissed lightly by theologians. His ideas, regardless of how fantastic they may seem now, were published and circulated.[49]

Eighteenth century Johann Wolfgang Brenk argued that Jesus' Christianity was merely a reformation of Judaism but never intended

---

Puritans in search of freedom of worship established a church in Frankfurt in 1554. By the end of the century, it had established a branch in Amsterdam; in 1610 this church had itself spawned a breakoff in Amsterdam. Patricia Caldwell, *The Puritan Conversion Narrative: The Beginnings of American Expression* (Cambridge, 1983), 52–53.

[45] P.T. van Rooden and J.W. Wesselius, "J.S. Rittangel in Amsterdam," *Nederlands Archief voor Kerkgeschedenis* 65 (1985): 131–152.

[46] *Bibliotheca librorum novorum* (Sept.–Oct. 1698), 674.

[47] *Nouvelles de la République des Lettres* (Amsterdam, August, 1699), 212.

[48] See Pierre Bayle's *Dictionnaire Historique et Critique* New Edition (Paris, 1820), vol. 12, 543–546, s.v. Rittangelius.

[49] Among his works relating to Jews, see *Irrendes Iśra'el wieder zurecht gebracht . . .* (n.p., 1704) and *Kurtzer Bericht an alle Puysancen von Europa, in deren Gebiet Juden sind: wo jetzt von **Oliger Paulli** geredet wird, betreffended seinen Beruff . . . dienende zur Vereinigung der Juden und Christen* (n.p., 1704).

to supersede it. Isaac la Peyrère stressed the reconciliation of Jews and Christians, and the imminent ingathering of Jews in the Holy Land. His *Praeadamitae*, published in Amsterdam, stressed the theological centrality of Jews in Christianity and disdained conventional theological categories, part of a larger phenomenon of Christian messianism and philosemitism typical of messianists who dismissed the role of the historical Jesus as they anticipated imminent messianic events.[50] Moses ben Avraham Avinu, the Moravian convert to Judaism, published the New Testament in Hebrew and sought the approval of Michaelis for a new Bible printing.[51] Paul Felgenhauer published his *Bonum Nuncium Israeli* in Amsterdam, advocating the reunion of Christians and Jews in one church. Peter Serrarius advocated a renewed Christianity united with a more Christianized Jewry.[52]

Within the diverse circles of these millenarians, sectarians, and missionaries who jostled for recognition in seventeenth-century Amsterdam there were many Germans.[53] Sebastian Jugendress, editor of convert from Judaism Paul Kirchner's *Jüdisches Ceremoniel*, cited as his source the Hebraist Lunden, who used a Jew from Amsterdam as **his** informant concerning what 'tzitzit' looked like.[54] The disciples of German visionary Jacob Boehme fled and established themselves in Amsterdam: Johann Georg Gichtel (1638–1710) published Boehme's *Der Weg zu Christo*[55] in Amsterdam and his disciple Ueberfeld founded the "Community of Brothers" there.[56] Another Boehme disciple, pastor Pierre Poiret, born in France, went to Germany, but

---

[50] On la Peyrère see Richard Henry Popkin, *Isaac La Peyrère (1596–1676): His Life, Work, and Influence* (Leiden-New York, 1987); on Christian messianism and philosemitism in this period see Jonathan Israel, *European Jewry in the Age of Mercantilism* (Oxford, 1985), 224–228.

[51] Max Freudenthal, *Aus der Heimat Mendelssohns* (Berlin, 1900), 177.

[52] According to le Roi, *Die evangelische*, 1:154, Serrarius went so far as to encourage the restoration of the Levitic cult among converted Jews.

[53] For an example of millenarians with an intense interest in Jewish matters who travelled to Germany, see Richard Popkin, *Spinoza's Earliest Publication?* (Assen, 1987), introduction.

[54] Paul Christian Kirchner, *Jüdisches Ceremoniel, das ist: Allerhand Jüdische Gebräuche welche die Juden in und ausser dem Tempel* ed. Sebastian Jugendress (Nuremberg, 1724), 7.

[55] (Amsterdam, 1682). English transl. and intro., Peter Erb, *The Way to Christ* (New York, 1978).

[56] Pierre Deghaye, "Jacob Boehme and his Followers," *Modern Esoteric Spirituality*,

found greater freedom, and spent his last forty years in Amsterdam, where in 1687 he published *L'Oeconomie Divine*. Germans from many different regions, including Bavaria, Silesia, Schleswig, and Swabia united in Amsterdam in the name of Boehme. They include his noted disciple Kuhlman, who was later burned at the stake in Moscow.

Collectively, these protean religious characters form a unique constellation in that each addressed Judaism as an ingredient in the religious complexes which they advocated.[57] Some personally ventured into these religious experiments and travelled through Judaism in at least one stage of their metamorphoses. A small but significant number remained Jewish. The most renowned of these converts, Johannes Peter Spaeth, had been a follower of German Pietist Jakob Spener. He came to reject the divinity of Jesus and in 1697, in Amsterdam, he converted to Judaism and took the name Moses Germanus. Even after his conversion, he continued to insist on the importance of Jesus as the greatest teacher. Opponents of the Pietists were quick to cite his example to prove that Pietism was one step away from Judaism. Spaeth had found a place where his ideas with their fluid religious boundaries could flourish.

The existence in Amsterdam of a conspicuous number of German Christians who had converted to Judaism along with numerous religious experimentalists and spiritual adventurers aroused scorn and dismay among conservative Christians throughout Europe.[58] The

---

ed. Antoine Faivre and Jacob Needleman, (New York, 1992), 210–247. This article imprecisely uses 'Holland', as a synonym for Amsterdam. On Gichtel see, Bernard Gorceix, *Johann Georg Gichtel, theosophe d'Amsterdam* (Lausanne, 1975). Gichtel happened to have been in Vienna during the height of the messianic movement of Sabbatai Zevi, and reported that the Viennese Jews tried to convince him to adopt their faith.

[57] Peter von Rooden, "Conceptions of Judaism as a Religion in the Seventeenth-Century Dutch Republic", in Diana Wood, ed. *Christianity and Judaism: papers read at the 1991 summer meeting and the 1992 winter meeting of the Ecclesiastical History Society= Studies in Church History*, 29 (1992), 299–308.

[58] See e.g. "Der getaufte Jude," p. 12, which cites the example of a Prague Jew who jocularly claimed to have converted to all three denominations to be found in the Holy Roman Empire to insure his salvation in at least one of them. After that, he would go to Constantinople [presumably to convert to Islam] and if he did not like what he found, he could always go to Amsterdam. The anonymous author concluded in alarm that nothing evil is beyond such people, for no law, no bond of religion ties them. Those who accept such converts without adequate preparation or test are doing more harm to the state than good because they create a class of people with no morals and values.

circles of academic Hebraists and philosemites, who counted many Germans in their ranks, complete the background against which we can understand Amsterdam as a beacon for German Jews who had converted from Judaism and now wished to return to their roots.[59]

---

[59] Of course, there were cases of conversion in the reverse direction, Jews who came through Amsterdam and converted to Christianity. See the case of Johann Nathan Hollander, *Die Wahrheit des eintzig und allein seeligmachenden Christlichen Glaubens, erkennet und bekennet durch Nathan Jacob, einem gebohrnen Juden aus Amsterdam, nach dem derselbe aus Trieb Gottes/nebst seiner Frau und dr—Kindern von seiner Jüdischen Familie ausgegangen und nach erlangten Unterricht in denen nothigen Glaubens=Articulin der Evangelsiche Lutherischen Religion . . . in Dohm Kirchen zu Riga by Heinrich Bruningst, Sept. 10 1717 getaufft . . . Nebst einem Bericht von denen Ceremonien und Aberglauben der Juden . . . aufs neue an sehr viel Orten vermehret und zum Druck gegeben* (Frankfurt am Main, 1738).

JUDAIZING IN THE SEVENTEENTH CENTURY: FRANCIS MERCURY VAN HELMONT AND JOHANN PETER SPÄTH (MOSES GERMANUS)

Allison P. Coudert

In the fall of 1661 Francis Mercury van Helmont (1614–1698) was arrested by soldiers of the Inquisition, escorted to Rome, and imprisoned on the charge of "judaizing." After a year and a half in jail, the charges against van Helmont were summarily dismissed without explanation and he returned to the very activities that had led to his imprisonment in the first place, the collecting, editing, and publishing of books dealing with the philosophy and theology of the Jewish Kabbalah.[1] At some point in 1696 Johann Peter Späth[2] (1642/5–1701) took the dramatic and dangerous step of converting to Judaism under the name Moses Germanus. Although these two events occurred more than thirty years apart, they were connected, for Späth's conversion was largely a reaction against van Helmont's kabbalistic philosophy.

It is ironic that Späth should have attributed his conversion to van Helmont, for the very idea of identifying with a single religion to the exclusion of all others was something van Helmont fought against his entire life. Ecumenism not exclusivity was van Helmont's life-long and constantly reiterated message. Although called a "Judaizer" and considered by many to be a secret Jew, van Helmont was neither. He described himself as a "Seeker," who, for all his wanderings across Europe during the many years of his long life, remained

---

[1] On van Helmont's arrest and imprisonment, see ch. 3 of my book, *The Impact of the Kabbalah in the Seventeenth Century: The Life and Thought of Francis Mercury van Helmont* (Leiden: E.J. Brill, 1998).

[2] Späth's name has been spelled in various ways (Späth, Speeth, Speath), but he himself preferred Späth. Cf. J.J. Schudt, *Jüdische Merkwürdigkeiten. vorstellende was sich Curiouses und denckwürdiges in den neuen Zeiten bey einigen Jahr-hunderten mit denen in alle IV. Theile der Welt/sonderlich durch Teutschland/zerstrueten Juden augetragen. . . .* (Frankfurt and Leipzig, 1714). *Jüdische Merckwürdigkeiten Vierdter Theil. Als eine weitere Continuation dessen/so in denen drey vorhergehenden Theilen vorgestellet worden. . . .* (Frankfurt am Mayn: Matthias Andreae, 1718), IV: 198.

intensely curious. While he had the courage to admit that neither
he nor anybody else knew, or could possibly know, all the answers,
this did not lead him to despair but to further searching. Not many
octogenarians plan, as van Helmont did, to travel to India to consult the Brahmins in the hope of obtaining new and better answers
to life's great existential questions![3] Späth's conversion was thus the
very antithesis of what van Helmont would have wanted or expected,
for to quote one of the Inquisition's charges against him, "Occasionally
he was heard to say that anyone is able to be saved in his own faith
according to his own inner light and the light of conscience."[4]

The bare facts of Späth's conversion and his life preceding his
conversion offer an insight into the agonizing spiritual dilemmas facing many people during this period of intense confessional warfare.[5]
Born in Vienna to a Catholic family around 1640, Späth grew up
in Augsburg, a first hand witness to the economic devastation caused
by the Thirty Years' War and the embittered religious divisions left
in its wake. By all accounts he remained within the Catholic community in Augsburg, which at that time represented a minority of
some four thousand out of a total population of sixteen thousand.[6]
As the son of a shoemaker, Späth was forced at an early age to
make his own living, and he became a tutor. His first extended contacts with Protestants came when he tutored a young Italian boy,
and the Protestant family with whom the boy was lodging challenged
Späth to defend his Catholic faith. His doubts about Catholicism
were heightened when he traveled to Stuttgart as secretary to a

---

[3] Furly to Locke, 19/29 May 1694, *The Correspondence of John Locke*, ed. E.S. De
Beer. 8 vols. (Oxford: Clarendon Press, 1976–1989), 54–5.
[4] "Informatio de Helmontio, May/June 1662; The Errors and Teachings of Helmont" (Archivio Segreto Vaticano, Archivio della Nunziatura di Colonia 81, n. 4).
Inquisitorial documents relating to van Helmont's case were printed as an appendix
to Klaus Jaitner, "Der Pfalz-Sulzbacher Hof in der europäischen Ideengeschichte
des 17 Jahrhunderts," *Wolfenbüttler Beitrage*, ed. Paul Raabe (Frankfurt am Main:
Vittorio Klostermann, 1988). I have included them (with a translation) in *The Impact
of the Kabbalah in the Seventeenth Century*, Appendix One.
[5] For a discussion of Späth's life and conversion, see N. Samter, "Johann Peter
Späth (Moses Germanus), der Proselyt", *Monatsschrift für Geschichte und Wissenschaft des
Judenthums* (1895), 178–87, 221ff. H.J. Schoeps, *Philosemitismus im Barock* (Tübingen:
J.C.B. Mohr, 1952), 67ff. The fullest account of his life can be found in the report
that J.T. Klumpf sent to J.J. Schudt, which Schudt included in his *Jüdische Merkwürdigkeiten*, I: 273–276; IV: 192–203.
[6] Wagenseil claims that as of 1635 there were 16432 Protestants and 4415
Catholics. *Geschichte der Stadt Augsburg*, vol. 3 (Augsburg, 1821), 108.

Prince von Oettingen. There he had the opportunity to debate with many Lutherans. Presumably as a result of these debates he at some point went to Tübingen, where he converted to Lutheranism. The exact date of his conversion is uncertain, but it occurred when he was an adult.[7]

Späth's conversion to Lutheranism was strange for several reasons, especially from the point of view of his later renunciation of Christianity altogether. By leaving the Catholic Church and embracing Lutheranism he essentially bucked a trend. For the prevailing current at the time of his conversion was the other way around, from Lutheranism to Catholicism. This was especially true in Germany, where some thirty-nine German nobles converted to Catholicism.[8] Furthermore, as will become apparent below, Lutherans were especially prone to a new and more virulent form of anti-Semitism that developed in the sixteenth and seventeenth centuries. The very virulence of this anti-Semitism appears to have been an important factor in Späth's ultimate rejection of Christianity.

After his conversion Späth returned to Augsburg and went immediately to his Jesuit teachers to tell them their religion was false.[9] His new-found faith was not, however, to the liking of orthodox Lutherans, for he favored the mystical works of Boehme and Weigel, a leaning shared by the Lutheran Superintendent in Augsburg, Gottlieb Spitzle or Theophilus Spizelius (1639–91), who became a close friend and admirer.[10] In 1680 Späth wrote a work in the spirit of Boehme entitled Σκιαγραφια Theologico-philosophico-aenigmata, which so captivated Spitzel that he recommended Späth to influential Protestants in Strassbourg, where he obtained another position with an apothecary named Greim, attended lectures at the university, and did some preaching. At his point in his life Späth's piety and enthusiasm was so strong that he described himself as a "second Luther."[11]

---

[7] Samter, "Johann Peter Spaeth", 180–81.

[8] Cf. Raab, Heribert, "Das 'discrete Catholische' des Landgrafen Ernst von Hessen-Rheinfels (1623 bis 1693): Ein Beitrag zur Geschichte der Reunionsbemühungen und der Toleranzbestrebungen im 17. Jahrhundert", *Archiv für Mittelrheinische Kirche-Geschichte* 12 (1960), 175–98; idem, "'Sincere et ingenue etsi cum Discretione.' Landgraf Ernst von Hessen-Rheinfels (1623–93) über eine Reform von Papstum", *Beiträge zu kirchlichen Reformbemühungen von der Alten Kirche bis zu Neuzeit. Festgabe für Erwin Iserloh*, hrsg. Baumer (Paderborn and München: Ferdinand Schöningh, 1980).

[9] J.J. Schudt, *Jüdische Merkwürdigkeiten*, IV, 198.

[10] Ibid., 193.

[11] *Sendschreiben eines gewesenen Pietisten, der sich selbst Moses Germanus nennt, und vor*

From Strassbourg Späth traveled to Frankfurt am Main to see Spitzel's close friend, Phillipp Jakob Spener, one of the founders of the pietistic revival movement. Spener took an immediate liking to Späth, treating him as a son. As Spener said later, he recognized Späth's ability as a scholar, and he responded to Späth's apparent religious conviction, sincerity, and commitment to truth. He even thought it a stroke of divine providence that Späth's name should begin with the same two letters as his own and Spitzle's.[12] Spener procured Späth a position as a tutor and gave him the hope of eventually obtaining a position as Rector.[13] But apparently even at this point in his career, Späth was plagued with doubts. He had reservations about such a basic Christian sacrament as communion: at the moment the cup was offered, and wholly against his will, he would think of Christ's words, "O my Father, if it be possible, let this cup pass from me" (Matt. 26:39). He communicated further doubts to Spener. How, he asked, could Lutherans claim to represent the true word of God when there was so much immorality and so little agreement among them?[14] He emphasizes this in a letter to Johanna Eleonore Petersen, the wife of the Lutheran theologian Johann Wilhelm Petersen, explaining the reasons why he became a Jew:

> ... we must finally come to the point, the point that ceaselessly vexed me and which I vexed you with many times: whether there might not be a touchstone or sign by which and by the power of which one could know who has the correct truth and knowledge since so many all over the world differ from each other, yet claim they are the best people and regard themselves as such. By way of example and evidence, Herr Spener will serve me before the seat of judgment. How often in distress and anguish did I ask him why he and Dr. Schutz and Hellmont never could agree since they prided themselves on the existence of a single truth, which in this case was as impossible as one can be two and two one.... May God will that you might not be so clearly reckless about these dangerous matters concerning the salvation of souls and that you would deliberate with great care for a quarter of an hour in spiritual soberness whether there is some

---

wenig Jahren ein Jude worden, mit nöthigen Anmerkungen publiziert von F. Chr. Bücher (Danzig, 1699), 2.

[12] P.J. Spener, *Theologishe Bedenken* (Frankfurt, 1692), III, 534; IV: 623; *Consilia ad Judicia latina* (1709), III: 427.

[13] Schudt, *Jüdische Merkwürdigkeiten*, IV, 193.

[14] Samter, "Johann Peter Speath", 184–5.

reason and truth for why you have such a great reputation for strife and turmoil.[15]

Things came to such a point that Späth regretted his conversion, claiming that one should remain in the faith into which one was born.[16] But before reconverting to Catholicism, he determined to consult Friedrich Breckling, the outspoken and divisive leader of the spiritualist, and chiliastic "left wing" Lutherans in Amsterdam. Breckling himself had decried "the Babel of today's Christianity," which he described as "a refuge of night owls, dragons, hedgehogs, wolves, basilisks, otters, sorcerers, ghosts [Feldgeister], whores, and living devils."[17] Späth wanted to understand how Breckling could remain a Lutheran given such a situation. He apparently received no help from Breckling, whom he referred to in his letter to Frau Petersen as "that irascible spirit" ("Der grimmigen Geister") and later derided as an "old squabbler" ("alte Zänker").[18]

Spener, aware of Späth's spiritual turmoil, wrote to Spitzel to enlist his help, but by this time all was in vain. In 1683 Späth reconverted to Catholicism.[19] However, his doubts about Catholicism did not vanish with his re-conversion. They only increased as he became more familiar with the writings of such mystical and radical sects as the Mennonites and anti-Trinitarian Socinians. It is at this point in his life, or perhaps some time earlier, that he came under the influence

---

[15] *Send-Schreiben*, 6–7: "Ja wir möchten enlich auff den Scruptel oder Nagel kommen/der mich unaufhorlich und ich euch verschiedene mal darmit vexirte/ob dest nicht ein Probstein oder Zeichten ware/an dem und Krafft dessen man erkenne könnte/wer die rechte Warheit und Erkäntnüß habe/da so viele undo wo Weltwit von einander differirende dieselbe profitiren/welche sonst die besten Menschen bey euch synd/und von sich selfst davon gehalten warden. Zum Exampel und Zeugen vor dem Richtstuhl der Warheit diene mir Herr D. Spener. Wie betrübt und ängstlich ich ihn offters angelangen/warum er und D. Schutz und Hellmont nimmer einig seyn können/da sie doch von einem Grund von einer Warheit sich berühmen/welches in her That denn so unmölich/als daß eines zwey/und zwey eins shyn können. Wolte Gott/daß ihr in diesen Seelen-Seeligkeit betreffenden periculeusen Punctun/nicht so gar fahrlässig sicher wäret/und eine viertel-stunde in geistlicher Nüchterheit bedäctet/ob auch etwas in der Sache Grund und Warheit sey/davon ihr so grosses Rühmens/strepitum und Turbam machet."
[16] Spener, *Consilia et judica latina*, III, 427; *Theologishe Bendenken*, III, 534.
[17] "Das Babel der heutigen Christenheit is eine Behausung voller Nachteulen, Drachen, Igel, Wölfe, Basilisken, Ottern, Zauberer, Feldgeister, Huren und lebendiger Teufel" (cited in Samter, "Johann Peter Speath", 185).
[18] *Send Schreiben*, 6; Samter, "Johann Peter Speath", 185.
[19] Spener, *Theologische Bedenken*, III, 534.

of Francis Mercury van Helmont and moved to Sulzbach to help
in the printing and publication of the *Kabbala denudata*.[20] The exact
chronology of subsequent events is unclear, but for some years before
his official conversion to Judaism in 1696, Späth resided in Amsterdam,
where he assumed the name Moses Germanus. After being initially
rebuffed by the leaders of the Portuguese synagogue, Späth was
officially converted and circumcised. He married a Jew, started a
family, and found employment as a teacher. According to the reports
of Christians, which will be discussed below, he lived in dire poverty
and died under mysterious circumstances.

The most complete account of Späth's life and conversion is found
in Johann Jacob Schudt's monumental four volume work entitled
Jüdische Merwürdigkeiten, or *Jewish Peculiarities*,[21] which was published
in Frankfurt and Leipzig in 1714. Schudt is a good example of a
Christian Hebraist whose very knowledge of Jews and Judaism makes
his attitude towards Jews problematic. While he is aware, as un-
educated Christians were not, of the kind of historical discrimination
practiced against the Jews and the way this forced them into trade
and money-lending, he still has to look for deeper motives to explain
why Jews engage in the business practices they do. And these motives,
in Schudt's opinion, can only lie in the peculiar and innate character of Jews:

> The reason the Jews practice usury so readily is partly due to Christians
> and partly to Jews. Christians are responsible because they do not
> allow them to practice any trades and because they do not allow them
> to possess any real estate or till the land or raise livestock. So, all that
> remains is trading, haggling, and usury. One of the greatest obstacles
> to their conversion is probably that they generally grow up and spend
> most of their lives in idleness and commonly earn their living through
> trading and haggling and yet really do not work. This is not altogether
> their fault since they do not have land to farm and in most places
> they are not allowed to learn or practice trades. Yet they can be faulted
> because even if they were allowed to work, they would not know how
> to go about it because of their laziness. Regarding those who are poor
> among them, whose number, as among Christians, is always the greater

---

[20] The exact dates of Späth's residence in Sulzbach are unkown. But it had to
be sometime between 1676 and 1684 because the first two parts of the *Kabbala
denudata* were published in 1677 and 1678 and the second volume in 1684.

[21] "Merwürdigkeiten" is a difficult word to translate since it can be taken in both
the pejorative sense of "peculiarities," "oddness," or "strangeness" or in a positive
sense implying things that are exceptional and worth investigating.

part, it is a sheer impossibility that anyone who has very little money can through trading turn this into enough to make ends meet and support a family without shady practices and fraud. As a consequence, these miserable people can ponder and think of nothing but how to maintain their poor lives through cunning, intrigue, fraud, and theft. . . .

It is on this account that the famous jurist from Halle, D. Böhmer . . . and some others are of the opinion that one should, on the contrary, encourage the Jews to learn trades so that they will have to earn their bread by the sweat of their brow. But since Christian craftsmen would hardly allow them to enter the guilds and to work with them, one should let them [the Jews] practice trades on their own. But, according to my humble opinion, this would cause many problems since the Jews would ruin the trades with their bungling as much as they have bungled trading.[22]

The example he gives of Jewish "bungling" brings us back to Späth, for Schudt takes obvious pleasure in the fact that Späth's circumcision was poorly done, causing him intense and prolonged pain:

For example, some Jews practice trades in Holland and it happened that a certain Jewish carpenter circumcised the apostate Speeth, but

---

[22] Schudt, *Jüdische Merkwürdigkeiten*, II, 168–170: "2. Die Veranlassung/daß die Juden so gern wuchern/ist enstanden theils von denen Christen/theils von denen Juden; Von denen Christen kommt die Veranlassung her/weil man ihnen keine Handwercke zu treiben erlaubet/und weil sie keine eigenthümliche unbewegliche Güther besitzen dürffen/können sie keinen Ackerbau noch Viehzucht treiben/bleibet also nichts als die Handlung/Schacherei und Wucher übrig; Eines der grössen Hindernüssen (ihrer Bekehrung) ist wol/daß sie insgemein alle von Jugend auf in Müßiggang aufwachsen/das Leben meistens in solchem zubringen/und sich insgemein alle von handeln und schachern nähren/hingegen zu keiner Arbeit kommen. Das theils ohne ihre Schuld geschiehet/indem sie eignes Land zu bauen nicht haben/auch an meisten Orten zu Handwercken/sie zu lernen/oder zu treiben/nicht gelassen werden/theils aber ists nicht ohne eigene Schuld/da ob sie zu arbeiten gelassen/aus Faulheit sich nicht darzu verstehen würden. Was nun arme unter ihnen sind/dero Anzahl so wol als bey den Christen allezeit den grössensten Theil machet/ists eine pure Unmöglichkeit/daß einer ohne Practiquen und Betrug/da er kaum wenige Thaler zum Capital hat/dieses durch Handlung also umsetzen könnte/daß er davon/wie genau er sich behilfft/mit einer Familie solte leben können; Daher die elende Leute Tag und Nacht auf nichts anders sinnen und dencken können/als wie sie mit List/Räncken/Betrug und also Diebstahl ihr armes Leben hinbringen. . . . 3. Dahero der berühmte Hallische Jurist Herr D. Böhmer. . . und andere mehr/der Meynung sind/man solle die Juden allerdings anhalten/daß sie Handwercker erlernen/und im Schweiß der Angesichts ihr Brod verdienen müssen/und da die Christl. Handwercker dieselbige wohl schwerlich für zünfftig passiren und als Mitmeister unter sich leyden würden/so solte man sie die Handwercker für sich treiben lassen; welches aber/meines wenigen Erachtens/eben so wol viele Beschwehrden würde nach sich ziehen/und durfften die Juden mit ihre Stümperey die Handwercker eben so sehr verderben/wie sie die Handlung verstümpeln."

rather unfortunately, as both Herr Diefenbach . . . and I were told by
a learned and noble friend, who heard from Speeth's own mouth what
great pain he had to suffer for a long time on account of such a
botched circumcision. It serves the apostate right![23]

Schudt returns to Späth's conversion to Judaism several times in his
work. The way the story escalates as he retells it is especially interesting in psychological terms. The first time he mentions Späth,
Schudt suggests that the Jews may actually have poisoned him because
he had doubts about Judaism:

> We have a completely new example in our own time of the wretched
> Johann Peter Speeth, who was born in Augsburg and raised in the
> Catholic religion, later converted to Lutheranism, then back to the
> Papists, and after that to the *novatoribus*, the newest and most eccen-
> tric sects of our time, and finally adhered to the Quakers and Socinians.
> (In book 6, chapter 29, paragraph 7 we will have more to say about
> this wavering spirit which led him to Judaism when he had himself
> circumcised and took the name of Moses Germanus in Amsterdam in
> 1697.). . . .
>   Speeth married an honest German Jewess and had children by her
> (since a noble friend saw a little son at his home). He led a miserably
> poor life because the Portuguese and other Jews cared little about him.
> Not only did he make very little money teaching Jewish children but
> he also begged in writing from a good Christian friend, who had vis-
> ited him previously in Amsterdam, for a single gulden to alleviate his
> extreme poverty, which he received. This friend assured me that, as
> one could clearly see from his conversion, the new Moses Germanus
> suffered from uncertainty, doubt, and anxiety, which caused the Jews,
> having certainly observed this, to worry about his return to Christianity.
> And because it happened that he was so opportunely plucked from
> the earth, having taken to his bed on April 26, 1701, dying on the
> 27th and having been buried by the Jews on the 28th, it is under-
> standable that doubt arose as to whether he died so quickly naturally,
> or took his own life, or whether his life was made shorter by the
> Jews.[24]

---

[23] Ibid., 170: "Gleichwol treiben einige Juden in Holland Handwercker/wie dann
ein jüdischer Schreiner es gewesen/der den abgefallenen Speeth beschnitten/aber
ziemlich unglücklich/davon Herr Diefenbach Jud. Convers. 15. p. 154 und mir aus
des Speeth Mund ein gelährter vornehmer Freund hier erzehlet/was große Schmertzen
er lange Zeit von solcher übel verrichteten Beschneidung ausgestanden; ist dem
abtrünnigen Vogel recht geschehen. . . ."

[24] Ibid., I, 273: ". . . Wir haben zu unsern Zeiten daß gantze neue Exempel des
unseeligen Joh. Peter Speeth, welcher von Augsburg bürtig/in Catholischer Religion
gebohren und erzogen/herrnachmahls Lutherisch worden/dann wieder zu den

In a later passage Späth's murder has become a reality, which proved to Schudt's satisfaction that even a reprobate like Späth finally recognized the truth of Christianity. In Schudt's mind Späth is a good example of what can happen if one becomes too immersed in Jewish literature. Späth had, as we have seen, assisted Knorr von Rosenroth in editing the *Kabbala denudata*, the largest collection of Hebrew Kabbalistic texts published in Latin up to that time:

> We have already said quite a bit about this rare bird and apostate Speeth . . . but we can now offer the gracious reader a further and even more curious report about him. Our highly esteemed patron Herr Professor Joh. Christoph. Wolffius has given a full report, especially of his published writings in his Bibliotheca Hebraea, p. 811 . . . and Herr de la Croze reports that Herr Knorr von Rosenroth employed Speeth in the publication of his *Cabbala Denudata*. Some years after his apostasy the Jews got him out of the way with poison because he would not condone all their Talmudic fabels. And one can read in Herr D. Spener . . . how hard he tried to get him away from the papists and later from the Jews.[25]

Papisten hernach zu denen *Novatoribus* und Sonderlingen unserer Zeit/ferner zu den Quäckern und Socinianern sich sehr gehalten/(wie wir von seinem Schwindel Geist unten Libr. VI cap. 29, para 7 ein mehres reden werden) die ihm den Weg zum Judenthum gebahnet/da er sich zu Amsterdam anno 1697 beschneiden und Moses Germanus nennen lassen. . . . Es hat der Speth auch eine saubere Teutsche Jüdin geheirathet/und mit ihr Kinder gezeuget/wie dann ein Christlicher vornehmer Freund bey ihm ein Söhngen gesehen; Er hat aber sein Leben/weil die Portugiesische und andere Juden sich seiner wenig angenommen/in socher kümmerlichen Dürfftigkeit zubringenmüssen/daß er nicht nur um ein gar geringes der Juden Kinder informiret/sodern auch von einem Christlichen guten Freund allhier/der ihn vormahls in Amsterdam besucht gehabt/durch Schreiben um einen eintzigen Gulden/zu Sublevirung seiner außersten Armuth gebetten/und auch erhalten/welcher Freund dann mich versicherte/daß der neue Moses Germanus, wie man aus seinen Reden deutlich abnehmen können/in lauter Ungewißheit/Zweiffel und Gewissens-Angst gewesen/welches dann die Juden wohl an ihm gemercket/und seinen Rücktritt zu der Christlichen Religion werden besorgen haben; und weil er . . . so gelingen von der Erden weggerafft/indem er den 26. April 1701 sich zu Bette gelegt/den 27 gestorben/und den 28. von den Juden begraben worden/so ist billig ein Zweifel entstanden/ob er natürlich/oder durch seine/oder der Juden Verkürtzung/so geschwind davon gefahren. . . ."
[25] Ibid., IV, 192: "Wir haben von diesem abtrünnigen Vogel dem Speeth schon in denen *Jüdischen Merkwürdigkeiten* Lib. 4. Cap. 18. par. 5. pp. 273ff. . . . angeführet/doch können wir jetzo dem geneigten Leser mit mehrer und curieuserer Nachricht von ihm an Händen gehen; Es hat unser hoch-geschätzter Gönner Herr Professor Joh. Christoph. Wolffius in seiner *Bibliotheca Hebraea* p. 811. sonderlich von seinen heraußgegebenen Schrifften gute Nachricht gegeben/auch aus des Berlinischen Bibliothecatii Herr de la Croze *Vindiciis Veterum Scriptorum* p. 61 seq. angeführet/daß Herr Knorr von Rosenroth den Speeth/bey Heraußgebung seiner *Cabbala denudata/*

Like many of his fellow Christians Schudt is obsessed by the problem of Christian converts to Judaism. He takes over and adds to the
examples given in Eisenmenger's intensely antisemitic diatribe to illustrate the dreadful consequences of allowing the Jews "too great freedom." Holland, of course, provided the worst example of this freedom.
The fact that Jews were allowed to practice their religion openly
there is something Schudt is resolutely against because he is convinced this openness encourages Christians to convert to Judaism:

> A second example of the too great freedom of Jews in Holland and
> especially in Amsterdam is the fact that Christians openly and with-
> out hesitation accept Jewish beliefs and allow themselves to be cir-
> cumcised, which is not permitted in the Holy Roman Empire but is
> punished by death. Although Herr Wülfer . . . deems such a forcing
> of one's conscience too severe, it is, however, proper and just because
> the apostasy from Christianity to Judaism cannot happen without blas-
> pheming the holy Trinity and without scandalous scorning of our
> blessed savior Jesus Christ (even and especially among Christians this
> behavior merits death). For this reason, the law demands death for
> those Jews who seduce a Christian to Judaism, as Herr Diefenbach
> shows in *Jud. Convers.*, para 14, p. 128. For this reason Nicol Antonius,
> a reformed minister, was hanged in Geneva in 1632 for converting to
> Judaism.[26]

Schudt's palpable worry about conversion is a leitmotif throughout
his enormous work.

---

gebraucht/es hätten ihn auch die Juden/einige Jahr nach seinem Abfall/mit Gifft
aus dem Weeg [sic] geräumet/weil er alle ihre Talmudische-Fabeln nicht billigen
wollen/wie sich Heer [sic] D. Spener bemühet/den Menschen von denen Papisten/und
nachmahls von denen Juden wieder abzuziehen/ist in seinen Teutschen *Consiliis
Theolog.* P. III. p. 534; P. IV. p. 623. und in *Consiliis Latinis Theol.* P. III. p. 430 zu
lesen."
  [26] Schudt, *Jüdische Merkwürdigkeiten*, I: 272: "Von den Juden in Holland und
Friesland: Eine allzu grosse Juden-Freiheit in Holland ist es/II. daß in Holland/son-
derlich zu Amsterdam/die Christen öffenlich und ohne Scheu den Jüdischen Glauben
annehmen und sich beschneiden lassen/welches im Römischen Reich nicht
gelidten/sondern am Leben gestrafft wird; Ob wohl solches Herr Wülffer *Animadvers.
ad Theo. Jud.* C. 3. para 16. p. 211 seq. für zu hart und einen Gewissens-Zwang
hält/ist es doch allerdings billig und recht/weil der Abfall vom Christlichen Glauben
zu dem Judenthum nicht ohne Gotteslästerung der Hochheiligen Dreyeinigkeit/und
schandliche Schmähung des gebennedeyten-Heylandes JESU CHRIST (so ja allerd-
ings/sonderlich bey einem Christen/den Todt verdienet) geschehen kan/dahero auch
so gar die Rechte denen Juden/die einen Christen zum Judenthum verführen/die
Todtes-Straffe setzen davon unterschiedlicher Juristen Zeugnüss anführen/Herr
Diefenbach im *Jud. Convers.* para 14. p. 128. So ist Nicol Antonius, ein Reformirter
Prediger in Genffer-Gebieth/als er ein Jud worden/anno 1632 erstlich gehenckt
und hernach verbrandt worden."

The fear that Christians will convert to Judaism if the Jews are not effectively silenced and prohibited from proselytizing is a constant theme in the work of many other Christians and Christian Hebraists as well. The Christian Kabbalah was singled out as especially dangerous and enticing in this regard because it was thought to undermine Christianity by presenting Judaism in a positive light. This was the view of Frederich Christian Bücher, a Lutheran who took great interest in Späth's conversion, going so far as to publish the letter written by Späth (under his Jewish name Moses Germanus) to Frau Petersen. In his annotations to this letter Bücher attributes Späth's conversion to his exposure to the Kabbalah, which he claims penetrated into Lutheran Pietism through Spener, who was for a period a close friend of van Helmont. Bücher's indictment of Spener, and by way of Spener, the Kabbalah, is worthwhile quoting at some length because it reveals the unsettling effect that biblical criticism and the recovery of Jewish and pagan sources were having on Christian beliefs. Bücher targets philological studies as especially detrimental to a true understanding of scripture:

> I will not mention philology, which in our time has reached such heights that the Pietists themselves complain about it and see it as a hindrance to true divine learning and the interpretation of scripture, especially of the books of Moses, Job, and Solomon because often more industry is applied to philosophizing than to explaining divine secrets....[27]

He reiterates Luther's claim that scripture is self-explanatory and decries the fact that theologians resort to traditions like the Kabbalah to explicate Christian texts:

> I might well ask a theologian whether holy scripture is not in itself a light to explain its own terms and words and build in us useful and necessary teachings about the natural things God wishes to reveal. Otherwise, where shall one find the explanation? Perhaps in the Rabbinic Cabbala? That is without doubt the *Keimelion* and precious treasure that D. Spener craves: because after I examined his Platonism I could easily imagine that above all other philosophies he liked the mystical

---

[27] *Send-Schreiben*, 2: "ich nicht sage von der herrlichen Philologia, die zu unsern Zeiten so hoch gestiegen/daß auch die Pietisten selbst sich darüber beschweren und sie für eine Hinderniß der wahren Gottsgelehrtheit ansehen/oder auch von einigen Auslegern der H. Schrifft/sonderlich in den Büchern Mosis/Hiobs und Salomonis/darin offt mehr Fleiß angewandt zu philosophiren/als göttliche Geheimniße zu erklähren...."

theology of the Jews, which is called Kabbalah, although it would be
better to call it a Cabale of Egyptian, Zoroastrian, and Pythagorean
garbage, through which the devilish teachings of the pagans were not
only introduced into the Jewish Church before the time of Christ but
also later into the Christian Church. We have sufficient evidence of
this not only in Reuchlin's *De Verbo Mirifico* and *De Arte Cabbalistica* but
in the devotional book of Henry More about the cabbalistic catechism
and a few other mystical books of the Rabbis, in which he points out
with ample evidence the very close relationship of Jewish teachings
with Pythagorean and Platonic philosophy.[28]

Bücher does not think it a coincidence that the Pietists became active
at the very time the first volume of the *Kabbala denudata* was published (1677). In his view the interest Pietists showed in the Kabbalah
was directly responsible for Späth's lamentable conversion: ". . . one
clearly sees what little fruit Pietists have gathered from Plato's bee
garden and that because of it one of the most zealous Pietists was
seduced into renouncing the Christian religion and taking up the
Jewish seal."[29]

Why Christians like Schudt and Bücher so feared Christian conversions to Judaism when the number of actual conversions was
miniscule becomes understandable when one appreciates the effect
Jewish criticisms of Christianity had in undermining Christian beliefs.
As we shall see when analyzing Späth's critique of Christianity, he

---

[28] Ibid., 2–3: ". . . möchte ich wohl einen Theologum fragen/ob denn nicht die
H. Schrifft an ihr selber ein Licht sey/ihre eigene Terminos und Wörter in denen
uns zur Erbauung nützlichen und nöthigen Lehren/von natürlichen Sachen/die uns
Gott darinn offenbahren wollen/zu erklären? oder wo soll man denn sonst die
Erklärung suchen? Vielleicht in der Rabbinischen Cabbala? Das wird ohen Zweyfel
das *Keimelion* und kostbahre Kleinoth seyn/was D. Spener verlanget: Denn nach-
dem ich seinen Platonismum untersuchet/kan ich leicht gedencken/daß ihm für
andern die Mystica Theologia der Jüden so wohl gefallen/die sie Cabbalam heis-
sen/viel besser aber einen Caballen vor den Aegyptischen/Zoraostischen und
Pythagorischen Dreck-Wagen nennen möchten/durch welchen die heidnischen
Teuffels-Lehren/nicht nur vor Christi Zeit in die Jüdische/sondern auch nachgehends in die Christiliche Kirche eingeführet worden/davon uns nicht allein des
Reuchlins Schrifften von dem Verbo Mirifico und der Arte Cabbalistica, sondern
auch des Henrici More Postill über den Cabbalistischen Catechsmum und einige
andere Mystische Bücher der Rabbinen/darinn er eine sehr genaue Verwandschafft
der Jüdishen Lehre mit Pythagorae und Platonis Philosophia angewiesen/satsam
Zeugnisß abstatten können. . . ."
[29] Ibid., 3: ". . . man klahr für Augen siehet/was für Früchtlein aus Platonis
Bienen-Garthen der Pietismus herfür gebracht/daß auch dadurch einer der eyffrigsten
Pietisten verführet worden/den Christliche glauben zu verleugnen/und das Jüdische
Siegel anzunehman. . . ."

repeatedly argues that Christians have misunderstood and misinter-
preted Old Testament prophecies. By showing that Old Testament
prophecies are not fulfilled in the New Testament, Späth along with
other Jewish critics of Christianity effectively separated the Old and
New Testaments, thus removing the historical and theological rationale for Christianity. Once this was done, it was possible for other
questions to be asked. For example, what was the historical and theological basis of the New Testament? Did Jesus really exist? And
was he anything more than a Jewish prophet preaching to mes-
sianically inclined Jews?[30] Späth makes all these points in his self
appointed role as biblical critic. His critique of Christianity, and
especially his characterization of Jesus as a "Roman animal . . .
adorned with all the predicates and characteristics of an idol"[31] was
so disturbing to Schudt and other Christians that they suspected
Bücher's motive in publishing it:

> The letter which he wrote to Herr Dr. Petersen's wife, describing his
> apostasy, was published by Herr Bücher in quarto in Danzig in 1699.
> I initially intended to insert it here, but with good reason I omitted
> it on account of the infuriating statements about Christ spewed out
> by this villain for fear that they might give the wrong idea to those
> with weak faith. . . . Herr Bücher was greatly suspected for printing
> this godless letter in Danzig and for allowing it to circulate in Saxony,
> since it happened both in Danzig and in other places that not only
> were various people led astray from Christianity by it but also had it
> in mind to deny the Christian religion. But those people were right-
> fully helped again by other pious Christians and given a stronger foun-
> dation [for their beliefs].[32]

---

[30] Richard H. Popkin, "Jewish Anti-Christian Arguments as a Source of Irreligion
from the Seventeenth to the Early Nineteenth Century", *Atheism from the Reformation
to the Enlightenment*, ed. Michael Hunter and David Wootton (Oxford: Oxford University
Press, 1992).

[31] *Send-Schreiben*, 9: "Der andere Respect, in welchem ich und viele andere diesen
Jesum von Nazareth unpartheyisch consideriren, is wieder [weder?] von Römischen
Thier zu einem Gott gemacht und auffgeworffen worden/und zugliech mit allen
Praedicaten oder Characteren eines Götzen außgezieret."

[32] Schudt, *Jüdische Merkwürdigkeiten*, I: 273: "Ein Brief/den er an Herrn D. Peterssens
Ehliebste/seines Abfalls wegen geschrieben/ist von Herrn Bücher aus Dantzig anno
1699 in 4 heraus gegeben worden/welchen ich anfänglich hier mit einzurucken
vorhabens war/allein wegen der ärgerlichen Reden von Christo/so der Böswicht
ausgegossen/aus Furcht eines Anstoßes bey Schwachgläubigen/billig habe unter-
lassen. . . . Herrn Bücher sehr verdacht worden/daß er den gottlosen Brief in Dantzig
drucken und in Sachsen divulgiren lassen/alldieweil sowohl an andern Orten/als
vornehmlich in Dantzig/wahrhafftig geschehen seye/daß unterschiedliche Menschen

Before discussing the reasons for Späth's conversion to Judaism, a word should be said about the drastic nature of such an act in seventeenth century Europe. In many places, such as the Holy Roman Empire where Späth was born and lived for the greater portion of his life, the conversion of a Christian to Judaism was a crime punishable by death.[33] This fact alone suggests that the characterization of the seventeenth-century, and indeed of the Renaissance and Reformation periods as a whole, as philosemitic is problematic.[34] Nonetheless, some scholars argue that the antagonism between

---

dadurch nicht nur an ihrem Christenthum irre gemacht worden/sondern auch die Christlicher Religion zu verläugnen im Sinne gehabt hätten/denen aber durch andere fromme Christen wieder seye zurecht geholffen/und ein besserer Grund angewiesen worden. Diefenbach *Jud. Convers.* para 15, p. 139."

[33] N. Samter, "Der Uebertritt zum Judenthum. Eine rechtsgeschichtliche Studie", *Allgemeine Zeitung des Judenthum* (1894), 509.

[34] The traditional view of the Renaissance and Reformation as periods of philosemitism has been qualified in recent years as scholars have increasingly revealed the very real limits to this phenomenon, together with the increasing hostility to Jews and Judaism. The attempt to distinguish between anti-Judaism and antisemitism made by Shimon Markish, for example, has been undermined by the work of Heiko Oberman, Jerome Friedman, Jonathan Israel and Po-Chia Hsia, among others. In the view of these scholars the enthusiasm of Renaissance Christians for Hebraica, characteristic of Pico della Mirandola and Johannes Reuchlin, was first dampened by the Reuchlin-Pffeferkorn controversy and then fundamentally distorted by the conflicts of the Reformation period. By the mid-sixteenth century "judaizing" became an all-too-convenient, pejorative epithet for Catholics in their fight against Protestants and for Protestants in their fight against each other. With the reaffirmation of the Vulgate as divinely inspired at the Council of Trent, the Catholic interest in Hebraica, which had always been less than the Protestant, diminished even further. The popular Catholic revival of the late sixteenth and seventeenth centuries further encouraged antisemitic sentiments by resuscitating charges of blood libel, which had largely been discredited. In such a situation the embattled Christian Hebraists who were left jumped on the bandwagon of antisemitism to prove that they were good Christians because they hated Jews like everyone else. On these issues, see Hans J. Schoeps, *Philosemitismus in Barock: Religions und geistegeschichtliche Untersuchungern* (Tübingen: J.C.B. Mohr, 1952); Shimon Markish, *Erasmus and the Jews*, trans. Anthony Olcott (Chicago: University of Chicago Press, 1986); Heiko Oberman, *The Roots of Anti-Semitism in the Age of Renaissance and Reformation*, trans. James I. Porter (Philadelphia: Fortress Press, 1984); Jerome Friedman, *The Most Ancient Testimony: Sixteenth-Century Christian-Hebraica in the Age of Renaissance Nostalgia* (Athens, Ohio: Ohio University Press, 1983); Jonathan Israel, *European Jewry in the Age of Mercantilism* (Oxford: Clarendon Press, 1985); R. Po-chia Hsia, *The Myth of Ritual Murder: Jews and Magic in Reformation Germany* (New Haven: Yale University Press, 1988). Miriam Yardeni, *Anti-Jewish Mentalities in Early Modern Europe* (New York: University Press of America, 1990); Ruth Mellinkoff, *Outcasts: Signs of Otherness in Northern European Art of the Late Middle Ages*, 2 vols. (Berkeley: University of California Press, 1993); R. Po-chia Hsia and Hartmut Lehmann (eds.), *In and Out of the Ghetto: Jewish-Gentile Relations in Late Medieval and Early Modern Germany* (New York: Cambridge University Press, 1995).

Christians in the post-Reformation era was so great that it deflected Christian hatred from the Jews and led to a lessening of tension and antagonism between the two groups.[35] Unfortunately the reservoirs of hate seem to have been limitless, and while attitudes towards the Jews may have been "disenchanted," to use R. Po Chia Hsia's phrase, and stripped of their magical and sacramental character,[36] new forms of anti-Semitism emerged predicated on overtly racial stereotypes. The revival of charges of ritual murder and the image of Jews as vampires "sucking" Christian dry with their usurious practices clearly illustrate that the practice of demonizing Jews continued. In fact, there is a great deal to suggest that the antisemitism of the early modern period was even worse than that of the Middle Ages; and nowhere was this more obvious than in those areas which roughly encompass modern-day Germany, especially among Lutherans.

The virulence of Lutheran antisemitism in the sixteenth and seventeenth centuries has been emphasized by historians. R. Po-chia Hsia gives the example of the Lutheran Pastor, George Schwartz, whose denunciations of Jews were even more violent than Luther's. In his diatribe *Juden Feind*, Schwartz resurrects all the old charges against the Jews—host desecration, ritual murder, and well-poisoning—and he makes it clear that Jews can never be anything else but Jews.[37] The promise of Galatians 3:28 is null and void in their case:

> A Jew is a Jew, baptized or circumcised, for all I care.
> Even if they are of diverse origins, they belong to a guild.
> They all serve one god, whom Christ named Mammon
> Who in the end with his servants, will go to the Devil's oven.[38]

Stephen G. Burnett, *From Christian Hebraism to Jewish Studies: Johannes Buxtorf, 1564–1629* (Leiden: E.J. Brill, 1996); Andrew C. Gow, *The Red Jews: Antisemitism in an Apocalyptical Age, 1200–1600.* Studies in Medieval and Reformation Thought, vol. 55 (Leiden: E.J. Brill, 1995); Allison P. Coudert & Jeffrey Shoulson (eds.), *Hebraica Veritas: Christian Hebraists in Medieval and Early Modern Europe* (Philadelphia: University of Pennsylvania Press, 2004).

[35] Amos Funkenstein, *Perceptions of Jewish History* (Los Angeles: University of California Press, 1993).

[36] R. Po-chia Hsia, *The Myth of Ritual Murder*, 131ff.

[37] Georg Schwartz, *Juden Feind, Von den Edelen Früchten der Tahlmyudischen Jüden/ so jetziger Zeith in Teutschlande wonen . . .* (n.p., 1570).

[38] Cited in R. Po-chia Hsia, "The Usurious Jew: Economic Structure and Religious Representations in an Anti-Semitic Discourse," *In and Out of the Ghetto: Jewish-Gentile relations in late medieval and early modern Germany*, 169.

For Schwartz, tolerating Jews "meant warming snakes in one's bosom and nurturing wolves in one's house."[39] This analogy of Jews to poisonous and dangerous animals was just one of the many tactics used by Schwartz to dehumanize them. Hsia identifies Schwartz's brand of antisemitism as something new and peculiar to Lutheran circles:

> The *Juden Feind* incorporated two traditions. First, it inherited the motifs of medieval anti-Semitism, which had focused on the religion of the Jews. The charge of blasphemy, stubbornness, arrogance, and avarice were all based on the fundamental charge of false religion. But this was an anti-Semitism that held out the promise of acceptance through conversion. Second, it bore the fruit of a new form of anti-Jewish polemic born out of the evangelical movement, which identified an innate, racial character to the Jewish refusal to convert, no doubt as a result of the evangelical clergy's anger with the fruitlessness of their Jewish missions. . . . The new Lutheran anti-Semitism drew its sources from several writers of the first Reformation generation. Schwartz invoked the works of Johann Reuchlin, Paul Ricius, Sebastian Münster, Martin Bucer, and, of course, Martin Luther. Although Lutheran anti-semitism assumed many motifs from the medieval polemical texts, a new emphasis was given to the immutable, essentialist, and, to employ an anachronistic concept, the racial character of the German Jews.[40]

As Hsia suggests, Lutheran antisemitism may have escalated because of the failure of Lutheran missionary activities among the Jews.[41] Given the hostility of the vast majority of Christians to Jews, and especially of Lutherans, what can possibility explain Späth's conversion?

---

[39] Ibid., 169.

[40] Ibid., 169, 171. To my mind the distinction between anti-Judaism and anti-semitism is untenable. As I have argued, race is not really the issue. The issue is the consistent way in which Jews from the earliest Christian centuries onwards were demonized and dehumanized to the point that they were as easy to kill as the dogs, swine, lice, and inhuman monsters with whom they were constantly identified. Even if before the nineteenth century Christians had unclear ideas about race (and who has a clear idea now?), hatred of Jews was directed as much, if not more, to their persons as to their beliefs (Coudert, "Christliche Hebraisten des 17. Jahrhunderts: Zu Johann Jacob Schudt, Johann Christoph Wagenseil und Franciscus Mercurius van Helmont", in: *Morgen-Glantz: Zeitschrift der Christian Knorr von Rosenroth Gesellschaft* 6 (1996), 99–132).

[41] Martin Friedrich is one of the few scholars to have studied the attitude of Lutherans to Jews in the seventeenth century. He rejects the prevailing view that the birth of the Pietist movement within Lutheranism heralded a new and more positive attitude towards the Jews, arguing instead that the opinions of orthodox and pietist Lutherans were indistinguishable when it came to Jews. While both groups appeared to encourage missionary activities among Jews, in actual fact they agreed across the board that conversion was less and less possible or even probable.

While Späth's conversion to Judaism was unusual, his pattern of conversion and reconversion between Christian denominations was not. Many Christians, especially in Germany where the notion of "cuius regio eius religio" held sway, were subject to forcible conversion as new rulers took over or old rulers changed their religious affiliations. One prime example of the way the fortunes of war and politics interfered with the beliefs and affiliations of individuals occurred in the territory of Sulzbach, where Späth came to work on the *Kabbala denudata*. By the time Späth arrived in Sulzbach, the Prince, Christian August, had proclaimed an unusual and widely disliked policy of religious toleration, going so far as to decree that the major denominations were required to share existing church facilities and divide Church offices and resources between them. Before this time the citizens had been forced to change their religion from Lutheranism to Catholicism and back again several times as a political battle for the control of the territories was fought between Christian August, who had been baptized a Lutheran, and his fiercely intolerant Catholic cousin, Philipp Wilhelm of Neuburg.[42] Christian August's tolerant policy, which he enacted after he gained full sovereignty over the Sulzbach territories, sprang from his own deeply held ecumenical views. These, in turn, had emerged from the spiritual crisis he experienced as a relatively young man (which caused him to convert from Lutheranism to Catholicism) and from his subsequent immersion in the Kabbalah.[43]

The degree to which Lutherans believed in the possibility of the conversion of the Jews readily correlates with their view of Jews as a whole. The majority, who thought conversion unlikely, if not out of the question, were overtly hostile to Jews and describe them in ways that can only be described as antisemitic. See Martin Friedrich, *Zwischen Abwehr und Bekehrung: Die Stellung der deutschen evangelischen Theologie zum Judenthum in 17. Jahrhundert* (Tübingen: J.C.B. Mohr, 1988), 6: ". . . die These eines absoluten Gegensatzes zwischen pietistischer und vorpietistischer Judenmission kann auf Anhieb kaum überzeugen." Elisheva Carlebach discusses other aspects of supposed "Jewish identity" that made their conversion suspect in Christian eyes. Especially important among these was the apparent inability of converted Jews to speak German rather than Yiddish. See Elisheva Carlebach, *Divided Souls: Converts from Judaism in Early Modern German Lands, 1500–1750* (New Haven: Yale University Press, 2001).

[42] For a thorough discussion of Christian August's difficult relationship with his cousin, see Volker Wappmann, *Durchbruch zur Toleranz: Die Religionspolitik des Pfalzgrafen Christian August von Sulzbach, 1622–1708* (Neustadt: Verlag Degener & Co., 1995).

[43] Wappmann describes Christian August's dramatic conversion.

The widespread incidents of conversions and reconversions during the sixteenth and seventeenth centuries were clearly a result of
the fragmentation of Christianity in the wake of the Reformation.
The Reformation encouraged conversion in another way as well, by
making it more possible for those Jews who had been forcibly converted to Christianity or who had professed to accept it while con-
tinuing to adhere to Judaism in secret (the so-called Marranos) to
revert to the faith of their ancestors. As many historians have pointed
out, the very fact of religious schism and the resulting religious pluralism, together with the conversion and reconversions of both
Christians and Jews, created a situation in which doctrinal purity
was undermined and skepticism, if not outright atheism, flourished.
In this climate, ecumenism could flourish as well. This was clearly
the case in Sulzbach.

As I have argued elsewhere, Sulzbach was perhaps the only place
where true philosemitism flourished, for here Jews were accepted as
Jews, not simply as possible converts.[44] Conversion was not an issue
among the Kabbalists at Sulzbach because they firmly believed that
the Kabbalah provided the means for uniting every kind of Christian
with every kind of Jew, Moslem, and Pagan in a single, universal
religion. I would suggest that it was in this atmosphere that Späth
gained the positive attitude towards Jews that eventually led to his
conversion. Christian August's policy towards the Jews was highly
unusual for a ruler of the time. Not only did he encourage the immi-
gration of Jews into the Sulzbach territories, but he protected the
Jews who came and never made his protection a means of extor-
tion, as did so many other Christian rulers. The Christian Hebraist
Johann Christoph Wagenseil gives a glowing picture of Christian
August's relations with his Jewish subjects. From his account one can
clearly see that Christian August's approach was unusual enough to
rate special mention, especially because of his dismissal of the charge
of ritual murder as an outright lie and his threat to punish any subject who spread such rumors:

> In this context we especially need to mention that the illustrious Prince
> Christian August of Pfaltz-Sulzbach, etc. has perfectly learned the sacred

---

[44] "The *Kabbala Denudata*: Converting Jews or Seducing Christians?" In *Christian-
Jews and Jewish-Christians*, eds. Richard H. Popkin and Gordon M. Weiner (Dordrecht:
Kluwer, 1994).

Hebrew language together with all the Jewish secrets, even the Cabbala, and that he delighted in such studies daily. Also after the rumor started for the second time in his territory, in 1682 and 1692, that the Jews had hanged Christian children, a rumor which was investigated and found to be totally false, he also had official proclamations nailed up everywhere to the effect that his subjects and inhabitants were strictly admonished under pain of mandatory corporal punishment not to believe this aforementioned vain fiction and lying rumor, much less to spread it further or to command or allow their children, servants or tenants to speak of it, let alone to verbally attack a Jew or ask, or allow, someone to attack a Jew because of these rumors. Whoever wishes to consider these important events bad, of minor importance, and unworthy should consider the words said by the wisest king of the Jews (Proverbs xxi:1): "The heart of a king and prince is in the hands of the Lord. Like a stream, he directs it where he will."[45]

The fact that so many Christians continued to believe Jews capable of murdering innocent children was an important factor in Späth's conversion to Judaism.

The volumes of the *Kabbala denudata* were published in 1677, 1678 and 1684. Späth did not officially convert to Judaism until 1696. It is therefore impossible to argue that Späth's experiences in Sulzbach were directly responsible for his later conversion. In fact, from the letter he wrote to van Helmont after his conversion, it is clear that

---

[45] J.C. Wagenseil, *Benachrichtigungen wegen einiger die Judenschafft angehende wichtigen Sachen. Erste Theil worinnen 1. Die Hoffnung der Erlösung Israelis oder klarer Beweiß der grossen und wie es scheinet/ allgemach herannahenden Juden-Bekehrung/ sammt vorgreifflichen Gedancken/ wie solche nechst Verheißung Göttlicher Hülffe/ zu befordern. 2. Wiederlegung der Unwarheit daß die Juden zu ihrer Bedürfniß Christen-Blut haben müssen. 3. Anzeigung/ wie leicht es dahin zu bringen/ daß die Juden forthin abstehen müssen/ die Christen mit Wuchern und Schinden zu plagen* (Leipzig, 1705), 32–33: "Hieher gehöret absonderlich/daß der Durchlauchtigste Fürst Christianus Augustus von Pfaltz-Sulzbach etc. die heilige Hebräische Sprach/sammt allen der Jüden Geheimnüßen/auch so gar der Cabbala, vollkommen erlernet/und mit solchen Studien sich täglich ergetzet. Er hat auch/nachdem in seinem Land zum zweyten mahl/als 1682 und 1692 der Ruf auskommen/als wenn die Juden Christen-Kinder aufgehangen hätten/nach genau untersuchter und Grund-falsch befundener Sache allenthalben öffentliche Mandata anschlagen lassen/durch welche Dero Hochfürstliche Durchl. Landes-Unterthanen und Ingesessenen bey unausbleiblicher Leibes-Straffe ernstlich geboten worden/den eitel erdichteten und lügenhafften Ausstreuen keinen Glauben beyzumessen/vielweniger aber davon weiter Ausbreitung zu thun/noch ihren Kindern und gebrodeten Leuten/oder Hintersassen davon zu reden/geschweig einen Juden deswegen anzufechten oder fürzuwerffen heissen oder gestatten. Wer wolte diese hohe Begebnisen für schlecht/gering und nicht würdig achten/daß ihnen beygeschrieben werde/was der weisseste König [p. 33] unter den Juden Prov. xxi. i. gesagt: Des Königs (und Fürsten) Hertz ist in der Hand des Herrn/wie Wasser-Bäche/und er neigets wohin er will."

while he was in Sulzbach and under the influence of van Helmont and Knorr von Rosenroth, he continued to believe that their kind of kabbalistic Christianity was the true religion. But as I have argued elsewhere, the kabbalistic convictions of the three people primarily responsible for the publication of the *Kabbala denudata*, Christian Knorr von Rosenroth, Francis Mercury van Helmont, and Christian August, undermined such basic Christian beliefs as the Trinity, the eternity of Hell, and even the notion that Jesus was the coequal and coeternal son of God. Thus the ecumenism and positive attitude toward Jews that Späth found in Sulzbach, together with the tendency of the Christian Kabbalists there to attenuate Christian doctrine by either explaining it allegorically or dismissing it altogether further undermined Späth's Christian convictions. Spener certainly believed this to have been the case. He singled out van Helmont as responsible for Späth's conversion on the grounds that he had made Späth's belief in Christianity "lukewarm."[46] Späth eventually came to the conclusion that if Christians disagreed so fundamentally among themselves and if Christian Kabbalists appropriated Jewish philosophy for their own purposes while discarding Christian fundamentals, perhaps the real kernel of truth lay in the Judaism, from which Christianity arose. Herman van der Hardt suggested that this was indeed Späth's reasoning when he described him as concluding after a long internal battle that, "everything is uncertain except this: God is certainly one."[47]

The other instrumental factor in Späth's conversion was his utter revulsion at the way Christians treated Jews and his sudden realization that the "suffering servant" in Isaiah, chapter 53 referred to the Jewish people as a whole. Schudt describes this decisive moment, which occurred in Amsterdam. He was out walking when a picture of Jesus covered with wounds and boils fell out of his pocket and onto the pavement. A Jew walking nearby picked the picture up and remarked, "That is Israel, the man of sorrows."[48] Späth abruptly realized that just as the Jews had suffered for the sins of the gen-

---

[46] P.J. Spener, *Consilia et judicia theologica latina*, III: 430.

[47] Van er Hardt made this observation in a conversation he had with Stolle. See G.E. Guhrauer, "Beiträge zur Kenntneiss des 17. u. 18. Jahrhunderts aus den handschriftlichen Aufzeichungen Gottlieb Stolle's", in: *Allgemeine Zeitschrift für Geschichte* 7 (1847), 403.

[48] Schudt, *Merkwürdigkeiten*, IV, 200.

tiles in the past, so they continued to suffer unjustly at the hands of Christians in the present. As he said:

> Even at the present time much of the same sort of thing happens in Poland and Germany, where circumstantial tales are told and songs are sung in the streets about how the Jews have murdered a child and sent the blood to one another in quills for the use of their women in childbirth. I eventually discovered this devilish lie and abandoned so-called Christianity in order to have no part in it nor be found with those who trample under foot Israel, the first begotten son of God, and shed his blood like water.[49]

All this and more is discussed in the letter Späth wrote to van Helmont after his conversion and under his new name, Moses Germanus. This letter offers an impassioned defense of his conversion to Judaism in terms of a searing criticism of what he regarded as an illegitimate appropriation and misinterpretation of kabbalistic thought by van Helmont and von Rosenroth. In the course of his denunciation of the Christian Kabbalah, Moses Germanus introduces arguments that reveal him to be a biblical scholar of considerable sophistication. His letter is written in German, a language which he never formally studied, as few Germans did in the Seventeenth century.[50] It is therefore not always easy to follow his train of thought or exact meaning.

From the opening paragraph, it appears that van Helmont had rebuffed Moses Germanus' attempts to arrange some kind of disputation. Van Helmont's reluctance may reflect his unwillingness to submit himself to the kind of polemical diatribe characteristic of the letter itself. But whatever van Helmont's motives in avoiding Moses Germanus were, the two men clearly had once enjoyed a close relationship before and perhaps even during the initial stages of Moses Germanus' conversion to Judaism, which apparently happened over several years. For Moses Germanus thanks van Helmont for his "love and faithfulness" and for providing him with used clothes, food, and money. His gratitude suggests that he was having trouble supporting himself after his conversion. But while Moses Germanus thanks

---

[49] The passage is quoted in H. Graetz, *History of the Jews*, 6 vols. (Philadelphia: The Jewish Publication Society of America,1967), V, 177. The original is cited in G. Wachter, *Der Spinozismus im Judenthumb* (Amsterdam, 1699), 29.

[50] Späth was educated by the Jesuits, who did not begin to instruct students in their mother tongue until 1703 (Samter, "Johann Peter Spaeth", 180 and n. 2).

van Helmont for his charity, he utterly rejects the "instruction" van Helmont tried to give him:

> Noble, highly revered and well-loved Herr von Helmont,
> Because I cannot be sure nor know whether I will succeed in speaking to you personally because you previously did not allow it and because I feel driven in my soul and conscience, I seek with these few lines or points to meet you face to face, and with that to derive satisfaction for my mind and free my conscience. First, I thank you once more and a thousand more times for you love and faithfulness and also for your generosity and good deeds, which you have shown me many times by giving me used clothes, food, money, and that well-meant teaching and instruction which I esteem above all, but which, in fact, I found very false and harmful when I went farther into the matter and continued, struggling to the source.[51]

Unfortunately Moses Germanus does not tell us what van Helmont's "well-meant teaching and instruction" was, but since he proceeds to criticize van Helmont's teaching about the *Zohar*, it would appear that he is referring to van Helmont's kabbalistic philosophy. In this section of his letter, Moses Germanus argues that van Helmont and Knorr von Rosenroth have "prostituted" the Kabbalah by misunderstanding and misinterpreting the doctrines of the *Zohar* in such a way as to produce "Grobian fantasies" worthy of Ovid's metamorphosis. At this point, Moses Germanus launches into a more far-reaching attack on the way Christians have distorted Jewish Scriptures in general:

> On account of such a teaching, I remind your illustrious self of the following: 1. As for the *Zohar*, which was published by Herr Rosenroth

---

[51] Moses Germanus to Francis Mercury van Helmont (Hamburg, Staats-Universitätsbibliothek, Suppellex. epistolica Uffenbaccii, v. 26, 67–68 (154), quoted by permission of the Staats- und Universitätsbibliothek Hamburg: "Wohledler, Hochgeehrter und vielgeliebter Herr von Helmont, Weilen nicht versichert seyn, noch wissen kan, ob mir gedeyen wird E. Edl. selbst persönlich anzusprechen dann auch das vorigmahl sie mir nun [68] solches nicht erlaubt und doch in meinem Seelen und Gewißen ich mich so getrungen finde, als ersuche ich mit diesen wenigen Zeilen oder Puncten doch vor E[ure] Angesicht zu kommen meinen Geist herinnen zu vergnügen oder mein Gewißen zu befreyen; Erstlich danke noch einmahl und tausandmahl für E[ure] Lieb und Treu auch Liberalitaet und Wohlthat so E. Edl. mir verschieden mahl mit angedienter Kleidung, Kost und Geld erweisen über alles aber, welches auch vor allem aestimire, die wohlgemeinte Lehr und Unterweisung, welche aber nach der Hand sehr falsch und schädlich habe [p. 67 (sic)/155)] gefunden, als ich weiter in derselben und darüber biß zum centro Brunnen fortgefahren und gerungen."

with your assistance: please, if only for the sake of the fear and love of God, consider what horror, sin, and injustice has been done with this. The figure of the matron in the dedication to the Prince of Sulzbach is indeed a sincere, pure Jewess of a very noble origin, from a very revered antiquity, from Palestine. Can greater injury and harm be done to her than was done to the Old Testament when it was handed over to the Roman people under Constantine and his successors, that band of spiritual gypsies, and prostituted? This indeed [can be understood] from the pages of the *Zohar* itself or from the laws of the mystical doctrine. The damage done to those into whose hands she has fallen is much greater than they suppose because they have something they are incapable of understanding. And, thus, they are defrauded to the highest degree, especially and inevitably when, following the harmful instruction given to the reader there, they often and at the same time read the Syrian New Testament and fill their poor skulls with your preconceived fantasies. Indeed, you can fabricate anything with your Grobian fantasies like Ovid's *Metamorphoses*. But you should leave this heavenly, pure nymph untouched and have no part of her.[52]

Interestingly enough, Moses Germanus' claim that the Christians began distorting the Hebrew Scriptures during the reign of Constantine is precisely what Knorr von Rosenroth and van Helmont believed. In the *Kabbala denudata*, Knorr argues that by delving into the Kabbalah, he is simply trying to return to the pure, apostolic Christianity of the early Christian centuries before Christianity had been corrupted by the spurious additions of Catholic Church Fathers, theologians,

---

[52] Ibid., fols. 67–69: "Derowegen aber solcher Lehr E. Edl. folgends erinnere. 1. Anbelangend den Sohar [forte Zohar] so durch H. Rosenroth mit E. Edl. Handanlegung und Beförderung ausgegeben worden. Bitte nur der Furcht und Liebe Gottes willen, sie bedenken was für Greuel, Sünd und Unrecht darmit angestellet werde. Ist solcher in der Figur eine Matron wie sie in der Dedication an Fürsten von Sulzbach stellen und zwar genere nobilissima, aetate gravissima, natione [fol. 68 (sic)] Palaestina, und also eine auffrichtige, reine Judinne kan ihr grössere Injurie und Schaden nicht geschehen als dem Römischen Constantischen Volk legitimis T.V. [Testamentum Veteris] in Regno Successoribus oder Geistl. [Geistlichen] Ziegeiner-Hauffen übergeben und prostituirt zu werden. Dieses zwar aus Seiten des gedachten Zohars oder mysticae doctrinae Legis selbsten. Auff den Seite der Participanten und in die Hände sie gefallen, ist der Schade noch viel grösser dann sie meinen werden, daß sie etwas haben, dessen sie doch in der That unfähig und also im höchsten Grad betrogen. Sonderlich und unvermeidlich wan sie nach der schadlichen Instruction dem Leser [fol. 69 [sic]/156] dort gegeben, sich verhalten und daß Syr. NT dabey zugleich und öffters lesen und also ihr armes Cerebell mit ihre vorgefassten Phantasie erfüllen, ja ein Büschel binden mögen sie mit ihrem Grobiantan in metam. Ovid. ergriffen. Aber diese himmlische reine Nymphen sollen sie wohl-unangetastet lassen und keinen Teil daran haben."

Popes, and Church Councils. And just as Moses Germanus says that
one can find evidence of these distortions in the *Zohar*—"This indeed
[can be understood] from the pages of the *Zohar* itself"—Knorr
looked to the same source for a more authentic apostolic Christianity.
Clearly, delving into Jewish sources could and did undermine the
beliefs of some Christians and produce "Judaizers" as well as outright Jews.[53] Moses Germanus went one step further than van Helmont
or Knorr, but in taking this step he effectively rejected their ecumenical vision.

Not only does Moses Germanus contend that van Helmont and
Knorr have misunderstood the Kabbalah, but he claims that the
Kabbalah they have is "more pagan than Jewish," and that, consequently, the kabbalistic proofs they offer to support the Christian
doctrine of the Trinity are invalid:

> The same applies to your *Kabbala denudata*. No more dreadful shame
> can happen to a married woman or daughter than to be stripped
> naked before such a horrible and abominable neophyte. Have not all
> honorable priests of the Pagans, Egyptians, Chaldeans, Greeks, Etruscans,
> and Romans been careful and taken pains so that their divine secrets
> would not be open to the unworthy rabble? But here the damage is
> even greater for the participants because they think they have a Cabbala
> which they do not in the least way have but only a heap of hastily-
> collected fragments which are more pagan than Jewish, just like D.
> Lupius' *Clavicula Solomonis* and many similar works. My soul will stand
> against yours in the balance before the judgement seat of the Almighty
> until you prove the persons in the Divinity on the basis of the Jewish
> Cabbala, although it is thought that these proofs were sniffed out
> from pagan delusions and misunderstood Rabbinical texts. To this
> day you and many others repeat the same things. It is absolutely not
> true that Psalm 50 can be understood to refer to a trinity of persons
> in the Godhead, or a triumvirate of praetors, through the words יהוה
> אל אלהים [El, Elohiim, Tetragrammaton] as you claim in your divine
> Cabbala, fol. 390.[54]

---

[53] David Katz, *Sabbath and Sectarianism in Seventeenth-Century England* (Leiden: E.J.
Brill, 1988).

[54] Moses Germanus to Francis Mercury van Helmont, 69–71 (156–157): "2.
Gleiches ist von E. Edl. Cabbala denudata zu bedencken, kein entsetzliche Schmach
kan eine ehelichen Matronen oder Tochter wiederfahren, als enblösst zu werden
vor so einem greulich und abscheulichem [70] Beginner hat sich alle erbare Heidnische
Aegyptische, Chaldaeische, Griechische, Hetrurische, Romische alte Priesterschafft
gehütet und geschert, daß sie ihr Göttliche Geheimnüße dem wilden Pöbel und
Unwürdigen nicht offenbahrten, ohne, daß auch hier auff der Participanten Seite

What Moses Germanus is referring to here is an argument made in the *Kabbala denudata* in which the members of the Christian Trinity are equated with three of the kabbalistic *sefiroth*, or emanations from the God-head. In Knorr and van Helmont's mind the fact that the Trinity could thus be discovered in the Kabbalah was ipso facto proof that the doctrine of the Trinity was not only an original part of apostolic Christianity but also something Jews were bound to accept once they clearly understood that it derived from their own sacred works. The problem with this line of argument from a Christian point of view was that it led to a conception of the Trinity that had very little to do with the kind of personalized Trinity of Father, Son, and Holy Ghost characteristic of most Christian teaching. The kabbalistic, rather than Christian, nature of Knorr and van Helmont's Trinity comes out clearly in the passage from the *Kabbala denudata* to which Moses Germanus referred above:

> Occasionally, the Tetragrammaton is written with the name *El* and *Elohim*, as in Psalm 50:1. The Psalmist of Asaph: "*El, Elohim, Tetragrammaton* has spoken and called the earth" (Compare Joshua 22:22: "God, God, the Lord, God, God, the Lord). Therefore, while these are joined together, you may perceive the sublime triumvirate of the Praetors seated upon the throne and determining whatever is necessary for the ordering of the world, either for good or bad, death or life. For *El* is mercy for those who are worthy; and יְדוֹד [I have taken this as a misprint for the *Tetragrammaton*, יְהוָה, since the meaning of יְדוֹד, "spark" or "flinging" makes no sense in the context, and the Psalm specifically refers to *El, Elohim* and the *Tetragrammaton* in the Hebrew] is fairness for those who were guided by it. From these three names come all laws or fairness, *Rachamim* or compassion, and *Din* or judgment. And this great testimony that the sons of Ruben and Gad and the half-tribe of Manassah made altars across the Jordan (Joshua

das Verderben größer ist, daß sie vermeinen einer Cabbalam zu haben, die sie doch auff keine Weiss und im geringsten nicht ist, sondern nur ein Hauffen zusammengeraffte und mehr Heidnisch als Judisch Scartequen, eben also D. Lupii Clavicula Salomonis und viel andern [71] dergleichen. Fast stehe meine Seele gegen E. Edl Seele vor dem Richtern Stuhl des Allerhöchsten in Gesichte, so lang protestando appelliunt, biß sie de personis in Divinitate aus der Juden Cabbala beweisen, wohl, wie schon gedacht aus heidnieschen Figmenten, so sie aus den nicht verstandenen Rabbinen hier und dar erschnuppert, wie auch E. Edl. gleichen Heut zu Tage noch vielen wiederfähret und zukommt. Es ist absolut nicht wahr, dass Ps. 50 durch die Wortter אל אלהים יוה eine dreiheit der personnen in der Gottheit oder triumvirate praetorium verstanden werde, wie E. Edl. aus Ihre Göttl. Cabbala den[udata] fol. 390."

22:22) has this meaning: if we make altars for the sake of memory alone, benedictions and beneficence will flow into us through *El*, which is a witness to our intentions. But if we build them for sacrifices, etc. *Elohim* is a witness and judge and punishes us for our grave sin. But יהוד [יהוה], which is the middle line and mediator tempers justice according to our intentions, either on the side of reward or punishment. For these three names are *Gedulah*, *Geburah*, and *Tipheret*. In this way, in the description of the creation of the world, the Psalmist of Asaph applies these three names. For God, having been about to create the world, clothed it in the appearance of a triple garment, one of which was the garment of great compassion, the second, the garment of perfect justice, and the third, middle garment consisting of compassion and judgment, all of which arise from that mystery of the created, some of whom are created in mercy, others in absolute judgment, and some in judgment and mercy. And just as wisdom has benevolence and mercy justice in their formation, so the same attributes are involved in the governing of the creatures. For at one time he proceeds with them with absolute mercy, at another wholly with judgment, and at another with both. And to this pertains the mystery of the three books which appear on New Year's day: The first of which is of the just, the second of the unjust, and the third of those in the middle. These correspond to the names אלהים אל יהוד [יהוה], all of which must be considered properly when they occur in Scripture.[55]

---

[55] In the reprint of the *Kabbala denudata* (Hildesheim: Georg Olms Verlag, 1974) the passage to which Moses Germanus refers appears in I, 1, 388: "Scribitur & interdum Tetragrammaton cum nomine El, atque Elohim, quemadmodum Psal. 50, 1. *Psalmus Asaphi: El, Elohim Tetragrammaton locutus est & vocavit terram.* Conf. Jehosch. 22, 22. Dum igitur haec sic jungi cernis sublime triumvirale praetorium super solium sedet, & pro cujusque operis necessitate mundi machinam dijudicat, sive in bonum, sive in malum, sive in mortem, sive in vitam. Nam El est Chesed, pro iis, qui eâ digni sunt; Elohim est retributio & poena pro iis, qui eâ digni sunt; & יהוד [יהוה] est aequitas vera pro iis, qui ea promerentur. Unde tria illa nomina continent omnia Mischpat seu aequum; Rachamim seu miserationem, & Din seu rigorem. Et Testimonium illud magnum, quod fecerunt Filii Ruben, & Gad, & dimidia tribus Menasche, altare nimirum trans Jordanem, Jehosch. 22. 22, hunc habet sensum: Si fecimus altare pro nuda memoria, influant in nos benedictiones & beneficia per mensuram El, quae testis sit intentionis nostrae. Si vero extruximus illud pro Sacrificiis, etc. Elohim sit testis & judex, & puniat nos ob grave hoc delictum: sed יהוד [יהוה], quae est linea media, mediatrix, judicium temperet secundum intentionem nostram, sive pro praemio, sive pro poena. Tria enim haec nomina sunt Gedulah, Gebhurah & Tipheret. Eodem modo in descriptione creationis mundi Assaph Psal. 50, 1. tria haec adhibet nomina. Deus enim creaturus mundum triplici vestium specie amictus erat; quarum una, vestis miserationum magnarum altera vestis judicii perfecti; & tertia vestis media, è misericordia & rigore consistens; quae omnia ex ipso creaturarum mysterio proveniunt, quarum aliae creatae sunt misericordiâ; aliae in rigore absoluto; aliae in judicio & misericordai. Et sicut se habuit sapientia illa & benignitas, misericordia & judicium in illarum formatione, ita eadem attributa se habent in creaturarum gubernatione: quandoque enim cum iis procedit in miseri-

The belief that key Christian doctrines such as the Trinity were implicit in the Jewish Kabbalah was the assumption of a long line of Jews who had converted to Christianity for precisely that reason.[56] In 1280 Abraham Abulafia says that some of his students converted because they had applied the kabbalistic practice of transposing letters to the phrase "I sit in the shade to which I aspire" (*Song of Songs*) in such a way that they came up with the phrases "I love his cross" or "in the shadow of the crucified one." Alfonse de Valladolid (Abner of Burgos) explicitly refers to the Kabbalah in discussing his own conversion in 1320. He maintained that the doctrine of the Incarnation was implicit in the concept of the *Shekhinah*, and he identified *Metatron* of the Kabbalah with Jesus on the grounds that some thirteenth-century Kabbalists had interpreted *Metatron* to mean "envoy." Although Jews began to argue strongly against this kind of Christian interpretation, even going as far as to argue that Christians were simply bad Kabbalists, who had derived such doctrines as the Trinity from a misunderstanding of the Kabbalah,[57] the practice continued. In 1512 Abraham Farisol, author of the anti-Christian polemic, *The Shield of Abraham*, described how Jewish converts to Christianity employed the idiom of the *Zohar* and other kabbalistic texts to justify the incarnation of God, his nativity, and resurrection. He pointed out that on the basis of the doctrine of the emanation of the *sefirot* Christians could argue that Jews already accepted the idea of multiplicity in God and that therefore the doctrine of the Trinity should not prove a stumbling block to conversion.

Farisol's point is well taken for the very good reason that Judaism and Christianity were both profoundly influenced by Neoplatonism, which described creation in terms of emanation from "The One" and encouraged the idea that this emanation occurred through triads or "Trinities." In explaining how The One became the many,

---

cordia absolutâ; quandoque in omnimodo judicio; quandoque in ambobus. Et huc pertinet mysterium trium librorum, qui aperiuntur die Novi anni, quorum unus est Justorum; alter impriorum; & tertius mediorum; qui correspondent nominibus אלהים אל ידוד [יהוה]. Quae omnia, quando in Scripturis occurrunt, probe sunt consideranda."

[56] Ernst Benz discusses these converts in "La Kabbale Chrétienne en Allemagne du xvie au xviiie siècle", *Kabbalistes Chrétiens: Cahiers d'Hermetisme*, eds. Antoine Faivre and F. Tristan (Paris: Editions Albin Michel, 1979).

[57] Benz gives the example of Profiat Duran, who argued in (1397) that Christians had obtained their doctrine of the Trinity from a misunderstanding of the Kabbalah.

Plotinus introduced the concept of the three *Hypostases*, a Greek term interpreted as meaning "origin," "substance," "real nature" or "first principle." According to Plotinus' formulation in his great work The *Enneads*, the first of these *Hypostases* was The One (*to hen*), the second, Intellect or Mind (*Nous*) and the third, Soul (*psuche*) (*Enneads* 5.1.) While Plotinus saw these as three separated entities, each one emanating from the previous one, Proclus tended to abolish any absolute distinction between them and "telescope" them into one. Christians were happy to see prefigurations of the Trinity in these triadic formulations (Proclus was especially helpful in this respect), and, indeed, it has been suggested that neoplatonic philosophy helped Christian theologians formulate the doctrine of the Trinity. Such triads made their way into Judaism and Islam through the infiltration of neoplatonic ideas, thus opening the way for Trinitarian interpretations of these rival religions by proselytizing Christians. Eventually Moses Germanus rejected this kind of reasoning, although he admits in his letter to van Helmont that much to his shame he had actually copied down van Helmont's explanation of Psalm 50:1 in his Psalter: "To my shame I wrote this down in my pocket Psalter, which I still keep today as a witness and testimony of such fruit."[58]

Moses Germanus is especially critical of the devotional hymns that Knorr von Rosenroth published in 1684 in his *Neuer Helicon*. He accuses van Helmont and Knorr of purloining these from Jewish sources and distorting them to fit a Christian message. His fury at this perceived desecration of authentic Jewish texts is so great that he relishes the thought of Knorr, who had died seven years before, rotting in his grave, forever barred from the face of God:

> What really and finally bothers me more than all the preceding things and which is also the real reason that I pour out my heart to you is the so-called Hecatomb or hundred panegyrics that you explained to me at that time in Frankfurt with the printed page in hand and, while doing so, dictated marginalia to me, which I have enjoyed for so many years and which finally appeared in von Rosenroth's *Neuen Helicon* and which I excessively recommended to others.
>
> But after I experienced the mercy and grace [of God], I made known the fraud with pain and heartache. Also, at that time in Cleve,

---

[58] Moses Germanus to Francis Mercury van Helmont, 72: "ich zu meiner Schandin mein Hand-Psalterlein notiert, alß auch Zeugnüss und Exempal solcher Früchten noct Heut au Tag bewahre."

when the two dreams or appearances of Herr Rosenroth to his daughter were described in a very credible fashion, sensitive thoughts came to my mind, that he would still be busy singing his blasphemous hecatombs and, in addition, his stinking corpse would daily be rejected and cast out from before the illuminated face of God.[59]

The references in this part of Moses Germanus' letter can only be understood in the context of the dreams that Knorr's daughter, Anna Dorothea (1669–1726), had shortly after her father's death in 1689. These dreams occurred after her marriage to a Catholic chamberlain, Marquard Leopold Freiherrn von Schütz, from Pfeilstadt, which had occasioned her conversion to Catholicism. They reflect her obvious desire to gain her father's approval for a step that he, as a Lutheran, apparently did not endorse. In fact, Knorr wrote a vehemently anti-Catholic polemic.[60] Walter Pagel and Friedhelm Kemp claim that there is absolutely no proof that Knorr wrote this because of his daughter's marriage.[61] However, the fact that his daughter had the dreams she had, in which her father appeared to her while in purgatory—which he as a Lutheran and a devotee of the Lurianic Kabblah would have rejected—and that in these dreams he did not say anything negative about Catholicism but implicitly assured her

---

[59] Moses Germanus to Francis Mercury van Helmont, 72–73/158: "3. Was mich eigentlich und endlich mehr als alles das vorige berührt, auch so ferner die eigenste Ursache ist mein Hertz also vor E. Edl. aus zu schütten, ist die sogenannte Hecatombe oder hundert Lob-Spruche, so mir neben dem gedruckten-Zettel E. Edl. da zumal in Frankfurt explicirt und marginalia dabey dictiret haben, dann ich mich auf viel lange Jahr erfreuret habe, endlich auch in KR [Knorr von Rosenroth] neuen Helicon ersehen und unmäßig andern recommendirt. Alß aber [p. 73/158] mir hernach Barmhertzigkeit und Gnade wiederfahren, habe den Betrug mit Schmertz und Hertzenleyd befunden, auch dazumahl in Cleve, als die beide Träume oder Erscheinungen des H. KR an seine Tochter sehr glaubwürdig erzelet würden, bey mir die empfindl[ichen] Gedancken kommen laßen, er werde wohl noch lang an seiner Gottes-lästerlichen Hecatombe singen müßen, auch darüber hinzu seinem stinckenden Cadaver täglich abgewiesen und von Gottes klarem Angesicht verstoßen werden."

[60] "Herrn Christian Knorrs von Rosenroth, Hochfürstl. Pfaltz-Sulzbachischen Hof-Raths und Cantzley-Direktoris Schreiben an seine älteste Fräulein Tochter, womit er sie für dem Abfall, als sie mit einem Catholischen Herrn von Schütz vermählet worden, wiewol vergeblich gewarnet." In: *Sammlung von Alten und Neuen Theologischen Sachen* . . . auf das Jahr 1738, 413–32.

[61] *Aufgang der Artzney-Kunst, das ist: Noch nie erhörte Grund-Lehren von der Natur, zu einer neuen Beförderung der Artzney-Sachen, so wol die Kranckheiten zu vertreiben als ein langes Leben zu erlangen. Geschrieben von Johann Baptista von Helmont* . . . (Sulzbach, 1683), reprinted and edited by W. Pagel and F. Kemp, 2 vols. (Munich: Kösel, 1971), xxxiii.

that she had earned a place in heaven, suggests Anna Dorothea was desperate for her father's post mortem approval.

Späth (for he was not yet Moses Germanus) was at Cleve when these dreams were discussed. They occured a year and a half after Knorr's death, or sometime around October, 1690 (Knorr died on May 4, 1689). Given the nature of these dreams, there is every reason to believe that Knorr's daughter would have been eager to communicate them to others as soon as possible. If that is the case, Späth may have begun to think about his conversion some six years before he was circumcised.[62] I quote Anna Dorothea's dreams because they explain the graphic reference to Knorr's "stinking corpse" in Moses Germanus' letter:

> Approximately a year and a half after the blessed passing away of my once dearest father, I dreamed as if I stood at a window in a room where once his library used to be at Alberhoff, his country estate. I heard a lovely voice, like that of my blessed father, as if he were coming from out of the wall. He appeared larger than he was in his life and he was singing his hundred songs of praise, which were in his hand. As I now rushed towards him, I was full of joy and said (according to my recollection, while sleeping): How happy I am to see my father in such a glorious state. He would be without doubt in heaven because he praises God so devoutly, which would not be expected of one who is wretched. Then he said to me, while sighing, that he was indeed blessed, but only in the hope of achieving perfect eternal bliss for which his soul thirsts. He was indeed in the best company of all holy and learned men, with whom he eats and associates, spending day and night in praise of God. But when he imagines that he has reached the supreme good, then his punishment, which he still has to suffer through, begins. Because the mercy of God is so inconceivable, it would not allow the smallest good that it finds in a soul to remain unimproved. However, it seems a fable to the world, how exactly everything is weighed there. Certainly, good will not remain unrewarded there and evil unpunished. His purification and punishment, however, consists in this, that often when he imagined that he praised God to the highest degree, then his soul had to return to his body in the

---

[62] The problem with this interpretation is that in a letter to Johannes Leusdens written in January or February of 1696 after his conversion, Moses Germanus says that the "burning desire" for his conversion "began two years ago when I was in Cleve." It is, of course, possible that Moses Germanus had been in Cleve at an earlier time as well and that his desire to convert already existed, for he says in the same letter that he "long pondered" "the reasons and decisions" that eventually led to his conversion (Hamburg, Staatsbibliothek, Suppellex. epistolica Uffenbaccii et Wolfiorum, v. 26, fols. 40ff.).

grave, which was so horrible that from that moment he anticipated such punishment continually with great trembling and fear. He had to suffer there for a certain time, and could I imagine what kind of torment this must be, to remain with a stinking corpse and to be in such darkness? Afterwards, while he was speaking, he began to show such fear and trembling that when I asked him whether the evil hour was about to come upon him, he answered me, yes, and said, shaking all over, when I [sic] begin to reform my soul and life, he [sic] hopes to receive the grace of God and to appear soon to me again and to tell me how things have been since his death. I wished to say much more, but both his horror and his whole account, as well as my fear and dread, made me unable to say more than that I asked him if he would bless my little child, who was being brought to me at that moment. My mother would have come as well, but he had scarcely touched the child and blessed him, when he began to hurry and shake and go back through the wall.[63]

---

[63] Hannover, Niedersächsiche Landesbibliothek, LBr 17: "Realtion von dem was Zwischen dem Herrn Knorr von Rosenroth und seiner Tochter nach seinem Tod vorgegangen seyn soll (asterick with the following written at the bottom of the page: Conte pour conte. Nous allons voir tantôt, qu'on avait payé Ch. de Helmont à Hanover de la meme moneye): von ihr selbst beschrieben. Nota: Mein seliger Vater ist gestorben den 4 May frühe zwischen 2 und 3 Uhr 1689.

Ungefehr anderhalb Jahr nach dem seligen Ableben meines liebst gewesenen vatters traumte mir, als wie ich zu Albershoffe auff sein Guth in einer stuben, wo selbsten seine Bibliothec zu stehen pflag, an einem Fenster stünde, und eben einer lieblichen stimme nachgehends aber meines seeligen vatters, als ob er aus der wand herausginge, gewahr wurde. Seine gestalt kame mir viel grösser, als in seinen Leben, vor, und hatte es seine hundert Lobspruche, daraus singende, in der Hand. Als ich nun voller freuden auff ihm zu eilete, und sagte meines bedunckens im schlaff: wie bin ich so gluckseelig, daß ich meinem Herrn Vattern also und in so glorwürdigen stande sehe; er wäre ja ohne zweiffel im Himmel, weil er Gott so inniglich lobe, welches denen Unseeligen nicht zuzutrawen were. Darauff sagte er mir, als seuffzende, er wäre zwar seelig, aber nur in der hoffnung [p. 17 v] und noch lange nit in der vollkommenen glückseeligkeit, warnach seine Seele durste; er wäre zwar in der besten gesellschafft lauter Heiliger und gelehrter Männer, mit denen er esse und umbgehe, und nacht und tag im lobe Gottes zubrächte; aber wann er im allerbesten vermeine zu sein, so komme seine straffe, so er noch aus zustehn; dann die barmhertzigkeit Gottes were so unbegreiflich, daß sie auch gar nicht das allergeringste gute, so sie an einer seele finde, ungebeßert ließe, und hingegen sey es der welt eine fabel, wie genau man dorten alles nehme und gewies weder gutes unbelohnet, noch böses ungestrafft bleibe: seine läuterung und straffe aber bestünde in diesem, daß er oeffters, wann er nun am allerbesten Gott zu loben vermeine, so muße seine Seele zu seinen Cörper, in das Grab; welches dann eine solche Ensetzung seye, daß er solche straffe allezeit mit großem zittern und angst vorhero ande. Da habe er seine gewiße zeiten auszustehn, und könne ich gedencken, was dieses vor eine Quall seyn müße, bey einem stinckenden Cörper zu wohnen, und in solcher Finsternis zu sein. Worauf er in währenden reden anfing solche angst und zittern spüren zulaßen, daß als ich fragte, nun würde gewies die böse stunde kommen, er mir mit ja antwortete und ganz zitterende sagte, wann ich es zu meines Seelen

Two weeks later Anna Dorothea had a similar dream, which reflects even more pointedly her concern to justify her conversion.

Approximately two weeks later I had the following dream of him again. It seemed to me as if I were in the Prince's house in which my blessed father died, in the company of other people. A small child of four or five years (as I remember) came and tugged on my skirt, saying: Come, I wish to speak to you. I immediately obliged him and went away from the group into a room with the child. I didn't yet think that the child was my father, but lifted him onto a chair. I myself sat on the floor. He began to speak. Don't you recognize your father, who returns by the mercy of God who especially loves your soul, to keep his promise to tell you how I have fared since the hour of my death? After such a welcome rebuke, which I did not take as empty and meaningless but for the good of my soul, to make me more zealous in the love of God, because God, through his special grace, had allowed him to come to me, which, perhaps, many wish for in vain. If I took this as a sign of certainty and did not reform my life so that he could look at me with joy sometime in the future, my judgment would be terrible. After such and similar beautiful speeches, he said, as soon as my soul was separated from my body, the angel of God was waiting by my bed and he brought me through the dark valley of death, where I had an uncommonly difficult journey. [On the journey I had to walk across] a slippery, round bar, under which was an open abyss and slough of steam and fog, where the damned wailed most horribly and the thick darkness and terrible stormy wind above me so injured my head that, as you see, I cannot go about with it unbandaged. Everything was so horrible to me and caused such fear and anxiety that I forgot that the angel of God was leading me. Then, with each step, I feared that I would fall into the slough, but God stood by me and the angel of God led me by the hand so that I did not fall and brought me into the land of the living and into the company of holy and learned men, about whom I recently spoke to you, where we praise God day and night and always study. My punishment still hung over me. I had to return to my grave until I became as little as a child, as you see me. I am now in a blessed condition, as is written: the just souls are safe and no torture can touch them. However, I am not yet perfect because

---

[p. 18] besten und beßerung meines lebens anwenden werde, hoffe er gnade von Gott zuerlangen mir bald wieder zu erscheinen und zu sagen, wie es ihm zeit seines Absterbens ergangen habe. Worauff ich noch viel sagen wollen; vor screcken und angst aber so mir seine Entsetzung und die gantze anhörung solcher sachen verursachte, mehr nicht zu wegen bringen kommmen, als daß ich ihn gebeten, er möchte mein kleines kind, so man eben hertruge, segnen; es wäre auch die frau mutter kommen aber er hat kaum dar kind berühret und gesegnet, so habe er geeilet und gezittert, und sey wider durch die wand getrungen."

much [of my sinful nature] has to be removed and I must be deprived of the perfect contemplation of God until I become as little as a light.

After this, I fell at his feet with joy and embraced him. I realized that for tears and joy I could not speak. Through his whole speech, I waited to see whether he would give me any warning about the Catholic religion. But because he did not mention it, I asked him whether there was any truth in the Catholic belief in purgatory or the third place, where the souls are cleansed. I believed that he would have to know about it now. I thought that because I had even named the religion that he would be able to say something certain either for or against that aforementioned religion, which I would have taken as the word of God. But he answered nothing further to my question, except that through this which he told me with God's permission I would have enough confirmation of the third place and of the purification of souls there, albeit not through fire. He had nothing further to say than that with repeated warnings I should give my heart to God alone, who would bless me and give me children and who would want me in heaven. I must not despise this [what he said] so that I would not be eternally damned. I did not dare ask any more questions but kept thinking about this. He became smaller and smaller before my eyes and finally went through the closed window as a bird. Before he was completely gone, I still asked whether I would see him again. He said he did not know but he thought that when his condition once again changed he would not think back but would then reach the desired perfection. I asked him not to stop remembering and entreating God [for me] and I wondered again whether he would not contradict me for this Catholic opinion. I heard him say nothing more and he went immediately through the glass as I went to the window to see whether or not he had broken the panes. But I found them untouched. Weeping, I said so loudly that my dearest husband heard: O God, how subtle is a spirit! The panes are not even broken! Having said that, my husband awoke me and asked me what the matter was. I immediately explained everything to him in all its detail.[64]

---

[64] Ibid.: "Nach ungefehr 14. Tagen aber traumte mir wider von ihme nachfolgendes: Es ware mir, ob wäre ich in dem Fürstlichen Hauß, in welchem mein seeliger Vatter gestroben, in Gesellschafft anderer leute; es kame aber ein kleines Kind, meinem beduncken nach von etwann 4 oder 5 Jahren, mit einer zugebundenen stirne, und zupfte mich bey dem rock, sagende: Komm, ich wil mit dir reden. Da ich nun solches gleich that, von den leuten mit dem Kinde in die Kammer gieng, und noch nit dachte, daß es mein vatter wäre, sondern das Kind auf den sessel hub, mich aber auf die erde setzte, fieng er an und sagte: Kennestu deinen Vatter [p. 18v] nicht, welcher aus großses Barmhertzigkeit Gottes, der deine seele sonderlich liebet, kommet, sein versprechen zuhalten dir zu sagen wie es mir von der stunde meines todes bis hieher ergangen? Nach einer sehr köstlichen Ermahnung, wie ich solches nit vor leer und nichtig sondern meiner seelen zu nutzen, und zur liebe Gottes desto eyferiger zu werden gebrauchen solte, dann Gott hette ihm zu

When listening to an account of these dreams it would be understandable if thoughts of his own religious anxieties and possible conversion to Judaism were aroused in Späth. The clarity with which
he remembers Anna Dorothea's description of Knorr rotting in his
grave suggests these dreams had a profound impact on him, an effect
they presumably would not have had he not already developed considerable antipathy towards Knorr and van Helmont's kabbalistic
philosophy. His description of his mental state while at Cleve certainly suggests that he was troubled and may well have developed
such an antipathy:

sondern gnaden erlaubet zu mir zu kommen, welches villeicht viele umbsonst wun-
scheten; würde ich es aber zur sicherheit gebrauchen, und nicht also leben, daß er
mich könte dermahleins mit freudenschauen, so wäre mein Gerichte erschröcklich.
Nach solchen und dergleichen schönen reden, sagte er so bald meine seele vom
leibe geschieden, wartete der Engel des Herrn schon bey dem bett darauf, und
brachte mich durch das finstere Todes thal, wo selbsten ich einen ungemeinen weg
zugehen hatte. Solcher war nicht anders, als eine glatte runde stange, unter mir
aber ein offener abgrund und pful von dampf und schwebel; das grausambste heulen
der Unglückseeligen. Die dickeste Finsterniße und der ershrecklichste sturmwint, der
ober mir war, und mich an meinem Haupt so sehr beschädiget, daß ich solches,
wie du siehest, nicht [p. 19] kan ungebunden tragen, war mir alles ein solches
Entsetzen und solche furcht und angst, daß ich vergeßen, daß mich der Engel des
Herrn fuhrete. Dann ich furchte mich jeden schrit in diesen pfuel zu fallen; aber
Gott ist mir beygestanden, und der Engel des Herrn führte mich bey der hande,
daß ich nit fallen konte, und brachte mich in das Land der lebendigen, und zu
der Gesellschafft des heiligen und gelehrten Männer, wovon ich dir neulich gesagt,
da wir Gott loben tag und nacht, und immer studieren. Da war aber meine straff
noch immer da, und ich muste zu meinem leib ins grab, bis ich so klein worden,
als ein Kind, wie du mich siehest. Ich bin zwar nun in einem viel seeligen stande,
und also, daß es heisse: Der Gerechtin Seelen seint in Sicherheit, und keine Quaal
rühret sie an; ich bin aber noch nit vollkommen; dann es mus noch viel weg, und
muß ich noch solange der vollkommensten Anschauung Gottes beraubet seyn, bis
ich so klein werde, als ein licht. Hiemit fiel ich ihm vor Freuden zu Füßen und
umbfieng ihn. Es dauchte mich auch, ich könte vor weinen und freuden nit reden.
Doch merckte ich durch seine gantze Rede immer zu auff, ob er mir keine warnung vor der Catholischen Religion thun wurde. Weil er aber gar nichts dergleichen gedachte, so fragte ich, was es dann mit der Catholischen Meinung von
[p. 19] Freyfeuer oder tritten ort, wo die seelen gereiniget würden, vor eine bewandt-
nus habe? Ich glaubte, daß er es nun wol wißen werde. Dabey war aber meine
Meinung, weil ich so gar die Religion nennete, er würde nur etwas gewißes etwan
vor oder wider gemeldete Religion melden, welches ich vor ein Außpruch Gottes
gleichsam gehalten hätten. Er sagte mir aber auf meine frag nit mehr, als daß ich
nun von dem dritten ort, und von der verbeßerung der Seelen aldorten, obschon
nit eben ein Feur seye, durch dies, was er mir auff zulaßung Gottes gesagt, gnugsame
Confirmation hätte, und hätte er mir weiter nichts zu sagen, als mit nochmahliger
warnung, daß ich mein Hertz solte Gott alle in geben, der mich zu segnen auch
mit Kindern zubegaben, und in Himmel zuhaben bedacht wäre, ich solte es nur

But because there and at that time I could not confide in anyone, as the outcome showed I would have made a bad impression and harmed myself, thank God that God's goodness protected me so well from this. Thus my sorrow was eating at my heart and I lamented so much more about Herr Helmont to myself, that he himself would at some time have to sing the same sad song and be bereft of God's presence, [God who is not] fooled by such fraud and hot air, that he will be relegated to such miserable places, etc., all of which I wanted to tell your illustrious self back then at the castle.[65]

Moses Germanus continues his letter to van Helmont on a note of obsequiousness that quickly turns to vituperative condemnation. He returns to the subject of Knorr and van Helmont's fraudulent publication of the "Hecatomb" and calls upon his God to imbue his words of warning with the supernatural force they deserve:

I come with no other armor but in the name of God and, indeed, as is known of him, he opposes the arrogant, but not with defiance or revenge or hard and harsh words, and he gives grace to those who are humble. Because of this, I approach you with the greatest humility. I put myself in the posture and likeness of a small dog at your noble feet, as I have done to my other worthy friends, especially at Cleve. I am obliged and owe it to you, your illustrious self, not only

---

nit selbst zu meinem äussersten verdamnus verachten. Ich trauete mir nun nichts mehr zu fragen, sondern blieb im Nachdencken, da mir dann nach und nach vorkam wie er vor meinen Augen so klein wurde, und endlich als ein Vogel durch das zugemachte Fenster drung. Ich fragte noch, ehe er allerdings von mir ware ob ich ihn nicht mehr sehen wurde; so sagte er erwuste es nicht, glaubte aber, daß, wan sein standt sich wieder verändere, er wohl nit mehr zuruck gedencken [p. 20] würde, sondern alsdan in die gewünschte vollkommenheit gelangen werde. Ich bat ihn, er solte bey Gott nit aufhören zubitten und zugedencken, und dachte wider, ob er mirs nit etwan, als eine Catholische meinung, widersprechen würde. Ich hörte ihn aber nichts mehr sagen, und war er gleich durch das Glass, als ich hin zum Fenster gieng und sehen wolte, ob er die scheiben nit zerbrochen. Ich funde sie aber unversehret, und weinete, und sagte so laut, daß es mein Liebster höret: Ach Gott wie subtil ist ein Geist! Ist doch die scheiben nit einmahl zubrochen! Daruber mich dann mein Liebster weckete, und fragte, was mir wäre: dem ich sofort gleich selbigen moment alles umbstendlich erzhelete."
[65] Moses Germanus to Francis Mercury van Helmont, 73/158–74: "Weil ich aber dort und dazumahl keinem mich vertrauen dürfen wie der Außgang auch bezeuget, daß ich übel angelassen und mich selbst [p. 74] beschädiget haben würde, da vor Gottes Güthe, so mich wohl bewahrt hat, danke. Habe ich also meinen Kummer in mich freßen müßen und um so viel desto mehr um meinen H. Helmont bey mir selbst gejammert, daß er dermahleins denselben Trauer-Thon nicht auch singen müße, nicht von solchen Schwindel und Windbrausen hingerißen, Gottes schönen Angesicht beraubt, in solche Jammer-Oerthen hingewiesen werde, und dergleichen, welches E. Edl. dazumahl zur Burg auch habe sagen wollen."

to kiss your hands and feet but also to lick the dust off your shoes
with my tongue. I wanted to offer my tears as a footbath and whatever other expression of subservience I could muster. But I have both
the truth and the word of God against you. It is not true that such
a Hecatomb was ever used by the Hebrews and, therefore, it is not
right that one cheats the world with such vain fantasies and provides
even more annoyance and offense to those blind ones. May God imbue
these words with the thunderous power of his own words, so that they
will go straight to your heart and through you to others. Amen. I,
through these many years of my own unfortunate experience, have
learned what damage can be done when one pretends to wisdom and
does not in fact possess it. Would God that others will heed this
warning.[66]

In Moses Germanus' opinion all of the kabbalistic works produced
by Knorr and van Helmont deserved censure because they are either
fabrications largely derived from pagan philosophy or vain and blasphemous speculations based on misinterpretations of Jewish tradition. He draws on the opinions of various experts to question the
accuracy of the biblical text and he ridicules various pagan philoso-
phies and even the work of Boehme, which he had previously revered,
for asserting that the one, true God could suddenly become many.
He ends his letter with the same mixture of obsequiousness and censure he displayed earlier. He begs van Helmont not "to push him
away" but at the same time adjures him to "banish, tear up and
burn" the *Kabbala denudata* as well as a number of his other books.

---

[66] Ibid.: "Ja ich komme doch mit keiner andern Rüstung, als im Nahmen Gottes
und zwar wie von Ihm bekannt, daß Er den Hoffärtigen wiederstehet, darum nicht
mit Trotzen oder Rachen oder harten, herben Wortten, und denen Demütigen
giebt Er Gnade. Darum in dem Grund der Demuth greiff ich E. Edl. an. Ich lege
mich in Positur und Gleicheit eines Hündleins zu E. Edlen Füßen, wie ich auch
zum andren an meine werte Freunde, [p. 77] sonderlich zu Cleve gethan. Ich
erkenne mich verplicht und schuldig E. Edl. nicht allein die Hände und Füsse zu
küßen, sondern auch den Staub von ihren Schuen mit meiner Zungen abzülecken.
Ich wollte wohl zu den Fußbad meine Trähnen offeriren, und was noch vor
Untertänigkeit durch einige Expression als kan bezeiget werden. Aber eine Wahrheit
als ein Wortt des Herrn hab ich wieder sie. Es ist nicht wahr, daß jemahl eine
solche Hecatombe unter den Hebraeren im Brauch gewesen und darum ists [ist es]
nicht recht, daß man die Welt mit solchen eiteln Phantasyen betrüge, [p. 78] jenen
blinden noch mehr Argenüß und Anstoß mache. Gott gebe diesen Wortten, als den
Donner seiner Wortten Krafft, daß sie an Eu Edl Hertz und andern durch sie,
durchdringend schneiden mögen. Amen. Ich durch mein eigene, so viel Jahr verderbende Erfahrung hab glernt, was für Schaden bringe, sich von Weißheit etwas einzu
bilden, da man in der That und Wahrheit nichts besitzet. Wollte Gott, daß andere
meine Warnüng sich dienen lassen wollen."

In his book *Spinoza im Judenthums*, Johann Georg Wachter made the preposterous claim that Moses Germanus did not convert to "real" Judaism but to a disguised form of Spinozism as a result of van Helmont's influence and the mistaken assumption that Spinoza's philosophy was the closest thing possible to the Kabbalah. Wachter also dates Moses Germanus' conversion to 1682. Wachter was wrong on all counts. As we have amply seen from his letter to van Helmont, Moses Germanus repudiated the Kabbalah in the form presented by Knorr and van Helmont. He also repudiated Spinoza for his betrayal of the Jewish belief in human free will and for his conviction that reason, not revelation, was the source of all knowledge.[67]

Moses Germanus indicted Christianity on the basis of both doctrine and practice. In important respects his criticism of Christianity reflected the conclusions of Christian Hebraists, whose biblical and textual criticism clearly promoted a skeptical attitude on the part of many Christians towards both the biblical text and many of the theological premises supposedly based on it. He makes this point in his letter to Frau Petersen in answer to her apparently "astonished" reaction to his conversion:

> . . . your Grace is astonished . . . that I so shockingly deny the history of this Jesus.
> . . . I learned such things by and by from these philologists, for whom, from the Gospel of Matthew to the Apocalypse, there is not one part sufficiently authentic or correct, as Herr Peterson and all those like him must know, to give one example of all these from Leusden's Philologo Hebraeo-Graeco.[68]

Drawing on the work of Johannes Leusdens (1624–99), Professor of Middle Eastern languages at the University of Utrecht (and one of his correspondents) as well as other Christian Hebraists, Moses Germanus

---

[67] Moses Germanus' refutation of Spinoza appears in *Sapientia in Israele*, which appeared as the second volume of *Diatribe de Ortu et Progressu Facultatis*, etc. (1697?), which Späth published anonymously. (The first volume is entitled *Salus ex Iudaeis*). The date 1670 appears on the title page, but this refers to the publication date of Spinoza's *Tractatus Theologico-Politicus*, not to Späth's critique of it.

[68] *Send Screiben*, 7: "Daß Euer Edl. . . . sich so verwundert . . . daßich die Historia von diesem Jesu so verschrecklich läugne. . . .ich solches nach und nach von denen Philologis erlernet/denen von dem Evangelio Matthaei biß an eurer Apolcalysis nicht ein Theil gut genug/authenticè oder richtig ist/wie Herr D. Petersen und allen seines gleichen nicht unwissend seyn kan: Nahmentlick und instar omnium aus des Leussdenii Philologo Hebraeo-Graeco."

dismissed the Christian Church as an invention from the period of Constantine. He claimed that the core of Jesus's teaching in the New Testament came from Jewish oral tradition, which was later deposited in the Mishnah and Talmud. Therefore everything valid in Christianity originated in Judaism. What was invalid—for example, the cult of Saints, adoration of the host, and worship of a human being—came from idolatrous Paganism.[69] Moses Germanus accused the Catholic Church of being a "God-maker" ("Gottermacherin") and dismissed the Papal throne as a "Seat of Pestilence" ("Stuhl der Pestilenz").[70] In his opinion the Christian martyrs of the early centuries were really Jews, and this included Ignacius and Polycarp. The Virgin birth was an "Ovidian metamorphosis and invented fable" ("Ovidianische Metamorphosis und erdictete Fabel"), and there were originally many more than four Gospels.[71] It was probably from reading Richard Simon that he came to reject the passage in 1 John 5:7–8 on the Trinity as a later interpolation because it was not found in the oldest Vatican Bible manuscript.[72] From Leusdens Moses Germanus learned that the incident of the adulterous woman in John 7:53–8:11 was a later addition.[73] Moses Germanus also realized that all the signs Jesus mentioned concerning the imminent Apocalypse were modeled on accounts of the destruction of the Temple in 70 CE.[74] He also argued that the author of the Book of Revelation interpreted the destruction of the temple as the beginning of the millennium.[75] In taking these positions Moses Germanus anticipated many modern scholars who claim that early Christianity represented a special form of Jewish eschatology. In Moses Germanus' view, it was only when millenarianism was renounced that Christianity become a separate religion.

---

[69] Schudt, *Jüdische Merkwürdigkeiten*, I, 694; Wachter, *Der Spinozismus im Judenthumb* (Amsterdam, 1699), 30.

[70] Hamburg, Staatsbibliothek, Suppellex. epistolica Uffenbaccii, v. 26, 57.

[71] Schudt, *Jüdische Merkwürdigkeiten*, IV, 194–5.

[72] The passage, which has been removed from modern scholarly translations of the bible, reads as follows in the King James version: "For there are three that bear record in heaven, the Father, the Word, and the Holy Ghost: and these three are one. And there are three that bear witness in the earth, the spirit, and the water, and the blood: and these three agree in one."

[73] Hamburg, Staatsbibliothek, Suppellex. epistolica Uffenbaccii, v. 26, 57.

[74] Schudt, *Jüdische Merkwürdigkeiten* I, 695.

[75] Ibid., IV, 195; *Das große Hosianna selfs van Joden uytgeroepen* (Amsterdam, 1701), 30ff.

It was for this reason that he regarded millenarian groups among Christians as essentially Jewish since they expected the millennium to occur on the earth. But for all the doctrinal fantasies and outright falsifications imagined by Christians, it was their lack of charity, mutual tolerance, and tolerance towards the Jews that bothered him the most. He ultimately decided that he wanted no part of a religion that permitted and even encouraged such atrocities.

Given the tremendous hostility to Jews and especially to Christian converts to Judaism, it is significant that Moses Germanus did not hide his light under a bushel. He actively proselytized among Christians, telling anyone willing listen how fraudulent and flawed the Christian religion was. (It must be admitted that after his conversion he remained in the safe haven of Amsterdam and thus enjoyed unusual freedom of speech.) In the face of all the laws against conversion, Moses Germanus saw himself as the forerunner in what he was convinced would eventually be a stampede away from Christianity and into Judaism. As he said, "Non vos deservui, sed praecessi" ("I do not dessert you, but preceed you").[76]

Appendix

Moses Germanus to Francis Mercury van Helmont (Hamburg, Staatsbibliothek, Suppellex. Epistolica Uffenbaccii, v. 26, pp. 67–90

Wohledler, Hochgeehrter und Seelengeliebter Herr von Helmont.

Weilen nicht versichert seyn, noch wissen kan, ob mir gedeyen wird E. Edl. selbst persönlich anzusprechen, dann auch das vorigmahl sie mir nun [68—sic] solches nicht erlaubt und doch in meiner Seelen und Gewißen ich mich so getrungen finde, also ersuche ich mit diesen wenigen Zeilen oder Puncten doch vor E[ure] Angesicht zu kommen, meinen Geist herinnen zu vergnügen oder mein Gewißen zu befreyen. Erstlich danke noch einmahl und tausendmahl für E[ure] Lieb und Treu, auch Liberalitaet und Wohlthat so E. Edl. mir verschieden mahl mit angedienter Kleidung, Kost und Geld erwiesen, über alles aber, welches auch vor allem aestimire, dero wohlgemeinte Lehr und Unterweisung, welche aber nach der Hand sehr falsch und

---

[76] Wachter, *Der Spinozismus im Judenthumb*, 28.

schädlich habe [67—sic] gefunden, als ich weiter in derselben und darüber biß zum centro Brunnen fortgefahren und gedrungen. Derowegen aber solcher Lehr E. Edl. folgends erinnere. 1. Anbelangend den Sohar [in margin: forte Zohar] so durch H. Rosenroth mit E. Edl. Handanlegung und Beförderung ausgegeben worden. Bitte nur der Furcht und Liebe Gottes willen, sie bedenken was für Greuel, Sünd und Unrecht darmit angestellet werde. Ist solcher in der Figur eine Matron, wie sie in der Dedication an Fürsten von Sultzbach stellen und zwar genere nobilissima, aetate gravissima, natione [68] Palaestina, und also eine auffrichtige, reine Judinn kan ihr grössere Injurie und Schaden nicht geschehen, als dem Römischen Constantinischen Volk legitimis T[estamento] V[etero] in Regno Successoribus oder Geistl[ichen] Ziegeiner-Hauffen übergeben und prostituirt zu werden. Dieses zwar auf Seiten des gedachten Zohars oder mysticae doctrinae Legis selbsten. Auff der Seiten der Participanten und in dero Hände sie gefallen, ist der Schade noch viel größer, dann sie meinen werden, daß sie etwas haben, deßen sie doch in der That unfahig und also im höchsten Grad betrogen. Sonderlich und unvermeidlich wan sie nach der schädlichen Instruction dem Leser [69] dort gegeben, sich verhalten und daß Syr. NT [Syriacum Novum Testamentum] dabey zugleich und öffters lesen und also ihr armes Cerebell mit ihrer vorgefaßten Phantasie erfüllen, ja ein Büschel binden mögen sie mit ihrem Grobian jam in metam. Ovid. ergriffen. Aber diese himmlische reine Nymphen sollen sie wohl-unangetastet laßen und keinen Teil daran haben. 2. Gleiches ist von E. Edl. Cabbala denudata zu bedencken, kein entsetzliche Schmach kan einer ehelichen Matronen oder Tochter wiederfahren, als enblößt zu werden vor so einem greulich und abscheulichen [70] Beginnen. Hat sich alle erbare Heidnische Aegyptische, Chaldaeische, Griechische, Hetrurische, Römische alte Priesterschafft gehütet und gescheut, daß sie ihr Göttliche Geheimnüße dem wilden Pöbel und Unwürdigen nicht offenbahrten, ohne, daß auch hier auff der Participanten Seite das Verderben größer ist, daß sie vermeinen eine Cabbalam zu haben, die sie doch auff keine Weiß und im geringsten nicht ist, sondern nur ein Hauffen zusammengeraffte und mehr Heidnische als Jüdische Scartequen, eben als D. Luppii Clavicula Salomonis und viel andere dergleichen. [71] Ja, es stehe meine Seele gegen E. Edl Seele vor dem Richter-Stuhl des Allerhöchsten im Gerichte, so lange protestando appelliunt, biß sie de personis in Divinitate aus der Juden Cabbala bewiesen, wohl, wie schon gedacht, aus heidnischen

Figmenten, so sie aus den nicht verstandenen Rabbinen hier und
dar erschnuppert, wie auch E. Edl. gleichen Heut zu Tage noch vielen wiederfähret und zukommt. Es ist absolut nicht wahr, daß Ps.
50 durch die Worte אל אלהים יוה [El, Elohiim, Tetragrammaton]
eine Dreyheit der personen in der Gottheit oder triumvirale praetorium verstanden werde, wie E. Edl. aus Ihrer Göttl. Cabbala
den[udata] fol. 390 [72] in voce יי n. 10 mir ad calamum dictirten,
ich zu meiner Schand in mein Hand-Psalterlein notiert, alß auch
Zeugnüß und Exempel solcher Früchten noch Heut zu Tag bewahre.
3. Was mich eigentlich und endlich mehr als alles das vorige berührt,
auch sofern die eigenste Ursache ist, mein Hertz also vor E. Edl.
auszuschütten, ist die sogenannte Hecatombe, oder hundert Lob-
Sprüche, so mir neben dem gedruckten Zettel E. Edl. dazumal in
Frankfurt explicirt und marginalia dabey dictirt haben, darin ich
mich auf viel lange Jahr erfreut habe, endlich auch in K[norr von]
R[osenroths] neuen Helicon ersehen und unmäßig andern recommendirt. Alß aber [73] mir hernach Barmhertzigkeit und Gnade
widerfahren, habe den Betrug mit Schmertz und Hertzenleyd be-
kunden, auch dazumahl in Cleve, als die beide Träume oder Erscheinungen des H[errn] K[norr von] R[osenroth] an seine Tochter sehr
glaubwürdig erzehlet wurden, bey mir die empfindl[ichen] Gedank-
ken kommen laßen, er werde wohl noch lang an seiner Gottes-
lästerlichen Hecatombe singen müßen, auch darüber hin zu seinem
stinckenden cadaver täglich abgewiesen und von Gottes klarem
Angesicht verstoßen werden. Weil ich aber dort und dazumahl keinem
mich vertrauen dürfen, wie der Außgang auch bezeuget, daß ich
übel angelaßen und mich selbst [74] beschädiget haben würde, da
vor Gottes Güthe, so mich wohl bewahrt hat, danke. Habe ich also
meinen Kummer in mich freßen müßen und um so viel desto mehr
um meinen H[errn] Helmont bey mir selbst gejammert, daß er dermahleins denselben Trauer-Thon nicht auch singen müße, nicht von
solchen Schwindel und Windbrausen hingerißen, Gottes schönen
Angesicht beraubt, in solche Jammer-Orthe hingewiesen werde, und
dergleichen, welches E. Edl. dazumahl zur Burg auch habe sagen
wollen. Aber da die Macht der Finsternüß eine allzugrosse turbam
wieder mich erreget, dabey gelegen, und letzlich noch allhier, haben
E. Edl. [75] anzuhören nicht beliebt, bin endlich auch soviel also
resolvirt gewesen, solche Hecatombe in Druck zu geben, mit dem
rechten, wahren Hebraeischen Original, wie solches nicht allein zu
der vermeinten Zeit Christus und die Apostel, sondern 1000 und

noch mehr Jahr vorher, item 1000 und noch mehr hernach, und dato würklich unter den Hebraeren täglich im Gebrauch (noch synd und jeder Zeit) gewesen, auch zu kräftigeren Nachdruck Ihr Hoch-Fürstl[ich] Edl. zu Sülzbach zu dediciren, welche aber in der Zeit auch Ihren Lauff vollendet zu haben höre. Uber alles nun E. Edl. selbst gegenwärtig hier [76] vernehme, alß begebe mich geraden Weges zu demselben (Gott gebe noch eins mündlich) aber doch in allem Fall, durch diese Zeilen schriftlich. Ja ich komme doch mit keiner andern Rüstung, als im Nahmen Gottes und zwar wie von Ihm bekannt, daß Er den Hoffärtigen wiederstehet, darum nicht mit Trotzen oder Rachen oder harten, herben Wortten, und denen Demüthigen giebt Er Gnade. Darum in dem Grund der Demuth greiff ich E.Edl. an. Ich lege mich in Positur und Gleicheit eines Hündleins zu E. Edlen Füßen, wie ich auch zum andren an meine werte Freunde, [77] sonderlich zu Cleve gethan. Ich erkenne mich verplicht und schuldig E. Edl. nicht allein die Hände und Füße zu küssen, sondern auch den Staub von ihren Schuen mit meiner Zungen abzulecken. Ich wollte wohl zu dero Fußbaad meine Trähnen offeriren, und was noch vor Unterthänigkeit durch einige Expression also kan bezeiget werden. Aber eine Wahrheit als ein Wortt des Herrn hab ich wieder sie. Es ist nicht wahr, daß jemahl eine solche Hecatombe unter den Hebraeren im Brauch gewesen und darum ists nicht recht, daß man die Welt mit solchen eiteln Phantasyen betrüge, [78] jenen Blinden noch mehr Aergernüß und Anstoß mache. Gott gebe diesen Wortten, als dem Donner seiner Wortten Krafft, daß sie an Eu[er] Edl. Hertz und andern durch sie, durchdringend schneiden mögen. Amen. Ich durch meine eigene, so viel Jahr verderbende Erfahrung hab gelernt, was für Schaden bringe, sich von Weißheit etwas einzu-bilden, da man in der That und Wahrheit nichts besitzet. Wollte Gott, daß andre meine Warnung sich dienen laßen wollten. Einige particularia der Hecatombe halte nicht nothwendig und zumahl ich noch nicht alle Hoffnung gäntzlich aufgehebet, E. Edl. selbsten zu sprechen, bleibt solches [79] auff erwünschte Gegenwart verschoben. Unterdeßen füge nur noch dieses an, daß unter andern Formalien, so im gedruckten hätten stehen sollen sich express diese Wortt befinden: E. Edl. samt H[err] K[norr von] R[osenroth] sollen ihre Hände unter die Füss Abrahams legende beschworen seyn zu sagen, ob und wo Sie ein Original von solcher Hecatombe angetroffen haben, solches an Israel zu communiciren und dergl. Irret nicht, Gott läßt sich nicht spotten. 4. Noch um Gleicheit der Materie willen

und aus endlicher Affection verfüge über E. Edl nechst herausgegebe
Cogitationes sup. 4 priora Cap. Genes. daß gleich p. 1 [80] c. 1
v. 1 eine grobe Gotteslästerung enthalten und per tout, was nicht aus
Aben Esra, Raschi und dergleichen andern Rabbinen Traditionen
hergenommen, nichts als ungegründete, eitel Hirn-Speculationes. Weil
ich aber E. Edl. schon so lang forigen kenne, daß ich mir und andern
versprechen kan, daß solches nicht aus Bossheit, oder Gottlosigkeit
geschehe, sondern nur aus unbedachter Untermischung heidnischer
Philosophie N[ota] B[ene] (daß ist Torheiten) in Erkäntnüß Gottes,
so habe nur eine parallel passage aus Platone hierbey referiren wollen,
weil man die Absurditaet am leichtesten an andern als an sich selbst
sehen kan. Die selbe [81] bringt Theodoretus Cyrens. Epist. de curat.
Graec. Affect. Lib 2 p.m. 17. N[ota] B[ene] Er zweiffelt zwar ob
die Familie von Socrate oder Platone, uter autem sit ipsorum ita
certe te Scriptum reliquit *muthon tina* hoc est fabulum mihi videtur
unusquisq[ue] illorum nobis tanquam pueri simus narrare. Nam alter
quidamm illorum quasi tria nobis facit rerum principia (N[ota] B[ene]
wie Jacob Böhm von den dreyen principiis Göttl[ichen] Wesens) quorum quaedam quodammodo inter se nonnunquam repugnant, (N[ota]
B[ene] der Vatter Grim, der Sohn Sanffte, etc.) interdum [82] vero
in amicitiam redeant, quasi nuptias celebrent, filiosq[ue] propagent
N[ota] B[ene] die ewige Geburth, Menschwerdung des Sohnes Gottes,
Ausgehen des Geistes. Alter, vero duo principia rerum asserens,
humidum videlicet et siccum, vel calidum vel frigidum copulat ea in
unum eademq[ue] educit. Gens vero Philosophorum, qui apud nos
Eclectici nominantur, a Xenophane atq[ue] altius initium ducens,
fabulas, nescio quas nobis explicuit, tanquam unum sint ea, quae
dicuntur omnia. Jam vero et Siculae quaedam Musae nobis com-
mentae sunt, tutius esse utraq[ue] rerum principia [83] complicare
ac subinde asserere id, quod est, unum esse ac multa. Alß hier gegenwärtig mein Herr auch saget. Wann dann E. Edl hieraus sehen, daß
sie allerlei dergleichen alte Heiden Grund nur mit neuen Farben,
produciren, auf die weise wie Coccejus in Hiob. Traeck. 1644. p. 3
bedenklich schreibet: Fuisse olim a Patriarchis traditam filiis suis et
aliis hominibus doctrinam, sed aliquando extitisse pios, quibus Deus
etiam se familarius revelaverit. Ex qua institutione plurimum sine
dubio exoticae sapientiae derivatum, quanquam [84] posteri in foedis-
simam idolatriam et reprobos sensus prolapsi et traditi sint etc. und
also biß dato ihren Theil noch haben mit den Abgöttern, oder wie
Ψ 50. 18 stehet: Wo du einen Dieb siehst (nehmlich einen solchen

Gottes Ehren-Dieb) so lauffest du mit ihm und hast Gemeinschafft
mit den Ehebrechern, nehmlich solchen Geistl[ichen] Zigeunern et
adulteris Scripturae etc. Denn welche nicht zur rechten Thür einge-
hen, sind Diebe und Mörder, die rechte Thür aber ist der Stuhl
Moses, da die Schriftgelehrten sitzen, die man hören soll und nach
ihren wortten thun. So wollte Gott, daß diese [85] meine treue
Warnungs-Wortte euch nicht zu verächtlich wären, neue Augen und
Gemüth mit Krafft daraus zu bringen, was eod. Ψ 50. v. 16 stehet,
was verkündigest du etc. und spielest damit nur nach deinem eigenen Belieben, prüfest oder richtest dich zuvor nicht selbst, daß du
also von diesem Brodt der Englen möchtest eßen. Dann dieses ist
wahrhafftig das lebendige Brodt, das von Himmel gekommen, der
ware Ostern oder süße Teig, davon kein Unbeschnittener darf eßen,
oder er nimmt sich nur selbst das Gerichte etc. und wie dergleichen
Wortte sonst gantz ungereimt verstanden [86] werden. Verstoßet
mich dann nur nicht sogar ungerecht von euch weg, ach lachet nur
nicht absolut heraus, wie soll uns dieser weisen was gut ist, bedencket
doch, so ungestallt, verächtlich, jämmerlich von Gott geschlagen ich
vor neuen oder anderen hohen Zeugen scheine, so bin ich doch ein
Glied am Leibe jenes Mannes der Schmertzen Es. 53 des Israël
Gottes und zu dem noch endlich alte Heiden werden kommen müßen
und bekennen, daß sie Torheit und Betrug von ihren Vättern und
10000 Lehrmeisten ererbeten, und alsdann sehen, in welchen sie
gestochen haben und dergleichen, [87] welches alle Schrift bezeuget.
Hört endlich aus den lieben Syrach meinen Hertzens Wunsch und
Seuffzer, den ich oft vor gute Freund gen Himmel sende c. 17.
v. 20. 21. 22. So kehre nun zum Hl. [Heiligen Schriften] und laß
die Sünde fahren (das unbefugte Umgehen oder Arbeiten in einem
fremden und verbottenen Garten, Acker oder Weinberg, thue dein
Gebeth vor Ihm und nicht vor, weiß nicht was, vor unerkannten Cabbalistischen Sephira) und ringere den Anstoß, der hirdurch dem blinden Hauffen wiederfährt, [88] komm wieder zum Höchsten und
wend die ungerechten Thaten von dir (verweiß, zerreiß, verbrenn den
falschen 1. Sohar, 2. Scandaleuse Cabbala denudata, 3. Gottesläterliche
Hecatombe, 4. Heidnische unreine Cogitationes in Genes. 5. auch
die Observationes circa hominem ejusque morbos de p. 32 vom
tollen Hund ins Wasser werfen p. 37 von der Juden Weiber Baaden,
auch ein Fundament der Christen-Tauff gesucht und observiert wird
und was dergleichen mehr) denn Er selbst wird dich leiten aus der

Finsternüß in ein heilsam Licht. Er selbst, [89] nicht ein ander Person, Character, Qualitaet oder Glantz, oderwie es Nahmen haben mag. Nicht stellet Er Christum vor. Er selbst ist gnädig, barmhertzig, langsam zu erzürnen, viel zu erbarmen. Seiner Eigenschafft ist, sich erbarmen und verschonnen, etc. Er tilget unsere Sünden um sein selbst willen, nicht um Christi oder eines andern Dinges willen, weder in Himmel noch auf Erden sondern um seines Heil[igen] Nahmes willen. Er selbst erbarmet sich, wie sich ein Vatter erbarmet über seine kinder etc. und haßet zum Schrecken hefftig allen Greuel, den [90] ich hirmit euch vor Augen stelle. Ich will euch aber noch ein köstlichern Weg zeigen, strebet nach der Liebe, welche das von Gott an Israël gegebene particulare und eigene Kleinod ist. Trachtet daß ihr mich in Liebe tragen und behalten konnet, der ich euch, weil mich die Liebe Gottes dringet mit solcher Liebe, Redlichkeit und Einfalt suche, auch zu finden wünsche, Amen. E. Edl. und der jenen sämtl. welche Gott in Hingabe ihres Hertzens erlich suchen

treuer Freund und Diener
    Moses Germanus
    ehemal
    Joh. Peter Späth

Moses Germanus to Francis Mercury van Helmont (Hamburg, Staatsbibliothek, Suppellex. Epistolica Uffenbaccii, v. 26, pp. 67 (154)–91 (167)

Noble, highly revered and soul-loved Herr von Helmont,

    Because I cannot be sure nor know whether I will succeed in speaking to you personally because you previously did not [68] allow it and because I feel driven in my soul and conscience, I seek with these few lines or points to meet you face to face, and with that to derive satisfaction for my mind and free my conscience. First, I thank you once more and a thousand more times for you love and faithfulness and also for your generosity and good deeds, which you have shown me many times by giving me used clothes, food, money, and that well-meant instruction which I esteem above all, but which, in fact, I found very false and harmful [67 sic] when I went farther into the matter and continued, struggling to the source. On account of such a teaching, I remind your illustrious self of the following: 1.

As for the *Zohar*, which was published by Herr Rosenroth with your assistance: please, if only for the sake of the fear and love of God, consider what horror, sin, and injustice has been done with this. The figure of the matron in the dedication to the Prince of Sulzbach is indeed a sincere, pure Jewess of a very noble origin, from a very revered antiquity, from [68] Palestine. Can greater injury and harm be done to her than to be handed over to the Roman people under Constantine, as the legitimate successors of the Old Testament, or that band of spiritual gypsies, and prostituted? This from the viewpoint of the mentioned *Zohar* itself or the mystical doctrines of the Law. From the viewpoint of the participants, those into whose hands she has fallen, the damage done is even greater, because they will think they have something, while in fact they are incapable of it. And, thus, they are defrauded to the highest degree, especially and inevitably when, following the harmful instruction given to the reader [69] there, they often and at the same time read the Syrian New Testament and fill their poor skulls with your preconceived fantasies. Indeed, they can bind a bunch with their Grobian—already captured in Ovid's *Metamorphoses*. But they should leave this heavenly, pure nymph untouched and have no part of her. 2. The same applies to your *Kabbala denudata*. No more dreadful shame can happen to a married woman or daughter than to be stripped naked before such a horrible and abominable undertaking. [70] Have not all honorable priests of the Pagans, Egyptians, Chaldeans, Greeks, Etruscans, and Romans been careful and taken pains so that their divine secrets would not be open to the unworthy rabble? But here the damage is even greater for the participants because they think they have a Cabbala which they do not in the least way have but only a heap of hastily-collected fragments which are more pagan than Jewish, just like D. Lupius' *Clavicula Solomonis* and many similar works. [71] My soul will stand against yours in the balance before the judgement seat of the Almighty until you prove the persons in the Divinity on the basis of the Jewish Cabbala, although, as I said, these proofs were sniffed out from pagan forgeries, that were fabricated from misunderstood Rabbinical texts. To this day you and many others repeat the same things. It is absolutely not true that Psalm 50 can be understood to refer to a trinity of persons in the Godhead, or a triumvirate of praetors, through the words יוה אלהים אל [*El, Elohim, Tetragrammaton*] as you dictated to my pen from your divine Cabbala, fol. 390 [72] in the section יה n. 10.[77] To my shame I wrote this down in my pocket psalter, which I still keep today as a witness and testimony of such fruit. 3. What really and finally bothers me more than all the preceding things and which is insofar the real reason that I pour out my heart to you is the so-called Hecatomb or hundred pane-gyrics that you explained to me at that time in Frankfurt with the printed page in hand and, while doing so, dictated marginalia to me, which I have enjoyed for so many years and which finally appeared in von Rosenroth's *Neuen Helicon* and which I excessively recommended to others. But after [73] I experienced the mercy and grace [of God], I made known the fraud with pain and heartache. Also, at that time in Cleve, when the two dreams or appearances of Herr Rosenroth to his daughter were described in a very credi-ble fashion, sensitive thoughts came to my mind, that he would still be busy singing his blasphemous hecatombs and, in addition, his stinking corpse would daily be rejected and cast out from before the illuminated face of God. But because there and at that time I could not confide in anyone, as the outcome showed I would have made a bad impression [74] and harmed myself, thank God that God's goodness protected me so well from this. Thus my sorrow was eat-ing at my heart and I lamented so much more about Herr Helmont to myself, that he himself would at some time have to sing the same sad song and be bereft of God's presence, fooled by such fraud and hot air, that he will be relegated to such miserable places, etc., all of which I wanted to tell your illustrious self back then at the cas-tle. But because the power of darkness has stirred up an all-too-great crowd against me, neither then nor eventually here did your illus-trious self [75] desire to listen, and I finally decided to print that Hecatomb with the correct and genuine Hebrew original, such as was in existence in the so-called time of Christ and the Apostles and also more than 1000 years before and more than 1000 years after and which is today, indeed, used daily among the Hebrews (it still is and always will be). I had decided to dedicate this edition to your Prince of Sulzbach, but then had heard that he had died. About all this you may now hear me, [76], as if I was traveling straight-

---

[77] In the reprint of the *Kabbala denudata* (Hildesheim: Georg Olms Verlag, 1974) the passage Moses Germanus refers to appears in vol. 1, 388, section 7: "Scribitur & interdum Tetragrammaton cum nominee El, atque Elohim, quemadmodum Psal. 50, 1. *Psalmus Asaphi: El, Elohim, Tetragrammaton locutus est & vocavit terram.*"

away to you. God grant me a personal meeting, but in any case, [I communicate] through these written lines. I come with no other armor but in the name of God and, indeed, as is known of him, he opposes the arrogant, but not with defiance or revenge or hard and harsh words and he gives grace to those who are humble. Because of this, I approach you with the greatest humility. I put myself in the posture and likeness of a small dog at your noble feet, as I have done to my other worthy friends, [77] especially at Cleve. I am obliged and owe it to you, your illustrious self, not only to kiss your hands and feet but also to lick the dust off your shoes with my tongue. I wanted to offer my tears as a foot bath and whatever other expression of subservience I could muster. But I have both the truth and the word of God against you. It is not true that such a Hecatomb was ever used by the Hebrews and, therefore, it is not right that one cheats the world with such vain fantasies and provides even more [78] annoyance and offense to those blind ones. May God imbue these words with the thunderous power of his own words, so that they will go straight to your heart and through you to others. Amen. I, through these many years of my own unfortunate experience, have learned what damage can be done when one pretends to wisdom and does not in fact possess it. Would God that others will heed this warning. I do not think some particular aspects of the Hecatombs are necessary. And, since I have not given up all hope of speaking to your illustrious self, such matters [79] will remain postponed until [I come into] your desired presence. Meanwhile, I would like to add one more point that in the dedication the following should have been expressly stated: both you and Herr Rosenroth should, having put your hands under the feet of Abraham, swear to say whether and where you found the original of such a Hecatomb, how it was communicated to Israel, etc. Do not be mistaken. God will not be mocked. 4. To treat everything equally and because of my never ending [unendlich for endlich] affection, I say that the book Cogitationes super quatruor priora capita libri Moysis, Genesis published by you contains on p 1 [80] c. 1 v. 1 gross blasphemy and throughout it whatever was not taken from Eben Ezra, Raschi, and the rest of the Rabbinic tradition is based on nothing but vain speculation. But because I have known you for so long and so well, I can promise myself and others that such things do not come from malice or godlessness but only from a thoughtless confusion of pagan philosophy (Nota Bene that is, stupidity) with the understanding of God. I only want to refer to a parallel passage from Plato because it is easiest to see absurdity in others than in oneself. Theodoretus Cyrens. says the same thing [81] in Epistola de Curat. Graec. Affect. Lib 2 p. m. 17. (Nota Bene he has doubts about the schools of Socrates and Plato concerning which of the two left writings or *muthon tina*, that is fables. It seems to me that each of them tells a story to us as if we were children. For a certain one of them made for us three prnciples of things. (Nota Bene as Jacob Boehme on the three principles of God's nature). Some of them disagree to a certain extent (Nota Bene the father wrathful, the Son gentle), meanwhile [82] they become friends again, as if celebrating a marriage, and they produce children (Nota Bene the eternal birth, the incarnation of the son of God, from which came the Holy Spirit). Another asserting the two principles of things, namely, moist and dry, or hot and cold, joins these things and brings them out. Indeed, these sorts of philosophers, who are called by us eclectics and begin with Xenophanes and even earlier, display to us I know not what fables, as if these things are one which are called all things. For certain Sicilian muses wrote that it was safer to [83] fold together two principles of things and immediately afterwards asserted that what is one is many. And you have said much the same. From this, you can see that they have painted new colors on the same pagan canvasses as Coccejus says skeptically in Hiob. Track. 1644, p. 3: Formerely doctrine was handed down from the Patriarchs to their sons and other men, but sometimes pious persons existed to whom God also revealed himself more intimately. From this custom, without doubt, many sorts of exotic wisdom was derived, although [84] afterwards they were handed down having fallen into a foul, idolatrous, and reprobate sense, etc. and thus until now still busy temselves with idols or as Psalm 50:18 says, where you see a theief (namely, the kind of person who steals God's honor), so you walk with him and are in the company of adulterers, namely the kind of spiritual gypsies and adulterers of Scripture. For those who do not enter through the right doors are thieves and murderers. However, the right door is the seat of Moses, where the scribes sit, whom one must hear and act according to their words. So God wishes [85] that you will not deem these my faithful words of warning as too contemptuous and that they will open your eyes and mind as the same Psalm 50 v. 16 says, what

do you proclaim, etc.[78] But you do as you wish and you do not test
and judge yourself so that you can eat heavenly bread. For this is
the true, living bread sent from heaven, the true Easter [i.e. Passover]
or sweet dough, which no uncircumcised person may eat, or he takes
the meal himself etc., and as passages like these otherwise are understood absurdly. [86] Do not push me away, especially not unjustly,
do not laugh at me. How should this one [Moses Germanus] direct
us to what is good, so oppressed, so scattered, and scornfully and
miserably afflicted by God, I who appear to have new and higher
reprimands. Yet I am a member of that body of the man of sorrows (Isaiah 53) of the God of Israel, to which body peace must
finally come. And they will know that they have inherited foolish-
ness and fraud from their fathers and the 10,000 teachers. And they
will see what a mess they have gotten themselves into, [87] just as
the Scriptures demonstrate. Finally, hear my heart-felt wish from the
beloved Syrach and my sighs, which I often send to heaven in the
presence of a good friend (chapter 17, v. 20, 21, 22).[79] So now return
to the Holy Scriptures and abstain from sin (like an unauthorized
person walking about and working in a strange, forbidden garden,
field, or vineyard, make your prayer to Him and not to who knows
what unknown kabbalistic *Sephira*). And lessen your offense, which
misleads the blind masses. [88] Return to the Highest and refrain
from all unjust deeds. Banish, tear up, and burn the 1. false Sohar
2. scandalous Kabbala 3. the blasphemous Hecatombe 4. the pagan,
unclean Cogitationes in Genes. 5. also the Observationes circa
hominem ejusque morbos, p. 32, the way a rabid dog is thrown in
water (p. 37), as the bath of female Jews has been sought out and
observed to be the basis for Christian baptism (and there are other
examples). Then He himself will lead you out of darkness into heal-

---

[78] "But unto the wicked God saith, What hast thou to do to declare my statutes,
or that thou shouldest take my covenant in thy mouth?"

[79] Ecclesiasticus, or the Wisdom of Jesus, son of Sirach, 17:20–22: "their mis-
deeds are not hidden from the Lord;/he observes all their sins./Charitable giving
he treasures like a signet ring, and kindness like the apple of his eye." Moses
Germanus clearly had the following verses in mind as well as one can see from
the continuation of his letter: "In the end he will arise and give the wicked their
deserts, /bringing down retribution on their heads./Yet he leaves a way open for
the penitent to return to him/and endows the waverer with strength to endure./Return
to the Lord and have done with sin;/make your prayer in his presence and lessen
your offence./Come back to the Most High, renounce wrongdoing,/and hate intensely
what he abhors" (23–24).

ing light. He himself cannot [89] have another person, character, quality, or splendor, or name. He does not need Christ. He himself is gracious, merciful, slow to anger, and abundant in mercy. His character is to be merciful and to spare, etc. He forgives our sins for his own sake and not for the sake of Christ nor for the sake of any other thing on heaven or earth, but for his own holy name. He himself is merciful as a father is merciful to his children. And he vehemently hates all the abomination [90] which I have put before your eyes here. I will show you a precious way: strive for the love which is the particular treasure God gave especially to Israel. Strive to keep and bear me in love, me who, because the love of God compels me with such love, honesty, and sincerity to seek you and wish to find you. Amen. Your and of all those who God in the devotion of their heart honestly seek

true friend and servant,
    Moses Germanus
    Formerely Joh. Peter Späth

CARTESIANISM, SKEPTICISM AND CONVERSION TO JUDAISM: THE CASE OF AARON D'ANTAN

Martin Mulsow

A couple of years ago during a visit to the Biblioteka Jagiellonska in Cracow, I ran into two long letters, which contain the confession of a convert to Judaism.[1] They bear no date, but it can be determined that they originated from around 1710. Their recipient was Mathurin Veyssière La Croze, librarian to the Prussian King. The letters appear in a French and Italian version, they have been copied into a beautiful cursive and it can be assumed that the original was written in French. Together with an introduction in Hebrew cursive, they were very neatly bound together into a tiny octavo volume. The letters constitute the remaining fragment of a philosophical-religious correspondence. They were written by a young Frenchman, who signed them with the name Aaron d'Antan.[2] These letters provide a detailed insight into d'Antan's motivation for conversion and

---

[1] Biblioteka Jagiellonska Kraków, Ms. gall. Oct. 38. These letters seem to have left only two little traces in scholarly literature, and were never examined closely. See Nathan Samter, "Ein französischer Proselyt aus dem Anfange des achtzehnten Jahrhunderts", in: *Magazin für die Wissenschaft des Judentums*, 20 (1893), 199–203; Cecil Roth, *Personalities and Events in Jewish History* (Philadelphia, 1961), 158. I thank Matt Goldish for the reference of the book by Roth. Compare also Samter's lecture, *Judenthum und Proselytismus: ein Vortrag* (Breslau, 1897).—I am grateful to Eli Alshech, who deciphered the Hebrew passages for me and who found the references to Bible verses; Adrian Offenberg, Richard Popkin, Jonathan Israel, Alain Mothu and Friedrich Niewöhner provided me with useful information; finally I thank Ulrich Groetsch for his translation into English.

[2] Hitherto I was unable to identify d'Antan from his French family. The fact that he was a student at the Collège de Navarre does not seem to be helpful to identify him, because there are no lists of the students at the Collège at that time (at least as far as I know). The difficulty to track d'Antan down in archival documentation consists in the fact that not only his first name was certainly changed by his conversion, but also his last name "d'Antan" may be adopted. It can well simply mean "of yesteryear" and allude to the the view backwards from his new life. It is also possible that d'Antan, like many converts of his time, used several names. He may have used "Aaron ben Abraham", since converts were usualy called "child of Abraham"; he may, in other occasions, still have used his original French name. Certainly here still more archival research has to be done, especially in Paris, and in Amsterdam, where circumcisions of adults normally have been recorded by

into his beliefs: they constitute a rare instance of ego-documenta-
tion[3] among the already rare cases of conversion to Judaism. Apart
from that, d'Antan's beliefs fit very well the purpose of illustrating
the connection of a line of themes, which according to Richard
Popkin, were essential to seventeenth-century intellectual history: the
idea of a skeptical crisis,[4] the overcoming of skepticism not only by
means of Cartesianism, but by means of religious conviction[5] and
finally the use of Jewish anti-Christian arguments in Enlightenment
deism.[6] Therefore, it is worthwhile to reconstruct the life-story of
d'Antan in its context.

Safeguards

Marthurin Veyssière La Croze was a learned man. He had belonged
to the Benedictine order and had worked as librarian of the Maurine
Abbey of Saint Germain des Prés with illustrious colleagues such as
Montfaucon, Mabillon, and Longuerue.[7] At around 1696, he felt so

---

the Jewish community. The hypotheis, however, that the lack of archival identification
could mean the d'Antan's letters are only fictuous, cannot claim much support. I
cannot see any motivs for forging these letters, nor see I any clues that the texts
are fictuous. I thank Maria Fusaro, Josua Fogel and William Connell for discussing
these problems with me.

[3] For the concept of ego-documents see Winfried Schulze (ed.), *Ego-Dokumente:
Annäherung an den Menschen in der Geschichte* (Berlin: Akademie Verlag, 1996).

[4] See Richard H. Popkin, *The History of Skepticism from Erasmus to Spinoza* (Berkeley:
UCP, 1979).

[5] See Richard H. Popkin, *The Third Force in Seventeenth Century Thought* (Leiden:
Brill, 1992).

[6] See Richard H. Popkin, "Some Unresolved Questions in the History of Scepticism.
The Role of Jewish Anti-Christian Arguments in the Rise of Scepticism in Regard
to Religion", in idem, *The Third Force* (footnote 5), 222–235; idem: "Jewish Anti-
Christian Arguments as a Source of Irreligion from the Seventeenth to the Early
Nineteenth Century", in: Michael Hunter und David Wooton (eds.), *Atheism from the
Renaissance to the Enlightenment* (Oxford: OUP 1992), 159–181.

[7] On La Croze see Martin Mulsow, *Die drei Ringe. Toleranz und clandestine Gelehrsamkeit
bei Mathurin Veyssière La Croze (1661–1739)* (Tübingen, 2001); idem: "Views of the
Berlin Refuge: Scholarly Projects, Literary Interests, Marginal Fields," in: Sandra
Pott, Martin Mulsow und Lutz Danneberg (eds.), *The Berlin Refuge 1680–1780. Learning
and Science in European Context* (Leiden: Brill, 1993), 25–46; see also Charles Etienne
Jordan, *Histoire da la vie et des ouvrages de Mr La Croze, avec des remarques de cet auteur
sur divers sujets* (Amsterdam, 1741). For the milieu see Anne Goldgar, *Impolite Learning.
Civility and Conduct in the Republic of Letters 1680–1750* (New Haven: Yale University
Press, 1995). For the milieu especially of the learned monks in Paris see Bernadette
Barret-Kriegel, *Les historiens et la monarchie*, 4 vols. (Paris, 1988).

enclosed by the world of the monastery and so antagonized by the religious policies of Louis XIV to an extent that he fled to Basel. From there he went to Berlin, where he was received by the Huguenot colony and where he found employment as librarian at the court of the Brandenburg Elector, who would assume the title "King of Prussia" just a short time afterwards. At a certain moment while he was in Berlin, a letter reached him, in which a young man informed him about his conversion to Judaism.

The letter was signed by a certain d'Antan—a name that sounded familiar to La Croze from his past years in Paris. This initial letter, which is lost, was apparently written from Amsterdam. A certain Baron von Staff, to whom d'Antan would later pay his regards in his letters, seems to have established the contact between Amsterdam and Berlin. Soon after writing the letter—even before he could have received a response from La Croze—d'Antan had apparently embarked from Amsterdam on a journey to Palestine and to the Holy Land. At least the introductory letter of the octavo volume states: "The nobles and leaders of the community extended their hands to him and he traveled lightly as a deer to the land of Israel (el erez ha-zvi)."[8] One can encounter this pattern of deciding to travel to the Holy Land after conversion to Judaism, in Amsterdam, in other cases as well. This is what Valentin Potocki, a count from Lithuania, and Zalumba, a Pole, did; after their conversion in the early eighteenth century, each of these two undertaking the long and arduous journey to Israel.[9] Maybe this was also what the rabbis had asked for as a proof of their sincerity.

D'Antan traveled from Amsterdam via Germany to Bohemia and then to Hungary. From Hungary, he turned westward to Bavaria and then southward towards Tyrolia. Eventually he crossed the Alps into Italy (I,1).[10] Perhaps he had initially tried to circumvent the Catholic Italian states with their inquisition tribunals all together by taking the land route to Palestine. The fighting, however, which occurred in the context of the Wars of the Spanish Succession, such

---

[8] Ms. gall. Oct. 38 (footnote 1), fol. 2v.

[9] See David Max Eichhorn: "From Expulsion to Liberation (1492–1789)", in idem (ed.), *Conversion to Judaism. A History and Analysis* (New York, 1965), 96–135, esp. 128ff. See as well the introduction to this volume.

[10] I cite the text given in the appendix according the number of the letter (I or II) and the respective paragraph.

as the invasions by the Curuzzes, and the continuous turmoil in progress in Hungary during these years may have forced him to turn around.[11] Eventually he then traveled via Italy.

Five letters from La Croze to d'Antan's address in Amsterdam were forwarded to him. In these letters, La Croze had argued extensively ("vos lettres peuvent etre appellées sans flaterie l'extrait d'un volume", d'Antan says in I,1) that d'Antan should reconsider his conversion and return to Christianity. D'Antan extracted the most important passages from them and burned the letters afterwards in order not to carry incriminating evidence with regards to the Inquisition along with himself. Traveling as a Christian, d'Antan nonetheless probably visited Italian Jewish communities and secretly practiced Jewish rituals. Did he ultimately plan to cross by ship from Venice to Palestine? At this time with the Venetian-Turkish war raging, this seems unlikely. Possibly, he turned towards Livorno in order to look for a ship there.

His fear of the Inquisition was certainly not unfounded then. If officials discovered that he carried anti-Christian documents with him, the consequences would have been serious.[12] Thus d'Antan responded to La Croze only shortly before he was leaving Italy— obviously to Palestine—when he believed himself to be safe from the Inquisition. Maybe he had just successfully passed through customs. At this point, only eight months had gone by since he converted.

It is striking how frequently d'Antan refers to the "inhumane Inquisition." It is possible that he had negative experiences with it. The introductory letter may confirm such assumptions, because it mentions that d'Antan lived through some hard times and that he

---

[11] See Peter Broucek, *Die Kuruzzeneinfälle in Niederösterreich und in der Steiermark: 1703–1709* (Wien, 1985). For the War of the Spanish Succession, see the bibliography by W. Calvin Dickinson, *The war of the Spanish succession, 1702–1713: a selected bibliography* (Westport: Meckler, 1996).

[12] On the situation of the Jews in Venice, see the fourteen-volume edition of sources by Pier Cesare Ioly Zorattini (ed.), *Processi del S. Uffizio di Venezia contro Ebrei e Giudaizzanti, (1548–1734)* (Firenze, 1980–1999), esp. vol. 12, and M. Luzzati (ed.), *L'Inquisizione e gli Ebrei in Italia* (Bari, 1994); on the Jews of Livorno see Patrizia Bonifazio, *Le tre Sinagoghe: edifici di culto e vita ebraica a Livorno dal seicento al novecento* (Livorno: Comune di Livorno, 1995); Renzo Toaff: *La nazione ebrea a Livorno e a Pisa: 1591–1700* (Firenze: Olschki, 1990); Lionel Lévy, *La communauté juive de Livourne: le dernier des Livournais* (Paris: Éd. L'Harmattan, 1996); Cristina Galasso, *Alle origini di una comunità: Ebree ed Ebrei a Livorno nel Seicento* (Firenze: Olschki, 2002).

showed tendencies to become a martyr.[13] Probably under great pressure and facing the danger of being exposed on his journey, he seemed to have entrusted his letters to La Croze to the Rabbi Joseph Baruch Salman,[14] who later gave them to Isaac Cohen Rafa.[15] Rafa then must have added the introductory letter at around 1720, which is now part of the Cracow Codex.

Rafa seemed very impressed by d'Antan's account. According to him, d'Antan came from a wealthy French family in Paris, which he described as a wonderful city, although full of idolaters. D'Antan, he wrote, was a young military man of tall and beautiful stature, who had converted to Judaism ten years ago. When Rafa saw d'Antans letters, he was tantalized. "I was amazed by this sight," Rafa points out, "and was startled and said in my heart that these things [d'Antan's letters] are worthy as if they were revealed on Mount Sinai."[16]

Apparently, Rafa's introductory writing was originally intended for a Jewish community. By forwarding d'Antan's letters to them, he wanted to urge them into some pressing action: "Now listen, I call upon you and you shall act without delay.[17] You shall take his morals, not silver, and his wisdom, and not choose gold."[18] Rafa apparently had a particular addressee in mind, whom he wanted to take d'Antan's behavior to heart. It remains unclear, whether the request was intended to support d'Antan or to admit other non-Jews into the community or something else.

There are numerous precautions and ciphers in the text. The introductory letter in Hebrew is written in a liturgical language, which is on a high scholarly level and filled with allusions. This circumstance indicated to the addressee that he corresponded with a

---

[13] Ms. gall. Oct. 38 (footnote 1), fol. 2v.

[14] This name can be infered from an acronym in the text. See Samter, *Ein französischer Proselyt* (footnote 1), S. 200. So far, I have been unable to identify Salman biographically. It is doubtful that he is identical with a certain Baruch ben Salman from Osterlitz in Moravia, who was mentioned in around 1705 (DBA I 58, 240).

[15] This name, too, has to be inferred. The writer of the introduction signs with a modified citation from Gen. 38, 25. The first word has been modified, so that the name Isaac Cohen Rafa or Refa emerges. I prefer the reading "Rafa", because this name occurs casually in the biographical dictionaries.

[16] Ms. gall. Oct. 38 (footnote 1), 3r; for the descriptions, see ibd. fol. 1r and v. See Samter, *Ein französischer Proselyt* (footnote 1), p. 200.

[17] Reference to Daniel 9:19: "O Lord, forgive me: O Lord, hearken and do; defer not, for thine own sake."

[18] Ms. gall. Oct. 38 (footnote 1), fol. 3r. Reference to Proverbs 8:10: "Receive my instruction and not silver, and knowledge rather than choice gold."

serious and erudite person; apart from that, this particular style opened up the possibility to encode messages among the numerous unspecified bible verses, which an uninformed third party could not decipher, even if one had adequate Hebrew. One technique used in the letter is acronymy. Even the name of the author of the introductory letter is hidden by an acronym within a biblical verse.

But d'Antan's two French letters contain odd moments of Hebrew insertions as well, which encode secret messages and comments. In the first paragraph of the first letter for example, where d'Antan refers to the Inquisition's inhumanity, which he fears in Italy, the Hebrew reads: "This is the work of the pure lamp stand that Afran evaluated in front of God for eternity." This is an allusion to Numeri 8,4, which recounts the building of the golden candlestick. But this candlestick was built by Aaron and not by Afran. The biblically versed Hebrew reader would recognize that the term "Afran" constituted an acronym, whose letters A, F, R, and N referred to something else. The Hebrew term "work" with the letter combination M, A, S (or Sh) and P (or F) was marked as an acronym as well. Other insertions tend to distance themselves from certain statements in the text. When in II,1 the possibility is raised that three personalities may very well be present in one God (even though he may not have three different names), it reads: "God forbid! This is of course only a hypothetical assumption." I doubt that the Hebrew passages in the French text came from d'Antan himself. I believe them to be commentaries written by Rafa, the Jewish editor and author of the introductory letter.[19]

The care involved in the transmission, however, poses a basic question: Why, after all, was it La Croze, to whom d'Antan turned and who thus became the first person entrusted with the secret of his conversion and with his personal motivations? He did not even reveal his motivations to those Jews, who had carried out his conversion: "I would like to go that far and tell you what I have never even revealed to another Jew so far: the reason for my conversion, in which no other Jew played a particular role, since Jews were only

---

[19] Even in the case of the names that occur in d'Antan's French letters, such as Abbé de Lior, with whom La Croze had conversed in Paris, or Baron von Staff, it is not certain, if they have to be taken by face value, or might be cover names. But my impression is that the French letters do not operate with concealments.

informed about it in Amsterdam." The secret commentary is inserted at this point then in Hebrew letters: "This was the law of the leper in the day of the cleansing and his coming to the priest (the so called high priest)."[20] This probably means that the Christian d'Antan— and insofar "leper"—went to the chief rabbi of Amsterdam to ask for the permission of conversion. A deeper meaning, however, may still exist behind this reading.

Why then La Croze? La Croze was an uncommonly tolerant person in his age. He used his erudition to hold up a mirror of other eras and cultures to the corruption of the Christianity of his time. He studied Nestorianism, which had been suppressed by the early Church, but which contained already numerous elements, which Calvinism would later bring back to the surface. He was interested in the Muslims, whose faith he rejected, but whose culture and tolerance he knew from reading their literature. He was even interested in the Socinians and Jews, whose oppression and persecution he rejected.[21] There were not many people throughout Europe at that time who knew to combine erudition and tolerance in a similar way. If then such a man happened to be a mentor from the past—and La Croze had been young d'Antan's mentor in Paris— then it could very well come to one's mind to initiate that person into the secret. Perhaps d'Antan thought that La Croze would be able to comprehend his motivations and applaud and embrace his risky decision. The letter from Amsterdam to Berlin may have served as an additional assurance to d'Antan's own conscience.

Beginnings in Paris

First of all, we should clarify the chronological context, since the letters contain no specific reference of time. When were they written? When was d'Antan born? When did he convert?

The letters suggest that d'Antan became acquainted with La Croze already at the age of ten. D'Antan, who was the offspring of a

---

[20] Reference to Leviticus 14:2: "This shall be the law of the leper in the day of his cleansing: He shall be brought unto the priest."

[21] See La Croze, *Dissertations sur divers sujets* (Rotterdam, 1707); idem, *Entretiens sur divers sujets d'histoire, de littérature, de religion et de critique* (Cologne, 1711); *Histoire du Christianisme des Indes* (La Haye, 1724). See on these works Martin Mulsow, *Die drei Ringe* (footnote 7), chap. IV–VI.

socially prestigious family, because his father served as an officer in
the royal army, was at that time a student in Paris. The Paris of
the late seventeenth century was full of scholars, erudite monks and
poets of all couleurs.[22] It was, however, a city with limited freedom.
The Protestants had been expelled, and one was going to suppress
the intra-catholic opposition, the Jansenists, as well. Many writings
that contained radical critique and new ideas were not allowed to
be published in France; they had to be smuggled into the country
from the Netherlands or from England. La Croze once got himself
into trouble when it was discovered that he had secretly translated
and distributed texts on transubstantiation by the English Protestant
Stillingfleet.[23]

In I,3, d'Antan recalls a particular moment from his past, when
La Croze had a conversation about him with a certain Abbé de
Lior[24] in the Library of Saint Germain de Prés in which they pre-
dicted a splendid future for the boy ("je serois un grand homme").
D'Antan was obviously a very gifted student. Since La Croze stayed
at the monastery from 1693 to 1696, one can conclude that d'Antan
must have been born between 1683 and 1686.

There is a particular story to this prediction. Apparently, somebody had cast a horoscope for the student and the two scholars
discussed the marvelous circumstance that the horoscope showed
significant similarities to the one that had been cast for Jesus Christ.
Yet, it was viewed as heterodoxy to cast Christ's horoscope, because
it meant that Jesus' divine mission was subject to a Siderian deter-
minism, which seemed to many incompatible with God's freedom.[25]
Nonetheless, the Benedictine La Croze was a scholar, who undoubtedly knew Pietro d'Abano's, Pierre d'Ailly's, and Cardano's attempts
to determine Christ's nativity. The question remains of course how
serious these types of calculations were taken at that time.[26] But these

---

[22] On the scholarly life in Paris see Bruno Neveu, "La vie érudite à Paris à la
fin du XVIIe siècle", in idem, *Erudition et religion aux XVIIe et XVIIIe siècles* (Paris,
1994), 25–92.
[23] See Mulsow: *Die drei Ringe* (footnote 7), 11ff.
[24] So far I have not been able to identify the Abbé de Lior.
[25] On the nativity of Christ see e.g. Erminio Troilo, "L'oroscopo delle religioni:
'Pietro d'Abano e P. Pomponazzi'", in: *Figure e dottrine di pensatori*, vol. I (Napoli,
1937), 137–169; Laura Ackerman Smoller, *History, Prophecy, and the Stars. The Christian
Astrology of Pierre d'Ailly, 1350–1420* (Princeton: PUP, 1994).
[26] On the role of astrology in late 17th century Paris see e.g. Renée Simon, *Henry*

discussions may certainly have led young d'Antan to believe that he was something special.

Around that time d'Antan apparently began to study at the renowned Collège de Navarre. No lesser figure than Bossuet himself had received his scholastic training there.[27] D'Antan attended the college obviously already by the time he was nine or ten years old, because in another episode, in which he claimed to have been twelve years old, he mentioned that it occurred three years after the episodes from his time at the college. This seems similar to the career of Louis-Ellie du Pin, who graduated from the same place at the age of fifteen with a master's degree.[28] But by no means should one mistake d'Antan's education for a university education. The training he received there is probably comparable to a college preparatory school. The Abbe Lior may very well have been his teacher at the college and may have brought him into contact with La Croze.

Skepticism

In his first letter, d'Antan describes how during his time at the College he learned to distinguish essence from appearance. A simple student prank, when d'Antan took the tobacco tin from an older student, proved providential. When the victim went to the dean's office to denounce him, he even stated that d'Antan would steal on a frequent basis. Outraged by these false claims and by the fact that the evidence brought forth seemed to confirm these accusations, d'Antan decided to remain silent. But at the same time, he pleaded to himself that he would never judge other human beings simply by their appearance ("nous ne pouvions juger personne par les apparences qui sont fort souvent trompeuses" I,3). [29]

---

de Boulainviller: historien, politique, philosophe, astrologue, 1658–1722 (Paris: Boivin, 1941). See as well her edition: Traité d'astrologie, par le Comte Henry de Boulainviller, 1717. Présentation par Mme Renée Simon, Introduction générale par M. l'abbé Blanchard. Étude particuliere par M.J. Duvivier, etc., Garches, Éditions du Nouvel humanisme (Boulogne-sur-Seine, 1947).

[27] The is no study of the early modern history of the Collège; on its medieval history see Nathalie Gorochov, Le Collège de Navarre de sa fondation (1305) au début du XVe siècle (1418) (Paris, 1997).

[28] See Pierre Féret, La faculté de théologie de Paris VII (Paris, 1910), 5ff.

[29] This episode seems to be comparable with the similar "comb"-episode in

From that moment on, d'Antan not only exposed the deceitful in
his social interaction, but became suspicious in religious matters as
well. In this process he made another crucial experience: at the age
of twelve, he knew a man, who lived in his part of the city and
called himself a Saint. This man claimed to be able to perform miracles. Obviously this person was one of those itinerant preachers
who attracted the lame and the sick and who were passing through
cities and villages.[30] D'Antan remarks dryly that he was never able

---

Rousseau's youth, in which he "lost his state of innocence". See on the latter Hans-
Robert Jauß, *Ästhetische Erfahrung und literarische Hermeneutik* (Frankfurt: Suhrkamp
1982), 311.

[30] It is not completely clear if the "saint" really called himself "saint Ovide"—
after the medieval French legend of a Saint Ovide—or if the phrase "nommé Saint
Ovide" refers to the quarter in which d'Antan grew up. Anyhow, this saint seems
to have been a forerunner of the Jansenist 'convulsionnaires' of Saint-Médard, who
were discussed vividy in Paris from the 1730s onwards. See Catherine-Laurence
Maire, *Les convulsionnaires de Saint-Médard: miracles, convulsions et prophéties à Paris au
XVIIIᵉ siècle* (Paris: Gallimard: Julliard, 1985); Robert Kreiser, *Miracles, Convulsions,
and Ecclesiastical Politics in Early Eighteenth-Century Paris*; Albert Mousset, *L'étrange histoire des convulsionnaires de Saint-Médard* (Paris: Minuit, 1953). Voltaire, born in 1694,
also knew the stories about Saint-Ovide (the medieval one?) well. He mentions him
several times as someone who had pretended to revive dead children. See Voltaire:
Article 'Philosophie' des Questions sur l'Encyclopédie, Section III: "Si la philosophie a fait tant d'honneur à la France dans l'Encyclopédie, il faut avouer aussi que
l'ignorance et l'envie, qui ont osé condamner cet ouvrage, auraient couvert la France
d'opprobre, si douze ou quinze convulsionnaires, qui formèrent une cabale, pou-
vaient être regardés comme les organes de la France, eux qui n'étaient en effet que
les ministres du fanatisme et de la sédition, eux qui ont forcé le roi à casser le
corps qu'ils avaient séduit. Leurs manoeuvres ne furent pas si violentes que du
temps de la Fronde, mais ne furent pas moins ridicules. Leur fanatique crédulité
pour les convulsions et pour les misérables prestiges de Saint-Médard était si forte,
qu'ils obligèrent un magistrat, d'ailleurs sage et respectable, de dire en plein parlement 'que les miracles de l'Église catholique subsistaient toujours.' On ne peut
entendre par ces miracles que ceux des convulsions. Assurément il ne s'en fait pas
d'autres, À MOINS QUE L'ON NE CROIE AUX PETITS ENFANTS RESSUS-
CITES PAR SAINT OVIDE. Le temps des miracles est passé; l'Église triomphante
n'en a plus besoin." See as well Voltaire, 'Fragments historiques sur l'inde' (1773),
article XXIX: 'Du Lingam, et de quelques autres superstitions': "Ovide ne parle
point de cette cérémonie dans ses Fastes; et nous ne connaissons aucun auteur
romain qui en fasse mention. Il se peut que la superstition ait ordonné cette posture à quelques femmes stériles. Nous ne voyons pas même que les Romains aient
jamais érigé un temple à Priape. Il était regardé comme une de ces divinités sub-
alternes dont on tolérait les fêtes plutôt qu'on ne les approuvait. Nous avons dans
nos provinces un saint, dont nous n'osons écrire le nom monosyllabe, à qui plus
d'une femme a quelquefois adressé ses prières. Le dieu Priape, le dieu Jugatin, qui
unissait les époux, le subjuguant Materprema, qui empêchait la matrice de faire la
difficile, la Pertunda, qui présidait au devoir conjugal, tous ces magots, tous ces
pénates n'étaient point regardés comme des dieux. Ils n'avaient point de place dans

to witness such a miracle or healing. "It provided me with the opportunity to examine the mysteries of religion in the same way as I had
examined human judgment before. That proved not very difficult
for me since at the occasion of what you now call first communion,
I had been entrusted to the hands of a cleric shortly before that."
(I,4) D'Antan thus appears to have pondered over the doctrine of
transubstantiation.

Transubstantiation, which preoccupied La Croze and some of his
brethren at around the same time as well, was one of those cases,
which together with the doctrine of the trinity, was an instance of
the theologians' apparently absurd claims: namely, that the exterior
properties of wine and bread would remain as such, whereas the
substance would turn into flesh and blood. When d'Antan turned to
his teacher to ask him about the reasons for this, he received only
ridiculous and superficial explanations in return (I,4). In face of the
explanations provided by his "superieur," he then plunged into blasphemy, because he could not and did not want to comprehend why
God would "serve his own body from a dreadful feeding bowl" and
why this God, who was supposed to be just, was equally distributed
among the good and the evil.

During these years, in the context of personal self-examination to
distinguish appearance from reality, the young student started to read
Descartes. The *Discours de la Methode* from 1637 and most of all
the *Meditationes* from 1641 were widely disseminated during that time
in France and had been intensely discussed for decades.[31] D'Antan
took especially the methodical doubt from the first and second medi-
tation as his model. "Sifting through everything, what I had seen
until then in my mind again, I decided to follow Descartes in his
use of doubt; within a short amount of time, I had acquired such

---

le panthéon d'Agrippa, non plus que Rumilia la déesse des tetons; Stercutius le
dieu de la chaise percée; et Crepitus le dieu pet. Cicéron ne s'abaisse point à citer
ces prétendus divinités dans son livre De la Nature des dieux, dans ses Tusculanes,
dans sa Divination. IL FAUT LAISSER A LA POPULACE SES AMUSEMENTS,
SON SAINT OVIDE, QUI RESSUSCITE LES PETITS GARCONS, et son saint
Rabboni qui rabonnit les mauvais maris, ou qui les fait mourir au bout de l'an-
née." I am grateful to Alain Mothu for the references.

[31] On the diffusion of Cartesianism in France see Henri Gouhier, *Cartésianisme et
augustinisme au XVIIe siècle* (Paris: Vrin, 1978); François Azouvi, *Descartes et la France:
histoire d'une passion nationale* (Paris: Fayard, 2002); Tad M. Schmaltz, *Radical Cartesianism.
The French reception of Descartes* (Cambridge, 2002).

solid grounding in it that I told a friend one day that this system did not seem unfounded to me, because I actually doubted that I existed (I,6)." It is quite surprising that d'Antan called this doubt Cartesian, because Descartes stops his methodological doubt at the very moment, when his "cogito ergo sum" provides him with the certainty of his own existence. The young student then must have either exaggerated or he referred to his own physical existence, because Descartes included it in his experiment on doubt in his meditations as well.[32]

It is tempting to interpret these "petites Histoirettes pueriles," as d'Antan himself called them (I,7), psychologically. Obviously, we are dealing here with a very talented boy, who retreated in some dramatic fashion into himself and who continued to live with the consciousness of being somebody special. He played with the idea that he did not even exist. Overall, the twelve year old boy is more interested in doubt than in its theoretical resolution as it occurs at a later point in Descartes' *Meditationes*. An actual slap on his thigh by one of his friends convinced him of his friend's existence, but not of his own.

At the same time, however, the contemporary discussions about Cartesianism and Skepticism could have possibly nourished his mind and shaped it accordingly. During the 1690s, when d'Antan was a student, the reverberations of the discussions between Simon Foucher and Malebranche could still be felt in Paris. Foucher, the skeptic, had already raised intelligent objections against Descartes.[33] On the other hand, there were also historians such as Father Hardouin, who taught at the Collège Louis Le Grand and who considered a large part of ancient literature as a forgery.[34] Thus there were intellectual cur-

---

[32] See Descartes, "Meditationes de prima philosophia", *Oeuvres* ed. Adam/Tannery, vol. VII (Paris: Vrin, 1964), Meditatio II, p. 24: "Suppono igitur omnia quae video falsa esse; credo nihil unquam extitisse eorum quae mendax memoria repraesentat; nullos plane habeo sensus; corpus, figura, extensio, motus, locusque sunt chimerae. Quid igitur erit verum? Fortassis hoc unum, nihil esse certi."

[33] See Richard A. Watson, *The downfall of Cartesianism 1673–1712: a study of epistemological issues in late 17th century Cartesianism* (The Hague: Nijhoff, 1966), and idem, *The breakdown of Cartesian metaphysics* (Atlantic Highlands, NJ, 1987).

[34] See Anthony Grafton, "Jean Hardouin: The Antiquary as Pariah," in idem, *Bring out your Dead. The Past as Revelation* (Cambridge, Mass.: Harvard University Press, 2001), 181–207; in general: Carlo Borghero, *La certezza e la storia. Cartesianesimo, pirronismo e conoscenza storica* (Milano: Angeli, 1983).

rents, whose skepticism went very far: a phenomenon, which Paul Hazard has called the "crise de la conscience européenne."

Did young d'Antan absorb any of these debates? Certainly not directly. His letters do not indicate an extensive philosophical training of any kind; in them, it is more the amateur philosopher who speaks. Evidently, d'Antan did not receive a university education at the Collège. The second letter to La Croze namely reads: "since I never received the kind of education, which Christians use to adorn the minds of their children, how then could I discover, what so many able theologians in your religion have not discovered so far?" (II,1). Yet, one has to be careful not to underestimate that the echoes of intellectual debates can keep on reverberating in the schools as well. The bright young boy, who listened to the conversations between his teacher and the librarian of Saint Germain des Prés, may very well have picked up bits and pieces on the debates about Skepticism and Cartesianism.

D'Antan overall used the skepticism he developed against religion. He explained to La Croze that his doubts brought him to a point "where he doubted not only religion but God as well." He stated more precisely: "Time favored me since it was—like my philosophy—full of ideas. I observed and studied the world as something deceiving. The pious were hypocrites in my eyes. Thieves seemed to have no other plan but to give, but simply in a less spectacular way." (I,7) This appears to be some kind of Robin Hood type of ideal, which he seemed to have developed. D'Antan maintained the point of view, which he himself phrased later as "a turning upside down if not the world then at least the order of nature" during the rest of his time as a student and during his subsequent military service.[35]

His spending some time—or beginning his career—in the military seems close at hand since his father served as a royal officer himself. Yet we do not know how much time d'Antan spent there. It is possible that he ran into like-minded people when he was a student in Paris, but also during his military service. Mersenne already complained during the 1620s about the sheer number of "libertins" and "atheists", and their number had certainly not decreased by the end

---

[35] I,7: 'que je fus à l'armée'; see also Rafa's description of d'Antans as a "warrior"; see footnote 16.

of the seventeenth century.[36] D'Antan entered a stage where he could
not believe anything at all ("je ne crusse rien", I,8). This phrasing
evokes thoughts about a clandestine manuscript, an *Ars nihil credendi*,
which was created exactly at this time, namely at around 1700. Its
unknown author, whose points of view are similar to d'Antan's but
who phrased his disbelief in a much more explicit form, also adopted
Descartes' methodological doubt. He wrote: "I do know to what
extreme position I could be pushed upholding my thesis: to being
uncertain, to doubting whether I doubt, to not knowing whether I
think and whether I am; but how absurd the consequences from
proper reflection may be, I reject the consequences only to embrace
reflection nonetheless with even more stubbornness; whatever turmoil I may encounter, all of these absurdities will not prevent me
from committing myself to a position, where no probability of any
kind seems to be able to keep me. These unavoidable contradictions,
which appear in everything, prove to me even more the changing
nature of reason and that everything remains uncertain, my own
uncertainty thereby included."[37]

The author of this passage, like d'Antan, considers delusion omnipresent as well. The senses in particular are "deceivers, which play
tricks on us." In this case, too, universal doubt leads eventually to
the doubt of God's existence. His piece was smuggled from Paris in
1705 and made its way via Germany into clandestine distribution.[38]

Incidentally, by studying d'Antan it becomes possible to examine
how quick-witted young people used contemporary histories of pagan
disbelief and of the frauds of heathen priestcraft[39] (with the fables,

---

[36] See Marin Mersenne, *L'impieté des deistes, athées, et libertins de ce temps* (Paris,
1624).

[37] [Pseudo-Vallée:] Ars nihil credendi, ou Le Fléo de la Foi, cited after Anthony
Mc Kenna, *De Pascal à Voltaire. Le role des Pensées de Pascal dans l'histoire des idées entre
1670 et 1734*, 2 vols. (Oxford: the Voltaire Foundation, 1990), vol. 2, 761f.: "Je
sais à quelle extremité on veut me réduire, dans la thèse que je soutiens, jusqu'à
étre incertain, jusqu'à douter si je doute, jusqu'à ignorer si je pense et si je suis:
mais quelles absurdes conséquences qu'on puisse tirer d'un juste raisonnement,
j'abandonne les conséquences, pour embrasser méme avec plus d'opiniátreté le
raisonnement; quelque orage qu'on me prépare, toutes ces absurdités ne m'em-
péchent pas de m'attacher où plus de probabilité semble m'attirer. Ces contradictions
inévitables, qui se rencontrent dans tout, me prouvent encore mieux la volubilité
da la raison, et que tout est incertain, jusqu'à mon incertitude méme."

[38] See Alain Mothu, "La beatitude des Chrétiens et son double clandestin", in:
Anthony McKenna and idem (eds.), *La Philosophie clandestine à'l Age classique* (Oxford,
1997), 79–117; Martin Mulsow, *Die drei Ringe* (footnote 7), 25–27.

[39] See e.g. the successful book by Fontenelle, *Histoire des oracles* (s.l., 1687); on this

"which priests have invented with regards to their deities" [I,13])
and applied them instantly to Catholic Christianity, which surrounded
them. "I would never have believed," says d'Antan, "what has been
said about pagan worship of images and miracles if I had not realized that Christians nowadays do the same thing." This is a comparison, which many authors of these books had certainly not intended
(with the exception of intellectuals like Fontenelle); but especially
among Protestant scholarly writing there was a significant body of
literature, which masked its attack of the Catholic Church with a
criticism of Greco-Roman religion. One unintended dynamic of the
Enlightenment—at least in France—was then that this criticism
amounted to a disavowal of Christianity as a whole.[40]

In addition to that, the diversity of confessions and religions undermined the claim to truth of each individual one.[41] Only the assumption that they were worldly creations remained: "rather, I concluded
that many different cults were invented by politicians from the start,
because in each case they adjusted to the inclinations of the peoples,
which they wanted to take advantage of." (I,15) D'Antan undoubtedly may have adopted the theory of the political character of religions, which had been common since the time of the libertinage
érudit, from many different sources.[42] In clandestine manuscripts such
as the *Ars nihil credendi*, the idea of "réligion de l'état, du pays,

---

book, see Frank E. Manuel, *The Eighteenth Century Confronts the Gods* (Cambridge,
Mass.: Harvard University Press, 1959), 47ff. See further on the impostor thesis:
Giorgio Spini, *Ricerca die libertini. La teoria dell'impostura delle religioni nel seicento italiano*
(Firenze: La nuova Italia, 1983), 2. Aufl.; Winfried Schröder, *Ursprünge des Atheismus.
Untersuchungen zur Metaphysik- und Religionskritik des 17. und 18. Jahrhunderts* (Stuttgart:
Frommann-Holzboog, 1998), 146ff., 424ff. and 445ff.

[40] For the desastrous consequences not only of the strife between the denominations, but even inside the denominations, namely between the catholic Aristotelians
and the catholic Cartesians, see Alan Charles Kors, *Atheism in France 1650–1729*,
Vol. I: The Orthodox Sources of Disbelief (Princeton: PUP, 1990).

[41] In I,17, d'Antan speaks of the desastrous consequences of the pluralization as
well, when he says, he never found two groups of people, which consented with
another. Some had talked philosophically about the immortal soul, others poetically
about the Elysium, a third group had spoken theologically about heaven, and a
fourth esoterically about transmigration of the souls. By adopting Alistair MacIntyre's
diagnosis of modern ethics to this field, one could say that there was no uniform
language of life after death left.

[42] On the thesis of the political origin of religion, see René Pintard, *Le liberti-
nisme érudit dans la première moitié du XVIIe siècle* (Paris, 1943); Giorgio Spini, *Ricerca
sui libertini* (footnote 39); Martin Mulsow, *Moderne aus dem Untergrund. Radikale Frühaufklärung
in Deutschland 1680–1720* (Hamburg: Meiner 2002), 161–260.

du prince, de mes parents, et non pas la mienne" is omnipresent.[43]
The thought that the various cults had been adjusted to the diverse
peculiarities of different people was widespread.[44]

Religion in Paris had reached a level of incredibility, of political
abuse and intellectual hypocrisy at around 1700, which could hardly
be surpassed at all. Repression reduced the chances of the Jansenist
alternative. Liberally minded clerics such as La Croze left France
and found a refuge among the exiled Huguenot communities. Individuals such as d'Antan, who had lost their faith entirely, chose the
avenue of introvert emigration and turned into clandestine atheists
such as the Abbé Meslier.[45]

D'Antan, however, did not keep his atheist points of view entirely
as a secret. In I,9–I,15 he recapitulates a letter, which he wrote at
that stage to his father confessor ("directeur de conscience"), who
was a man, whom he called disdainfully an "alleged scholar ("pré-
tendu Docteur") and whose explanations of the transubstantiation
had already driven him crazy before.[46] This father confessor held
very orthodox points of view about the existence of devils, with whom
he threatened his flock, and his orthodoxy seems to have played a
significant role in d'Antan's turning from Christianity. Alluding polem-
ically to the stories about Catholic martyrs among the Jesuit missionaries in Japan and China, who then were frequently told to the
pious, d'Antan mockingly pointed out that if their attempt to Chris-
tianize was not more successful than his father confessor's attempt
with d'Antan, then they might very well just remain sweating in the
corner of their stakes (I,10). For he could not possibly believe in the
devil. Even if one accepted the Bible as a basis, one could not prove
the existence of devils. D'Antan's choice of words and the use of
terms such as "fables" and "erroneous ideas from childhood" shows

---

[43] Ars nihil credendi (footnote 37), cited after Mc Kenna (footnote 37), 760.

[44] See the contemporary argumentations against accommodation theory, e.g.
Friedrich Ernst Kettner, *Exercitationes historico-theologicae de religione prudentum* (Leipzig,
1701); Daniel Clasen, *De religione politica* (Magdeburg, 1655).

[45] See Jean Meslier, "Mémoire de pensées et des sentiments", in idem, *Œuvres
complètes*, ed. Roland Desné, Jean Deprun and Albert Soboul (Paris, 1970–72).

[46] On the practices of confession in 17th century France, see Alois Hahn, "Zur
Soziologie der Beichte und anderer Formen institutionalisierter Bekenntnisse: Selbst-
thematisierung und Zivilisationsprozeß", in: *Kölner Zeitschrft für Soziologie und Sozial-
psychologie*, 34 (1982), 407–434; Jean Delumeau, *L'aveu et le pardon: les difficultés de la
confession XIIIe–XVIIIe siècle* (Paris: Fayard, 1990).

that he phrased his rejection from a Cartesian mode of thinking as Balthasar Bekker did before him between 1691 and 1694.[47] Again this might have been a debate, whose echo made its way into d'Antan's thinking. It was since Bekker if not indeed before that the belief in the devil came under massive attack throughout Europe. The rejection of the belief in the devil then is for d'Antan one aspect among many others. It is the result of a rational examination of religion. D'Antan's credo in this phase is that one could not simply stop using reason when it came to questions of religion.

Overcoming Skepticism

But how did d'Antan overcome his skeptical crisis? How did it happen that he turned to Judaism? Before we examine his case, it may be instructive to look at a surprisingly similar one: the case of Johann Peter Späth.[48] The following has been recorded about Späth's motivations to convert to Judaism: "Since he did not encounter any agreement among one or the other and each person always said something that was contrary to the opinion of the other, he eventually concluded: omnia esse incerta, nisi hoc: unum scilicet esse Deum and, in order to ease his conscience, he converted to Judaism, which had owned and cultivated truth from the beginning."[49] According to this report, Späth experienced a pyrrhonic crisis as well; it was nourished by the plurality of religious points of views. His solution was a double reduction: first, a return to the only common and therewith only certain aspect of all religions he had explored, namely the belief in one single God. The emphasis has to be put here on "one single"

---

[47] Balthasar Bekker, *De Betoverde Weereld*, Amsterdam 1691–94; on the debates following the publication of that book see Jonathan Israel, *Radical Enlightenment. Philosophy and the Making of Modernity 1650–1750* (Oxford: OUP, 2001), 375–405; Andrew Fix, *Fallen Angels. Balthasar Bekker and the Spirit Controversy in Seventeeth-Century Holland* (Dordrecht: Kluwer, 1999). Jean Le Clerc had printed a 29 page review of the first two volumes of Bekker's book in his Bibliothèque universelle in 1691.

[48] On Späth ("Moses Germanus") see Hans J. Schoeps, *Philosemitismus im Barock* (Tübingen, 1952); Allison Coudert, "Judaizing in the Seventeenth Century. Franciscus Mercurius van Helmont and Johann Peter Späth (Moses Germanus)", in this volume.

[49] This is the report of the Helmstedt theologian Hermann von der Hardt to Gottlieb Stolle in 1703; cited from: Günter E. Guhrauer, "Beiträge zur Kenntnis des 17. und 18. Jahrhunderts aus den handschriftlichen Aufzeichnungen Gottlieb Stolles", in: *Allgemeine Zeitschrift für Geschichte*. 7 (1847), 385–436 and 481–531; here 403.

God, because monotheism was considered incompatible with the doctrine of the trinity. The second reduction pertained to time: only
the first monotheistic religion could be the true one. This, however,
was Judaism.

Did d'Antan have similar thoughts? Certainly not at a first glance.
His Pyrrhonism was in its essence, unlike Späth's, rooted in his philosophical subjectivism. He first needed to go beyond that. D'Antan
referred to this process, when, after philosophical debates with his
friends, he went to bed at night and continued to dwell on his
thoughts. The thought that religion was nothing but the outcome of
education and upbringing kept popping in his head. He may have
asked himself then, what remained of it once one eliminated the
educational aspect: "Then, all of a sudden, when I came across
Descartes' system again, I told myself that 'I think, therefore I am',
but this teaches me nothing. It remains an undeniable fact that I
am, but who am I? Once I fell asleep and after I believed to be a
monarch at several instances, I imagined that all of my thoughts
were just dreams and that I myself was nothing but an idea; I imagined that human beings only maintain the illusion to exist, and finally
that everything we see was just a grand chimera or masked noth-
ingness" (I,17). This shows again d'Antan's obsessive idea not to be
real; this idea certainly draws from the Cartesian Meditations, but
also possesses deeper psychological roots. Already his dream image,
in which he viewed himself as a monarch, provides some psychological clues: it exposes an egocentric mindset and elements of desire
for omnipotency.

This time, however, d'Antan's train of thought did not remain on
a surreal level. The reality principle—to speak in Freudian terms—
takes over. D'Antan awakens from his somber sleep: "I could easily
have been convinced by these vain ideas, if not, after these gruesome
thoughts, my senses had returned by the sensation of a present color
or a present feeling of joy, which for instance awaken my dormant
desires whenever I experience hunger, thirst, or when I am hot or
cold. Thus, through experience I found that I am an actual thing,
which is more than a bare thought, which one dreams, but rather
a compound, which is in need of meat, soup, clothes, and refreshments.
Therefore, I simply concluded without venturing into vain explo-
rations and without wrongful shrewdness that I am what one calls
a human being" (I,18). D'Antan discards his pyrrhonism; he "humblement" accepts to be a simple man. He has overcome his crisis.

But overcoming it has not yet anything to do with Judaism. For the time being, d'Antan has to start with the "sensualist" or "biological" fundament, which he has reached, by becoming conscious of being a simple creature.[50] In an entirely Cartesian method, but under a slightly different circumstance, he concludes "that, since I owe gratitude to other creatures for experiencing sensations, I owe gratitude to something different from me for my being as well. I examine my origin and I find that those who have brought me into this world are human beings similar to myself, they are subject to similar kinds of reflections, and they come from human beings as well, and so on to infinity. The infinite, which has passed, confuses me not very much, but I have to admit that what lies ahead in the future does some." (I,19) D'Antan's thought is here close to the third of Descartes' Meditations and he implies in his train of thought that there must be a creator outside of the biological chain of creation, upon which one's own Being depends. At the same time, however, he inserts reflections of the kind as they appear in Cartesian "provisional morale," namely that one has to deal with circumstances of uncertainty.[51] But he does not apply these reflections to morale, but to questions of faith. "What conclusions can I draw for my present affairs, I asked myself. Faith is lower than reason, but not to believe is still lower", he muses in a Pascalian manner. "I would like to find the golden mean and derive my faith from reason."

During these years, another man was in search of a "golden mean": he was stuck between universal doubt on the one hand and superstition on the other. He is the author of another clandestine work. This type of text comes in fact closest to d'Antan's confessions, because it is not geared to an audience and is a direct image of private thoughts. In this case it is the work *Réflexions morales et métaphysiques sur les religions et sur les connaissances des hommes*, which presents us with a parallel. Its' unidentified author goes back to the "I" as well and he, too, does not find security in the Cartesian Cogito. Like d'Antan, this author ponders sentiment: "I feel that I am and I know that I exist, but feeling is the only thing responsible for that and

---

[50] It is not quite clear, if one could describe d'Antan's affirmation of the sensation of pleasure as an influence of Epicureanism, perhaps by writings such as Saint Evremont's "Sur les plaisirs"; on this subject see McKenna (footnote 37), 689ff.

[51] See Descartes: Discours de la méthode, Œuvres (footnote 32), vol. 1. See Dezsö Kalocsai, *Le problème des règles de la morale "provisoire" de Descartes* (Budapest, 1973).

that proves exactly that this type of knowledge does not really constitute a science. [. . .] I feel internally that I do not see anything
clearly; this feeling has never been knowledge, since I have remained
entirely unsure about its nature. I am only affected by its presence,
that is all."[52] But despite the similarities to d'Antan's thoughts, it is
not so much the consciousness of brutish needs here, that rescued
the author from his self-doubt, but rather an indefinable feeling of
the Pascalian kind.

D'Antan's "golden mean" was supposed to be a reasonable faith.
Thus he arrived at the idea of a harmony between reason and faith,
which means a "reasonable" religion. The instruction to faith by
means of reason could of course be interpreted in multiple ways,
ranging from a very scholastic form to deism.

How then does he conceive this instruction? Worshiping external,
natural objects, Cartesian reason tells him, was not sensible, because
then one may just as well worship one's own sensual organs, which
perceive these external objects (I,20). Only an infinite Being, which
does not have a beginning or a creator, remains a possibility. This
is how d'Antan arrived at an abstract definition of a supreme Being,
which he intends to worship: "It is a being, which has no similarities, which is neither divided nor is limited in any way, whose center is everywhere, whose circumference is nowhere and which is a
single potent whole, from which everything originates ("emanent")
and to which everything returns."

This constitutes a highly philosophical definition of God and it
reflects the education, which d'Antan has now already obtained. The
pseudo-hermetical metaphor of God as "sphaera infinita cuius cen-
trum ubique, circumferentia nusquam" has been used by Nicholas
of Cusa and several other thinkers.[53] Around 1700, it was common
among people who wanted to distance themselves from the dogmas

---

[52] Réflexions morales et métaphysiques sur les religions et sur les connaissances
des hommes, Ms. Rouen 1569; the author is possibly a certain Delaube; I quote
from Mc Kenna (footnote 37), 754: "Je sens que je suis, je sais que j'existe, mais
ce n'est ce qui prouve que cette espèce de connaissance n'est pas véritablement une
science [. . .] je sens intérieurement que je ne vois rien de clair: ce sentiment ne
fut jamais une science puisque j'en ignore entièrement la nature: je suis seulement
affecté de sa présence, voilà tout."

[53] This definition is inspired by Plotinus, but orginates from the medieval Liber
XXIV philosophorum; on the reception see Dietrich Mahnke, Unendliche Sphäre und
Allmittelpunkt. Beiträge zur Genealogie der mathematischen Mystik (Halle: Niemeyer, 1937).

they had learned about in their catechism and who preferred over it a philosophical approach to religion.[54] Pascal had used this metaphor also in his *Pensées*—a book, which had appeared posthumously in 1670 and which had a great impact in the late seventeenth century.[55]

D'Antan thus had become a philosophical worshipper of God. After he turned his back to skeptical atheism, he lived through a euphoric phase, in which God "revealed to his imagination the greatness of his Being." The need to worship this God was so great that the desire arose to know the right ceremonies ("voeux et [. . .] obbeissances" I,23), which were necessary for such worship. At this point, the same type of reflections, which we had observed in Späth's case, become d'Antan's guide: he identifies the oldest religion as the one, which possesses the greatest degree of dignity. That was Judaism.[56] It was the avenue that lead from the "God of the philosophers" to the "God of Abraham, Isaac, and Jacob," from the abstractness to a living faith. It was the spirit of a Pascal without Christianity.

His turn towards Judaism provided d'Antan at the same time with the possibility to draw the consequences from his negative experiences with Christianity and to keep his distance from it. Since as a Frenchman, d'Antan had rarely had any contacts with living Judaism, it presented itself as a perfect project ground, on which he could apply all of his theoretical considerations.[57]

---

[54] See e.g. Martin Mulsow, "Ignorabat Deum. Scetticismo, libertinsmo ed ermetismo nell'interpretazione arpiana del concetto vaniniano di Dio", in: Francesco Paolo Raimondi (ed.), *Giulio Cesare Vanini e il libertinismo*. Atti del convegno si studi Taurisano 28–30 ottobre 1999 (Galatina, Lecce, 2000), 171–182.

[55] On the reception of the Pensées see Mc Kenna (footnote 37).

[56] See Pascal: Pensées, publiés suivant l'ordre chronologique, ed. Léon Brunschwicg (Paris, 1925), vol. III (= Œuvres XIV), No. 619: 'Mais, en considérant ainsi cette inconstante et bizarre varieté de mœurs et des créances dans les divers temps, je trouve en un coin du monde un peuple particulier, séparé de tous les autres peuples de la terre, le plus ancien de tous, et dont les histoires précèdent de plusieurs siècles les plus anciennes que nous ayons. Je trouve donc ce peuple grand et nombreux, sorti d'un seul homme, qui adore un seul Dieu, et qui se conduit par une loi, qu'ils disent tenir de sa main. [. . .] La rencontre de ce peuple m'étonne, et me semble digne d'attention. Je considère cette loi qu'ils se vantent de tenir de Dieu, et je la trouve admirable. C'est la première loi de toutes [. . .].'

[57] Judaism as non-Christianity, as an external point of view, from which Christianity can be viewed critically, appears also in La Croze's *Entretiens* (footnote 21), and later in d'Argens' *Lettres Juives*.

The Road to Judaism

Despite the fact that d'Antan in I,3 claimed that he had not talked
to another Jew about his conversion before his journey to Amsterdam,
that does not mean that he never before had any kind of social
interaction with Jews. On the contrary, in I,8 he admits that already
as a young man (about the time of his military service, which was
approximately in the years after 1700), he had "experienced some
sort of strange feeling in places, where he met Jews." Since there
were no Jews in Paris at that time, his military service may have
brought him to cities such as Metz or Avignon, where one could
have encounters with Jews. If he fought with the French troops in
the Wars of the Spanish Succession, then it could even have been
possible for him that he encountered Jews outside of France. But
even in Paris itself it was still possible to come in contact with Jewish
culture, at least with Jewish intellectual culture. This is what we learn
from the life-story of the Lithuanian Count Valentin Potocki, who
became fascinated on his peregrinatio academica in Paris (just a few
decades after d'Antan) by an old man, whom he met in a tavern
and who spoke Hebrew.[58] Potocki learned Hebrew, which convinced
him so much about Judaism that he moved to Amsterdam later and
converted. Perhaps there is a similar intellectual background as
d'Antan's behind this episode, shaped by the "crise de conscience
européenne", an episode from which we do not possess any Ego-
documentation.

Thus d'Antan's rationally motivated move towards Judaism could
build upon an early feeling of "je ne sais quoi." D'Antan, like Potocki
later on, started to study the Pentateuch. We do not know if he did
that on his own or if he got some help from somebody else as was
the case with Potocki; neither do we know if he began to learn
Hebrew at this point or if he was able to build on what he had

---

[58] On Potocki see David M. Eichhorn, *From Expulsion to Liberation* (footnote 9),
128–131. On the "crise" see Paul Hazard, *La crise de la conscience européenne* (Paris:
Boivin, 1935).—There was at least one known Jew in Paris towards the end of the
17th century: Jonas Salvador, who was a friend of Father Richard Simon. Salvador
had a monopoly on the tobacco industry in France and was Sabbatai Zevi's agent
in Paris. He and Simon were working on a French translation of the Talmud. I
am grateful to Richard Popkin for this information.—If d'Antan experienced Jewish
culture outside of Paris, Metz would be a probable place. It was as well a city with
military camps and with a Jewish community that was in contact with these camps,
since it provided the soldiers with material goods.

already learned at the Collège de Navarre. In any case, his admiration of the style of the Pentateuch ("sacré stil", I,24) alone suffices to chase away his earlier thoughts about Moses' priestly deception. D'Antan may even have adopted this point of view from Pascal and Filleau de La Chaise as well, who regarded the "simplicité" of the style of Holy Scripture as a proof for its authenticity.[59] But he may also have taken it from a Jewish source.

In his study of Hebrew Scripture d'Antan finds fulfillment and confirmation: "While I was reading these sacred symbols, I discovered the joy of this people and I concluded that God must still wish for what he had in the past since his will remains unchanging. He loved Israel and consequently always will" (I,24). At this point, d'Antan recognizes the political laws in Leviticus as basis for the laws of all subsequent people[60] and discovers the predictions of the prophets, which leave a considerable impression on him (I,24).

At the same time, d'Antan examines Christian arguments used to support their religion, which were viewed critically from the Jewish side. He focuses solely on the central question such as the advent of the messiah and not on "choses inventées" and "fables" like the legends of the saints (I,26). What are the qualities adherent to the messiah, he asks. To answer this question one has to, according to d'Antan, understand the punishment ("chatiment") God has inflicted upon his beloved people:[61] he struck them with the plague, starvation and war, let the temple be destroyed in order to make them understand that the temple becomes respectable solely through his, God's presence. This God, which d'Antan presents here, is the divine educator that the tradition starting from Maimonides with their rationalist idea of accommodation had represented. The following arguments refer to key passages, which were under dispute between Jews and Christians and which concern the value of Old Testament prophecies as evidence. The prophecy of Jacob in Genesis 49,10 reads for example: "The schebet shall not depart from Judah [. . .] until tribute comes to him; and the obedience of people is his."

---

[59] Filleau de La Chaise was the influential author of the *Discours sur les Pensées de Pascal* (Paris, 1672). On him see Mc Kenna (footnote 37), passim.

[60] See the numerous 17th century writings on the Respublica Hebraeorum. A survey can be found in Adam Sutcliffe, *Judaism and Enlightenment* (Cambridge, 2003), 42–57.

[61] D'Antan refers to the French proverb "Qui aime bien chatie bien" (I,24).

Controversial was the meaning of the term "schebet". Christian inter-
preters translated the term as "scepter." but it could also signify
"tribe" or "rod". D'Antan rejected the Christian translation as "scepter"
on philological-exegetical grounds and chose "rod, whip" as the correct translation (I,30). For "we are vagabonds and we are wandering
aimlessly through the entire world" (I,31). He viewed the Jews as a
suffering people. "I therefore finally conclude that the messiah will
be similar to the sad remnants of the children of Jacob and that he
will lead them back into the land, which God had promised to their
fathers and where they will settle in peace and where they can collect the fruit, which nourishes them if they serve God in spirit and
truth" (I,31).

The characteristics of the messiah are determined according to
Deuteronomy: he will be of the kind of Moses, he will lead Israel
out of captivity and he will eradicate idolatry (I,32). He will come
solely for the Jews (I,34). D'Antan claims that Jesus Christ ("votre
legislateur") does not match these criteria. His mission as atonement
for the Fall does not correspond with the biblical narrative about
Eden, since Adam, according to Scripture, already had to pay for
his disobedience: by being nude, ashamed and with death. Apart
from that: "If the founder of your religion had eliminated this sin,
then this would mean that we would reenter our original state of
innocence and we would enjoy the privileges of Paradise, as did our
parents before the Fall," which means that we would live in plenty
and become immortal. But obviously that did not happen (I,36).

D'Antan's attack on the doctrine of the Trinity follows right after
that. How can it be that Father, Son and the Holy Spirit are one
single God? That may still be possible (the Hebrew commentator
exclaims here: "God forbid!"), but Father, Son and Holy Spirit are
three names and it is written in the Bible that God had also just
one single name (I,36). D'Antan will repeat the same argument later
on in his second letter (II,1).

From where did d'Antan get these arguments? One can barely
assume that they all grew from solitary biblical studies. D'Antan was
aware that these questions "were often debated," but since the Jews
were afraid in their Christian environment, only weaker arguments
were used (I,26). This means that he claims to have an overview
knowledge of the literature of the Jewish-Christian controversy.[62] But

---

[62] The best survey is provided by Samuel Krauss, *The Jewish-Christian Controversy*

did he know clandestine Jewish anti-Christian polemical writings as well? These polemics were hardly available in France—they were more likely to be found in Amsterdam. Some, however, had been printed in the meantime. The first of these manuscripts that was printed and translated into Latin was Isaac Trokis's *Hizzuk Emmunah*, which Johann Christian Wagenseil published in his collection *Tela ignea Satanae* in 1681.[63] Johannes Müller from Hamburg, who had made an unpublished translation of the *Hizzuk Emmunah* himself and who collected similar texts, complained that the Jews would seduce Christians with their arguments into conversion.[64]

This is why it would be important to know if d'Antan received guidance in his Jewish anti-Christian studies. He characterized his thoughts as those of a "young man, who is inspired by God to search for truth" and not as those of a "philosopher, who reasons" (I,27). But he may have had his reasons not to mention the people who provided him with guidance.

All these studies of the Pentateuch rendered d'Antan an enthusiastic philosemite, but not yet a Jew. There still remained a great difference between developing sympathies for Judaism in spirit and within the four walls of a study and taking the avenue to full conversion. The latter would mean abandoning all professional career plans, one's domestic security and homeland and exchanging them for an uncertain future. Indeed, beyond all that it meant risking one's life since in many countries Apostates from Christianity who became Jewish were still customarily burned at the stake in 1700.

Another personal crisis needed to occur to render d'Antan willing to accept even these risks. "The dread of making a mistake

---

from the earliest times to 1789. Vol. I: *History*. Edited and revised by William Horbury (Tübingen, 1995).

[63] See Johann Christian Wagenseil, Tela Ignea Satanæ: Hoc est: Arcani, & horribiles Judæorum adversus Christvm Devm, & Christianam Religionem Libri Anekdotoi; Sunt vero: R. Lipmanni Carmen Memoriale. Liber Nizzachon Vetvs Avtoris Incogniti. Acta Dispvtationis R. Jechielis Cvm Qvodam Nicolao. Acta Dispvtationis R. Mosis Nachmanidis Cvm Fratre Pavlo Christiani, Et Fratre Raymvndo Martini. R. Isaaci Liber Chissvk Emvna. Libellvs Toldos Jeschv. . . .; Additæ sunt Latinæ Interpretationes, Et Dvplex Confvtatio. Augustinus Justinianus Episcopus Nebiensis in Præfatione præmissa Victoriæ Porcheti . . .; Accedit Mantissa De LXX. Hebdomadibus Danielis Adversus V.C. Johannis Marshami Eqvitis Avrati Angli novam & incommodam earundem explicationem. Altdorfi[i] Noricorvm Excudit Joh. Henricus Schönnerstædt, Academiæ Typographus . . . Prostat Noribergæ apud Johannem Hofmannum, & Francofurti ad Mœnum apud Ioh. Davidem Zunnerum, 1681.

[64] Johannes Müller: *Judaismus, oder Judenthumb. Das ist Ausführlicher Bericht von des jüdischen Volckes Unglauben, Blindheit und Verstockung* (Hamburg, 1707), 1387.

restrained me for at least another three years, but these years did
not pass without my conscience stinging me. Finally I fell ill and it
was believed that I would die. This is when I swore to abandon
everything and to follow the Jews" (I,37). D'Antan seems to have
undergone a similar process as the Pole Zaremba, who also needed
to fall sick first before his conscience gave in and he went to Amsterdam
to convert.[65] "I wished nothing else," as d'Antan describes his state
then, "but Jacob to come down from heaven at the time, when he
fled from his brother to hide with Laban. I do not tell you about
visions, which I had during my illness, but about how I regained
my health." Three months after his recovery, however, he took a
carriage to Amsterdam.

During these decades, Amsterdam was well-known as a place where
the Jewish community could risk accepting even converts who were
not marranos. The city experienced a period of great intellectual
and economic prosperity; the Jews—many of them Sephardim—were
often traders, physicians, and scholars, dressed in fashionable clothes,
who spoke Spanish or Portuguese; they were of course often well-
versed in the French idiom as well and were able to live relatively
freely.[66] Of course they also had to be careful that anti-Christian
polemics, which had been written by scholars such as Orobio de
Castro and Saul Levi Morteira, did not leak out so they would not
provoke the anger of the host society.

In spite of all this Jewish cosmopolitanism, it had been the
Amsterdam community which excommunicated and expelled Spinoza
and Juan de Prado. Therefore, it was certainly a good idea for
d'Antan to entrust the Amsterdam rabbis with his biblicist motivations and not to explain his philosophical thoughts. We do not know
how quickly the elders of the community accepted his petition to
become a member of the community by means of conversion and
circumcision.[67] Eventually they did and d'Antan, in solemn mode,

---

[65] See David Max Eichhorn, *From Expulsion to Liberation* (footnote 9), 128–131.

[66] On Amsterdam see Jonathan Israel, *European Jewry in the Age of Mercantilism 1550–1750* (Oxford: OUP, 1985); Henry Méchoulan, *Être juif à Amsterdam au temps de Spinoza* (Paris: Michel, 1991); Carel ter Haar, *Jüdisches Städtebild Amsterdam* (Frankfurt am Main, 1993); Yosef Kaplan, *From Christianity to Judaism. The Story of Isaac Orobio de Castro* (Oxford: OUP, 1989); Miriam Bodian, *Hebrews of the Portuguese nation: conversos and community in early modern Amsterdam* (Bloomington [u.a.]: Indiana Univ. Press, 1997), and the contribution of Elisheva Carlebach to this volume.

[67] There seem to be no records on d'Antan as a member in the files of the

refers to his time in Amsterdam: "It was there that I sealed the covenant with our fathers Abraham, Isaac, and Jacob with my blood" (I,37). The Hebrew introduction to the letters gives a similar description: "And he left his house and homeland and traveled to the holy community of Amsterdam to worship God and offer his sacrifice there; the heart and blood."[68] Around that time d'Antan must have accepted his Jewish first name. We do not know his original first name. However we know that it must have been about that time that d'Antan decided to write a book about his "miraculous conversion" (I,38), not unlike converts to Christianity, who often wrote justifying this step in a public report. D'Antan's book never seemed to have been published. Was it ever written? If so, then it may still remain untouched without a name on its cover among the collections of the Amsterdam community.[69]

It is hard to determine from the available information when the conversion precisely occurred. If one adds to his time at the Collège, which must have been during the mid-1690s, a few years of military service, which may have overlapped with the three years of indecision, then one arrives at around 1705 as the year of his conversion. D'Antan would then still only have been about twenty years old. The unknown variable in this calculation, however, remains the precise time and duration of his military service. If it is taken into consideration that d'Antan's second letter—as we shall see—was written after 1711 then it may very well be that we have to presume his conversion for approximately 1710 or even later. It could even be that only the publication of La Croze's *Entretiens* in 1711 served as the impetus for d'Antan to contact his old mentor. In this work, La Croze uses a fictional Sephardic Jew as a mouthpiece to criticize the intolerant and corrupt conditions in Christianity. He endows the Jew—quite uncommon for this time—with very benevolent character traits. The Jew is a cosmopolitan, educated and eloquent figure.[70] D'Antan may have heard, possibly from Baron von Staff, that the

---

Amsterdam Jewish community. I thank Adrain Offenberg of the Bibliotheca Rosenthaliana for the information.

[68] Ms. gall. Oct. 38 (footnote 1), fol. 2v.

[69] On the manuscripts, see above all L. Fuks und R.G. Fuks-Mansfeld, *Hebrew and Judaic Manuscripts in Amsterdam Public Collections* (Leiden, 1975).

[70] See La Croze, *Entretiens* (footnote 21); on that book see Jonathan Israel, "Philosophy, Deism, and the Early Jewish Enlightenment" (forthcoming).

author of the anonymously published book was his old mentor, who worked by that time as librarian in Berlin. This may have motivated him to entrust this man, whom he could picture with sympathies for the Jews, with the story of his conversion.

With regards to von Staff, his identity remains a mystery. The archives in Berlin have records of a certain Nathanael von Staff, who was director-in-chief of the Berlin Fürsten-und Ritterakademie (Academy for Princes and Knights) and from 1706 on became civil servant or the *Herolds-Amt* (Office of Heralds) there.[71] Another line of the family leads us into military circles. In 1709, Carl von Staff, who was a royal Prussian major, died. In 1729, Thomas Ernst von Staff died, who probably was also a descendant from a Prussian family and who had served as lieutenant general in the imperial Russian military.[72] A connection between d'Antan and von Staff seems possible through the military service of both men. The years preceeding 1713/14 were characterized by intensive military movements against the background of the Wars of the Spanish Succession. At the time of the peace negotiations in Utrecht, numerous ambassadors and military officials arrived in Holland;[73] it is possible that von Staff knew La Croze from Berlin and that he made the acquaintance of d'Antan either when d'Antan served in the military or after his conversion in Amsterdam. But it is impossible to speculate more than that. The question of von Staff's religious views remains a speculation as well. Could it have been possible that von Staff harbored anti-Trinitarian sympathies? In II,6, for example, where d'Antan developed his cabbalism, operating with ternary distinctions, he hints: "Please show this letter to Baron von Staff and he will be equally stunned to see a Trinitarian Jew as I would be if I saw a Unitarian Christian." It is not clear if the "I would be" has to be taken purely hypothetically or if it indeed referred to von Staff's beliefs.

---

[71] See Geheimes Staatsarchiv Preussischer Kulturbesitz, I. HA Geheimer Rat, Rep. 7 Preußen, Nr. 13 Fasz. 83x von Staff, 1708; I. HA, Rep. 176 Heroldsamt, S Nr. 312 v. Staff/Reitzenstein. A title "Baron" cannot be found in the archivalia. I am grateful to the GSTA PK for the information. The first name Nathanael is rather unusual. Might this von Staff have any connection to Judaism?

[72] See *Genealogisches Handbuch des Adels*, vol. 26 (Limburg/Lahn, 1961), 396.

[73] On the milieu see Max Braubach, *Geschichte und Abenteuer: Gestalten um den Prinzen Eugen* (München: Bruckmann, 1950); on the diplomatic life at the Utrecht peace negotiations see Lucien Bely, *Espions et ambassadeurs au temps de Louis XIV* (Paris, 1990).

Only one aspect remains certain: Shortly after his conversion, d'Antan embarked on his journey to Israel.

Kabbalah

D'Antan's biography as a whole suggests that he is a self-reflecting philosophical amateur. Therefore, any analysis of d'Antan's points of views cannot make the mistake of looking for their sources as if he had been a professional scholar. Rather, his ideas seem to be a mélange of many different influences—sometimes not even consistent with each other—from which d'Antan constructs his worldview.

D'Antan's religious-philosophical convictions during his life among Jews seemed to have changed considerably, which may partially be explained by his exposure to Hebrew literature, which he now read and the interaction with Jewish scholars. In his second letter to La Croze, which we possess, he talks about these convictions. Whereas an exact dating of the first letter is not possible, the second letter provides us with a clear *terminus post quem*. D'Antan namely refers to a conversation with La Croze that he had with him some time after the publication of the latter's *Entretiens*, which were published in 1711 and which contained in their fourth part a treatise about atheists: "that what I had the honor of telling you on the subject of your treatise on the atheists in the garden of your King and in his library" (II,5). How could d'Antan have come to Berlin? Was it on his return from his trip to Israel? Or did he come directly from Amsterdam?

This Berlin talk at least confirms our assumption that the *Entretiens* must have been a book with a certain significance for d'Antan. In his letter he expresses thoughts that have preoccupied him "for more than a year" (II,1). This suggests that some time may have passed before he addressed the topics raised in the conversation as well as the questions in La Croze's letters. The letter does not seem to have been written before 1712 or 1713.

The reason for d'Antan's long silence lay in his difficult situation. He admits that until then he "had been living like an animal, which eats and drinks and worries little about the future" (II,1). Rafa's Hebrew introduction to the text also reports that d'Antan had a difficult time after his return from the Holy Land: "When he returned to [. . .], where his house is after leaving it in order to find a living, we observed him when he was in dangerous times, [surrounded]

by an ocean of confusions. [He was] like a person who found a
great spoil[74] and one who is in calm water. He was willing to become
a martyr when they were conspiring to take out our skin and put
in on fire." It remains unclear to which threat Rafa here refers.
Where there any fears about progroms? Which location did Rafa
mean by "where his house is?" It is unlikely that he feared for progroms in Amsterdam. Had d'Antan temporarily returned to France?
Or does Rafa refer to the Italian circumstances?[75] Yet, it does not
seem surprising that d'Antan was prepared to become a martyr given
his belief that he had been selected and that he was lead by a divine
providence.

Unclear, however, remains what d'Antan did for a living. This
was certainly not an easy task for a convert with only military training. In his first letter already, d'Antan had hinted that he had little
time and practice for intellectual pursuits: (I,2: "n'ayant pas beaucoup de tems, ny mesme l'usage d'écrire sur cette matière."). In II,8
he repeats the justification for the poor level of sophistication of his
words: "But the number of visits, which overwhelms me, in combination with my low level of experience in the art of writing serve
me well as a justification with respect to you." That could only mean
that d'Antan had to spend all his time with more practical labors—
perhaps as a trader—so that he would earn enough money to be
able to live. Beyond that not much was left.

In the second preserved letter—we do not know if there were
more than just these two—d'Antan responds to further inquiries by
La Croze, who urges him with "beautiful and pleasant, but difficult
questions" to rethink his position. D'Antan seems obviously disappointed by La Croze's response—especially about La Croze's attempt,
despite d'Antan's long biographical explanations, to convince him
convert to Protestantism. Therefore, he makes it clear that this would
be his last letter: "I herewith appeal to you, Monsieur, that you
should be convinced that I will not abandon the faith of my fathers
for yours; in order not to waste time with useless pursuits, I will not

---

[74] Reference to Psalms 119:162: "I rejoice at thy word, as one that findeth great
spoil."

[75] There are still other possibilities. The years of d'Antan's journey undoubtedly
featured many heavy attacks by Christian soldiers on Jewish communities in Poland,
Ukraine, Hungary (beginning with the sacking of Budapest in 1686), and Serbia.

provide you with any different response than to refer you, Monsieur, to the content of my previous letter." (II,1). D'Antan in a provocative way, calls Judaism "the faith of his fathers" despite the fact that he grew up a Catholic, because his reference goes much further back to the "fathers" Abraham, Isaac, and Jacob.[76]

Since La Croze in his conversion attempts mentioned that it would be a shame if such a beautiful soul as d'Antan's would be subject to damnation, d'Antan picks up this topic and explains his thoughts on the soul. But, as he points out, he would restrict himself to answering La Croze's questions and not elaborate on everything he thinks about the subject. He begins by stressing that a general consensus existed about the existence of the first principle. According to d'Antan, differences arise with regards to the attributes and especially the question of providence. The "naturalists" or "atheists" deny a divine providence with regards to the particular circumstances ("gouvernement particulier"), whereas the "Religionaires" presume the existence of one. The Jews, so believes d'Antan, constitute a specific group among these "Religionaires": they presume that God, the first principle, is only one. "I would say that that first cause, which was capable of creating beautiful things, must be above all of these beautiful things; it must be completely preoccupied with the task of guiding and maintaining its opus, in which nothing can exist by itself." (II,2).

Perhaps, we have here again the reverberating echo from scholarly discussions. D'Antan's categorization of religious beliefs according to their relationship to providence and the notion that Jews would accept providence down to its greatest detail, because the single detail could not exist by itself, is reminiscent of the theses of the chief

[76] At this point we have to consider the possibility that d'Antan was of Marrano origin. Not only his expression of "the faith of my fathers" seems to support this possiblility, but also the fact that he went to the Collège de Navarre, a Collège with traditional ties to southwest France. In southwest France, there lived communities of Marranos, some of them still with strong interests in Judaism. (See Jonathan Israel, "Crypto-Judaism in 17th-century France: An Economic and Religious Bridge between the Hispanic World and the Sephardic Diaspora", in idem, *Diasporas within a Diaspora. Jews, Crypto-Jews and the World Maritime Empires (1540–1740)* (Leiden: Brill, 2002), 245–268.) I find, however, this hypothesis not covincing, since it would not be intelligible, why d'Antan in reconstructing his own intellectual itinery until his conversion should not have mentioned such an important fact and motiv. The moment in which he would have become aware of his origins must have had in such a case been of tremendous emotional power, and he would certainly not have omitted the report of this experience. I am grateful to Benjamin Binstock for discussing this point with me.

rabbi David Nieto, which were vehemently debated in London and Amsterdam in the years after 1703. Sounding strongly like Spinoza, Nieto had expressed the provocative thought that God and nature were the same. But he explained his theses in his tractate *De la Divina Providencia* in 1704, in which he emphasized that no natura universalis existed, since God alone assumed the functions of directing and maintaining the universe.[77] Nieto was able to show that his point of view was inherent already in classical Jewish texts such as the *Kuzari*.

The neoplatonic philosophy of religion in Jehuda Halevi's *Kuzari*—which was used at that time to teach Hebrew[78]—may very well have influenced d'Antan's following remarks.[79] Especially since d'Antan claims that the cause, which guides and directs everything, must be the "soul of all things." One had to assume that "the universe harbored one single fire, which nourished all of the other fires in this world." It consumes bodily substance and revives all bodies, which contain a part of it. This "ame universelle", as d'Antan points out, "is the Supreme Being and the God of the Hebrew people" (II,2).[80]

Of course this constitutes a very unusual thesis. Even in neo-Platonism, in which it is widespread, the concept of the world-soul is generally viewed as a hypostasis below the One, which is however not identical with it. But d'Antan's concept may constitute a crude and abbreviated version of Kuzari's teaching, mingled with materialist ideas.

---

[77] See David Nieto, *De la Divina Providencia, o sea Naturaleza Universal, o Natura naturante* (London, 1714); see Jakob J. Petuchowski, *The theology of Haham David Nieto: an eighteenth-century defense of the jewish tradition* (New York, 1970). This debate in some respect reminds to a contemporary debate: the debate "De ipsa natura", which was started by Boyle and which triggered a great response in Germany, notably from Leibniz, Sturm and Schellhammer. In this case, the possibility of an active nature in the things was at stake. See Heribert M. Nobis, "Die Bedeutung der Leibnizschrift de ipsa natura im Lichte ihrer begriffsgeschichtlichen Voraussetzungen", in: *Zeitschrift für Philosophische Forschung*, 20 (1966), 525–538.

[78] See José R. Maia Neto, "The Struggle against Unbelief in the Portuguese Jewish Community of Amsterdam after Spinoza's Excommunication", in: Silvia Berti et al. (eds.), *Heterodoxy, Spinozism and Free Thought in Early-eighteenth-Century Europe. Studies on the "Traité des trois imposteurs"* (Dordrecht: Kluwer, 1996), 425–437.

[79] On Juda Halevy's Kuzari see Yochanan Silman, *Philosopher and prophet: Judah Halevi, the "Kuzari", and the evolution of his thought* (Albany: State Univ. of New York Press, 1995); Diana Lobel, *Between mysticism and philosophy: Sufi language of religious experience in Judah Ha-Levi's Kuzari* (Albany, NY: State Univ. of New York Press, 2000).

[80] But see also the contemporary clandestine writings, in which the soul resp. world-soul is conceived as material fiery soul. See esp.: *L'ame materielle*. Édition cri-

Hence, d'Antan had arrived at that topic of the soul, towards which he was heading. Understandably, this problem remains inseparably linked for him to the problem of the animal soul, since the Cartesian provocation had rendered the question of the existence and fate of the animal soul into one of the most heavily debated controversies during the seventeenth and early eighteenth centuries.[81] This question was decisive, because it determined whether man constituted a gradual component of nature or whether he was radically different from it. D'Antan chose the continuity thesis. Continuity seemed to make sense to him under the impression of fire, light, and radiation. "The comparison, which I viewed as most suitable for the existence of being is the sun. Just as the sun is the most distinguished among the planets, our body as well as the body of animals constitutes the earth, upon which the rays of the sun, the divine Being, shine. If now the sun shines on a diamond, it is more pure than as if she shines on dirt. Does this sun, I ask, shine less on this inferior and common object than on the brilliant and glittering object? Undoubtedly not, but the deficient nature of the substance is responsible that the sun shines brighter on one than on the other, or more precisely, that appears like that. Now, as I understand it, the sun is the Being whose perfection is little known to human beings. Human beings are the diamonds, animals are copper, and trees are just like plain stone—or, to use a comparison that fits more to the dignity of Man: Man is the fire of that fire, animals are water, trees are earth, which are the three basic elements of nature if we do not take, as you know, air as an element as well" (II,4).[82]

However nice this world of different reflections from the absolute may appear, already in the next sentence d'Antan confesses that within this world nothing seems stable. Everything is coming and going, becoming and extinguishing, even the main religions. This indicates that d'Antan perceived this world as a large organic whole, whose radical change affects entire cultures and religions. It is a

tique avec une introduction et des notes par Alain Niderst (Paris, 1973). Alain Mothu has noted that spiritualistic-hermetic conceptions on the one hand and materialistic conceptions on the other hand during that time were often intertwined— especially with respect to the nature of the soul. See Alain Mothu, "Hermétisme et 'libre pensée'. Note sur l'esprit universel", in: *La lettre clandestine*, 1 (1992), 11–13.

[81] See Leonora Cohen Rosenfield, *From Beast-Machine to Man-Machine. the theme of animal soul in French letters from Descartes to La Mettrie* (New York, 1940).

[82] See Kuzari IV,15.

world similar to the one naturalists such as Campanella have portrayed during the late Renaissance.[83] Key terms such as animal soul,
fire, and the three basic elements suggest that d'Antan's view of the
world may obviously have come to him via hermetic-alchemical
sources.

This however means that d'Antan's ideas were not exclusively
Jewish in nature. Rather, they can be found in that kind of Jewish-
hermetic-neo-Platonic syncretism, which prevailed in the Amsterdam
of 1700. This impression becomes stronger once we take a look at
d'Antan's thoughts on a solution to the problem of just reward and
punishment. "Philosophically, everything has to return to its corresponding center, just like the fire strives to the top and the stone to
the bottom. This is truth which cannot be denied by anyone; I would
even say that according to my system, the soul is an emanation without being separated from the whole, which is the highest Being, as
long as we can claim that a candle remains equally connected with
its main body. If then it is the case that everything in nature has
to return to its center, this would then mean that the soul has to
return to its center as well, which is the Supreme Being, from which
it emanated. Since nothing, however, returns to its center before it
acquired a certain degree of perfection, the soul equally cannot return
to its center before it has been purified, because its center, God, is
purity. But how do we reach this purity, how do you think? In order
to understand this process properly, one only needs to know that it
remains impossible for the soul, since it is spiritual, to pertain to any
physical medium and suffer with it, if it is possible to say it that
way. This is where the punishment through metempsychosis comes
in, because how could you then explain otherwise that we do see
poor people who have the spirit of a great king and kings who are
as ignorant as shepherds? On the other hand, do not believe what
the Christians do, namely that all people will be transferred to an
eternal imaginary paradise, because I have destroyed the gruesome
torment, which the Christians teach. I am neither flatterer in this
nor am I forgiving. The reward like the punishment consists according to my own point of view solely in that the substance, which is
for the second time hit by a ray of light that illuminates or more

---

[83] See e.g. John M. Headley, *Tommaso Campanella and the Transformation of the World*
(Princeton: PUP, 1997); Nicola Badaloni, *Tommaso Campanella* (Milano: Feltrinelli,
1965); Germana Ernst, *Tommaso Campanella* (Bari: Laterza, 2002).

precisely revives the body, is in a state of greater or lesser purity, depending on how we have led our life in these days. I would however not say that the rational soul leaves its center, as the philosophers of Antiquity believed, because just like mountains and valleys will always remain mountains and valleys, the human soul will always remain a human soul and so will his sensitive and vegetable soul" (II,6).

This passage allows us for the first time to identify d'Antan's sources. The teaching of the center of the souls, their perfection and their metempsychosis was put forward for the first time during the 1690s by Franciscus Mercurius van Helmont, a physician and philosopher from Amsterdam. In cooperation with Christian Knorr von Rosenroth, Van Helmont had collected works from the Lurianic Kabbalah and had edited them in the work *Kabbala denudata*.[84] Van Helmont's own philosophy was based very much on this Kabbalah and he had connected it with the Paracelsian theory of his father Johann Baptist.[85] Works such as *De revolutione animarum*, which appeared in 1690 in Amsterdam—as well as the work of Anne Conway, that he edited—, promoted the idea of the kabbalistic migration of the soul, the "gilgul," as an alternative to the eternity of hellfire, which was rejected as barbaric.[86] Still during the late

---

[84] [Christian Knorr von Rosenroth, ed.:] Kabbala Denudata Seu Doctrina Hebraeorum Transcendentalis Et Metaphysica Atqve Theologica: Opus Antiquissimae Philosophiae Barbaricae variis speciminibus refertissimum, In Qvo Ante ipsam Translationem Libri difficillimi atq[ue] in Literatura Hebraica Summi, Commentarii nempe in Pentateuchum, & quasi totam Scripturam V. T. Cabbalistici, cui nomen Sohar Tam Veteris, quam recentis, ejusque Tikkunim seu supplementorum tam Veterum, quam recentiorum, praemittitur Apparatus (Sulzbach, 1677–84).

[85] See Allison Coudert, *The impact of the Kabbalah in the seventeenth century: the life and thought of Francis Mercury van Helmont (1614–1698)* (Leiden: Brill, 1999). On Johann Baptist van Helmont see Walter Pagel, *Johan Baptista van Helmont: reformer of science and medicine* (Cambridge, 1982).

[86] Franciscus Mercurius van Helmont, *De revolutione animarum humanarum, quanta sit istius doctrinae cum veritate Christianae religionis conformitas problematum Centuriae duae* (Amsterdam, 1690); idem, *Seder olam: or, the order of ages* (London: Howkins, 1694); see as well [Anne Conway:] *Opuscula philosophica quibus continentur: Principia philosophiae antiquissimae et recentissimae* (Amstelodamum, 1690). On the Lurianic idea of metempsychosis see Gershom Scholem, "Gilgul: Transmigration of Souls", in: *On the Mystical Shape of the Godhead*. Trans. by Joachim Neugroschel (New York: Schocken, 1991), 197–250. See also Helmut Zander, *Geschichte der Seelenwanderung in Europa: alternative religiöse Traditionen von der Antike bis heute* (Darmstadt, 1999). On the rejection of eternal torment in Hell, see Daniel P. Walker, *The Decline of Hell. Seventeenth-Century Discussions of Eternal Torment* (Chicago: CUP, 1964).

eighteenth-century, this basically Origenist concept was propagated as a "rational metempsychosis."[87]

Even if d'Antan may have learned about van Helmont's teaching only once he got to Amsterdam, the fertile soil for his interest was already there. Already during his early years in Paris, d'Antan, then still an atheist, interacted with circles ("companies"), which speculated about the fortune of the soul after death; in these circles, the idea of "transmigrations" was one among several that was talked about (I,17; I,18). And he already knew from Parisian hermetic-libertine circles even the pseudo-hermetic definition of God and the idea of emanation, which were both shared by van Helmont.

Still, all of these ideas were debated intensively in Amsterdam around 1700 and they found a positive response in him. They combined Judaism and philosophy. More than ten years before that, they had captivated the convert Johann Peter Späth, but Späth based his final move towards Judaism precisely on his turning away from this kabbalistic-alchemic philosophy. Eventually, Späth considered van Helmont as an "old pagan," because Späth had absorbed the historical critique to such an extent that he came to view the Lurianic Kabbalah as a late doctrine, corrupted by Platonism.[88] Späth thus had distanced himself from what fascinated d'Antan.[89] This is why we could apply the harsh criticism of Johann Georg Wachter, of Späth, much better to d'Antan. Wachter considered this version of Kabbalah, which was popular in Amsterdam at that time, to be a sort of Spinozism.[90] That seems understandable if we consider d'Antan's words, when he claims that everything is an emanation of the sin-

[87] See Georg Schade, *Vernünftige Metempsychosis*, reprint in idem, *Die unwandelbare und ewige Religion*, ed. Martin Mulsow (Stuttgart: Frommann-Holzboog, 1999); see Martin Mulsow, "Vernünftige Metempsychosis. Über Monadenlehre, Esoterik und geheime Aufklärungsgesellschaften im 18. Jahrhundert", in: Monika Neugebauer-Wölk (ed.), *Aufklärung und Esoterik* (Hamburg, 1999), 211–273; idem, *Monadenlehre, Hermetik und Deismus. Georg Schades geheime Aufklärungsgesellschaft* (Hamburg: Meiner, 1998).

[88] See the contribution by Allison Coudert to this volume. I intend to publish a study on Späth's reception of the theory of corruption of the Church Fathers by Platonism.

[89] D'Antan's plea to La Croze not to talk about his opinions to "our Jews" ("Ne divulguez point, Mr., mon sentiment à nos Juifs" II,6) resembles the situation of Späth, who did not appreciate the "rabbinic fables," and about whose death in 1701 there is even the rumor that he was poisoned by hostile Jews of his Amsterdam community. See von der Hardt according to Stolle (footnote 49).

[90] Johann Georg Wachter, *Der Spinozismus im Jüdenthumb, Oder, die von dem heütigen*

gle fire, to which it is connected. Späth had abandoned this teaching even before Wachter charged him with it. But d'Antan, ten years later, supported this semi-pantheistic "Spinozism in Judaism" in a certain way.

Of course, he did that solely "philosophiquement parlant," when he abstracted from revelation. In the course of their conversation in the garden of the royal library, d'Antan had extracted from La Croze the concession "that the Jewish religion constituted the most probable religion for a person who does not accept Scripture" (II,7). That was a far-reaching concession: it implied that La Croze believed that the "theologia naturalis" came close to monotheistic Judaism. D'Antan then in turn tried to build some connections for him to Christianity. Although Christianity, which had historically speaking been erected on the ruins of Judaism, made efforts to destroy its divine character, he stated, there still had to be something good within it, since God himself had created it (II,5). In this respect, one could try, as d'Antan points out, to explain baptism as the process of purification, which he had described from a kabbalistic point of view, and the trinity with the three souls: the soul of the human being, of the animal and of the tree, which exist inseparably within the universal soul (II,5). This of course constitutes a risky speculation and it demonstrates once again how simple-minded and amateurish d'Antan remained in his thinking as "Juif Trinitaire." In return, it certainly also reflects the Trinitarian motivations of the philosemitic assimilation towards Judaism among authors from Reuchlin to Pico and from Rittangel to Rosenroth, a tradition that belongs to his sources.[91]

We do not know what La Croze thought about d'Antan's last letter. From what we know about him, the speculations may barely have inspired him. But he kept silent. He never talked to anybody about his old protégé, who had become a Jew.

* * *

Juedenthumb, und dessen Geheimen Kabbala Vergoetterte Welt, an Mose Germano sonsten Johann Peter Speeth, Amsterdam, 1699, reprint ed. Winfried Schröder (Stuttgart, 1994). See Gershom Scholem, "Die Wachtersche Kontroverse über den Spinozismus und ihre Folgen", in: Karlfried Gründer and Wilhelm Schmidt-Biggemann (eds.), *Spinoza in der Frühzeit seiner religiösen Wirkung* (Heidelberg, 1984), 15–25.

[91] On the trinitarian convictions of Christian Kabbalists see François Secret, *Les kabbalistes chrétiens de la Renaissance* (Paris: Dunod, 1964); Wilhelm Schmidt-Biggemann: *Philosophia Perennis* (Frankfurt: Suhrkamp, 1998).

Much research is still needed to explain d'Antan's intellectual background and the context of his conversion. Much will always remain
in the dark. But I still dare to say that highly personal decisions and
beliefs like these, however rare and unlikely they may be, constitute
precisely for that reason important examples for testing certain theses about the course of the modern era. In this case it is Richard
Popkin's thesis of a skeptical crisis during the seventeenth century, in
the course of which new certainty has been ensured either in its philosophical form of the Cartesian cogito or in its religious-historical
form of infallible biblical exegesis and pansophy. Does this then mean
that d'Antan's as well as Späth's intellectual development constitute
an extreme but living confirmation of Popkin's thesis, since it went
against all resistance? Don't we have a case here where the Cartesian
search for certainty is surpassed by a Jewish-Deist one?

Appendix

The text is preserved in Ms. Gall. oct. 38 of the Berlin State Library.
It is presently kept in the Biblioteka Jagiellonska in Cracow. This
octavo manuscript is part of a bound volume and consists of sixty-
seven sheets. It is a handwritten copy of two long French letters, a
beautifully written French version on the left-hand side and an Italian
translation on the right. The Italian text contains marginalia, which
document or summarize the topic of the corresponding passages.
The actual text is superseded by a five-page introduction in Hebrew.

The manuscript, which is located in Cracow since the Second
World War, had been purchased by a certain D. Fränkel from Vienna.
The manuscript's earlier history remains unclear. It appears that the
slim volume circulated in Jewish circles in Italy. The Hebrew introduction, the Italian translation with the marginalia and the calli-
graphical style, which makes the text appear like a precious circular
letter and finally little drawings on the last page of an eagle under
which the words "Aquila" and "Figlio del'Aquila" appear, all of that
suggests that.

The manuscript described by Nathan Samter[92] seems to be of
identical content with the one in Cracow except that it contains only

---

[92] See above footnote 1.

the Italian version without the French text next to it. It could very well be that it is a copy of the Cracow manuscript or that they both have a common source. The manuscript described by Samter had been acquired by Abraham Berliner on one of his travels to Italy some time before 1893. He then donated it to the Alliance israélite universelle in Paris. My inquiry there about the present whereabouts of the manuscripts have remained unanswered so far.

Principles of Transcription

The transcribed text constitutes a reproduction only of the French original. In order to facilitate a reading of the text, I have occasionally inserted a missing apostrophe (for example il n'y aura instead of il ny aura, or c'est instead of cest) or added or modernized accentuation (à instead of á or a). But basically, the often inconsistent style has been maintained, even if there were obvious spelling mistakes so that the text's authenticity would not be distorted. Punctuation has been added only whenever missing breaks would have made the text illegible. In the original virtually no breaks appear, only commas.

I have numbered the letters as I and II and I have numbered the paragraphs in order to make references easier.

Copie des Lettres de Monsieur Aáron D'Antan

[I.]

A' Berlin Monsieur De la Croze Bibliothequier du Roy.

[1] J'aj recu vos lettres que vous adressiez à Amsterdam dans les diferents sejours de mon long, et penible voyage par l'Alemagne, la Boeme, Hongrie, Baviere, Tirol et Italie. elle sont au nombre de 5, que j'ay brulé apres en avoir tirez un extrait dans la crainte de'l Inquisition dont vous n'ignorez pas la cruaute, elle est mesme cause que je ne me sui pas donné l'honneur de vous faire reponse avant que d'être seur que mon prompt depart d'Italie, me metroit hors de sa juridiction inhumaine ([in Hebrew:] *This is the work of the pure lampstand that Afran evaluated in front of God for eternity*). vous vous etonné dites vous Mons., que j'aye abbandonné a la fleur de mon aáge la Religion de mes Peres pour en embrasser une qui est la plus meprisé de toutes celles que Dieu ou les hommes ayent jamais

inventé. Vous la comparé aux Schytes qui errant et vagabons sans chef, et sans loix battoient tous les deserts les plus affreux de l'orient, n'ayant conversation ny negoce qu'entreux, abhorrant la compagnie des autres hommes meprisant leurs Loix, et leurs gouvernement &c. Apres cela vous vous écriéz que ma jeunesse m'a trompé, &t aveuglé et que voulant sortir d'un bourbier, c'est l'Epithete dont vous honoré la religion Catholique, je me suis precipité dans une Abisme, vous ne pouvez pas vous immaginer, ditte vous, que cela vienne de moy, mais il faut que quelque Juif m'ait seduit; Et qu'estant jeune j'ay aimé la nouvaute, Enfin qu'estant François j'ay sans refléxion ny examen, suivis une vaine lueur qui se rencontre dans quelque passage de l'escriture que semblent favoriser l'aveuglement & l'obstination des Hebreux. Il me faudroit plus de papier que vous n'en avez employé dans vos lettres pour repeter toutes vos apparentes raisons, car vous ecrivez avec tant d'elégence don qui vous est naturelle que vos lettres peuvent être appellées sans flaterie l'extrait d'un volume.

[2] Je serai court en réponce n'ayant pas beaucoup de tems, ny mesme l'usage d'écrire sur cette matiere. Je pouvrois vous contenter en deux mots en vous disant que Dieu qui n'a pas plus été ingrat envers moy qu'envers les autres hommes m'a donné le libre arbitre, et qu'ainsi ma volonté, sans rendre compt à personne du sujet, a été d'abbandonner une religion que vous appellez idolatre ([in Hebrew:] *This letter is sent to the book keeper of the part of Prussia. He is from Athens* [= Berlin?]. *The Lutherans thought of the Christians of Spain, France and those in Ashkenaz and Italy as idol worshipers or bowing down to figures*) pour une qui n'adore qu'un seul Étre le Createur de toute choses. Mais comme j'apprehendrois de vous confirmer dans votre prejugé que je l'aye fait par jeunesse, par nouveauté, par le naturel bouillant d'un François, tant pour ma justification dis-je, que pour l'honneur de la nation Israelite dont par la grace de Dieu despuis 8 Mois je suis membre. Je m'abbaiseraj jusqu'à vous dire ce que je n'ay pas encore fait non pas mesme à aucun Juif le sujet de ma conversion à la quelle nul Juif n'a part n'en ayant jamais connú qu'à Amsterdam pour la premiere fois ([in Hebrew:] *This was the law of the leper* [the author misspells here the word leper] *in the day of his cleansing and his coming to the priest (the so called high priest).*)

[3] Vous scaurez ma naissance qui quoi qu'elle ne soit pas d'un rang fort ellevé, ne laisse pas d'être honnorable, par l'honneur que mon Pere a d'être officier du plus grand Monarque de la Terre. Cela servira de reponce à ceux qui ignorant qui je suis pourroient croire par leur zel indiscret que l'interest est le principal motif de mon changement. Vous n'ignorez pas non plus mon education et la molesse avec la quelle je suis parvenú en âge de raison. Vous vous souvenez bien je pense de ceque vous dites à Mr. L'Abbé De Lior dans votre Bibliotheque de S. Germain de Prez qu'un jour je serois un grand homme quoique pour lors je n'eusse que 10 ans. Il ne vous est pas non plus passez de la memoire le recit qui vous fist ce fameux Astrologue sur l'observation de ma naissance qui ariva à la mesme minute selon la plus probable opinion que votre Legislateur, apres cela Mr. je m'estonne que vous m'accusiez de legereté. Il est inutile pour ma justification de vous rapporter tous les passages de l'Ecriture Ste., tant de la loy que des Prophetes puis qu'il faudroit inserer dedans tout la Bible. Mais je montrai à la scuree, et vous verrez pourveu que vous vous depouillé de tous prejugé pendant la lecture de cette presente, que c'est plus tost une grande Prudence derigée par Dieu qu'une neuveauté naturelle au genie françois qui m'a fait faire cette demarche. Comme j'estudiois au College de Navarre il ariva que voulant faire un tour d'Écolier à un de mes Cammarades je luy pris sa Tabatier pour luy faire chercher. Il êtoit plus vieux que moy et consequement plus sage au lieu de divúlguer le pretendu vol, il ne dit mot, mais en fist toute la perquisition requisé pendant l'heure de la recreation tems ou un chacun est occupé à se delasser de la fatigue de l'estude, il ne luy fut pas dificil de trouver ce que je n'aurois pas à coeur de cacher puisqu'elle êtoit sous le chevet de mon Lict. sans examiner la chose il s'en fut à mon Precepteur et luy conta ce que l'apparence luy permit de dire, et mesme exagerant il adjouta que ce n'êtoit pas la premiere fois que pareille chose luy avoit êté fait tant à luy qu'à ses cammarades. Estant appellé par mon Precepteur et ayant veu que l'apparence l'avoit prevenu j'aimay mieux me taire que d'âvouer un crime dont j'estois innocent ou de nier ce que l'apparence prouvoit si evidement; mon silence confirma donc mon pretendu crime du quel j'ay receú le chatiment, mais comme si Dieu eut ordonné cette chose pour me conduire dans la verité, J'examine le prejugé que les hommes ont par l'apparence qui les trompe le plus souvent, et j'apris de la

à ne juger personne par quelque apparence que ce soit, je me sentois innocent du crime dont on m'accusoit, et cespendent je n'osois m'excuser de peur de tomber dans l'inconvenient de parroin doublement coupable en parroissant menteur refuge ordinaire des vouleurs. ces sentiments ne me resterent pas seulement en l'esprit pendant le tems de mon injuste punition mais plusieurs tems apres mesme jusqu'à present, en sorte que j'ay conclus qu'equitablement nous ne pouvions juger personne par les apparences qui sont fort souvent trompeuses; Comme c'estoit un fait qui m'avoit touché de si près, j'en fut tres sensiblement touché, et tous les Docteurs du Monde ne m'eurent pas fait revenir de cette oppinion.

[4] Persuadez donc que c'estoit de l'injustice des hommes de juger par l'apparence, il ariva un autre cas environ trois ans après. Il y a un St. dans notre Quartier nommé St. Ovide, dont un chacun rapportoit avoir vú des miracles, remplie du prejugés que les hommes jugent sur l'apparence j'ay voulu en jeune homme, ou en libertin si vous voulez, voir quelqu'un sur qui ces faveurs celestes s'estoient fait sentir, mais quoique cela ce fut fait à ma porte, jamais je n'en peut trouver un. Et quoique je visse parfaictement bien l'augumentation des Bequilles neantmoins je n'en trouvois pas un seul qui y reconnut la sienne. Cela me donna lieu d'examiner les misteres de la religion comme j'avois cy devant examiné les jugemens des hommes, cela ne me fut pas deficil en ce que peu tems après on me mit entre les mains d'un Eclesiastique pour ce que vous appelle la premiere Communion, entre tant de sotises qu'on fait passer pour mystheres l'on me demanda. Nota, je n'avais que 12 ans. Si après les parolles sacramentalles les especes restoient encore, je ne manqué de rendre selonque mes maistres m'avoient apris, sçavoir que non, mais que le corps de votre Legislateur en avoit pris la place, mais me dit mon Docteur s'il arivoit par hazard Dieu garde qu'un Plat poussé par la faim entra dans ce qu'on appelle Tabernacle, et mangea les Hosties consacrées mangeroist il le corps de vostre legislateur? Un autre que moy auroit esté embarrassez n'estant point instruit sur cette matiere, mais moy qui suis un Brouillon François, et jeune comme vous me reproché je ne me consulte pas mesme et reponds qu'ouy adjoutant que cela ne se pouvoit pas faire autrement, puis qu'ayant fallut quattre parolles pour changer les Especes du Pain et du vin au corp, et au sang du Legislateur, et encor qu'il falloit que se fut un Prestre ordonné qui les pronnonça, il s'ensuiveroist que le Plat feroist un

plus grand miracle s'il ne mangoit pas le corps du Legislateur puis qu'il feroit sans le secours d'aucune parole une seconde transsub-stanciation, d'autant plus facil de croire qu'il seoit ignominieux à la Divinité de s'enfuire d'ou il êtoit venú pour eviter la morsure d'un (Plat) si vil animal.

[5] Qui n'eut crut avoir pour le moins un mois de vacance pour une si belle reponce.

[6] Cespendent comme il Dieu m'eut voulu punir d'avoir oublié ma premiere maxime de ne pas juger sur l'apparence j'entendois avec estonnement le crúel commandement de me preparer au suplice qui meritoit un si pretendu horrible blaspheme en soufrit avec une patience qui pour un Enfant de mon âge pouvoit passer pour hero-ique. Je songea long-tems à la bisarerie du Destin qui m'avoit abbaissé dans le tems que je pensois devoir être exalté, mais je ne fus cespen-dant pas si porte à me condamner que je ne voulusse examiner la raison pour quoy j'eu beau me vouloir par resignation à la volonté de mon Superieur donner le tort, j'ay eu beau faire reflexion qu'il n'estoit pas de la Justice d'un Chrestien de donner le corps de son Dieu qui se donnoit volontairement à luy 'a manger à un Plat infect Domestique. Je me le serois mesmes facilement persuadez. Si je ne me fusse pas resouvenú que ce mesme Docteur (qui m'avoit asscuré que les scelerats receuvoient le corps, et le Sang du Legislateur de la mesme maniere que les bons, diferement il est vray les premiers comme Juge, et les derniers comme Pere, mais disois je en moy mesme quelle difference entre un scelerat, et une bétte, il n y a que la connoissance de Dieu qui distingue l'homme de la bétte, donc le scelerat ne croyant rien, ne differe rien de la Bêtte, et qui plus est Dieu ne peut il pas être aussi bien Juge de la Bêtte, comme il l'est du pecheur. Je vous avoue que cela m'inquieta jusques en fin. repas-sant tout ce que j'avois vú despuis ma connoissance j'ay resolú de suivre le sentiment de Decartes sur son doûte, et en peu de tems je m'y confirme si bien que je peut dire avoir doûte de mon existence jusque la qu'ayant dit un jour à un de mes Camarades que ce sis-teme ne me parroissoit pas insoutenable, puisque veritablement je doubtois que je fússe. Il tacha de me vouloir ramener à son oppin-ion, et mesme pour y parvenir il me donna d'une Espingle dans la Cuisse; et comme je me mis à crier, il me dit existez vous presen-tement? je luy repondis tant il est vray que j'estois persuadez de

mon oppinion tu ne me preuve pas mon existence mais bien la tienne.

[7] Il ne vous ay racconté ces petites Historiettes pueriles que pour vous faire voir que mon changement n'est pas sens fondement, et que les fondements ne son pas nouveaux. Il ne vous est pas dificile de croire par ce que je vien de dire qu'il me fût aisé de doûter non seulement de la Religion, mais aussi de Dieu. Le tems me favorisoit êtant celluy de ma Philosophie remplis des idées je regardois et estudiois le Monde comme trompeur. Les Devots à mon avis me parroissoient Hypochrites. Les vouleurs me parroissoient n'avoir que le dessein de donner, mais avec moins d'éclat, enfin je renversois si ce n'est pas l'ordre du Monde au moins etoit ce celuy de la Nature. J'ay passé tout le tems de mon cours et mesme plus d'un an après dans cette oppinion. Ce qui me confirma fut que je fus à l'armée, et voicy à peu près la lettre que j'escrivis à ce pretendú Docteur, qui m'avoit voulú persuader que Dieu êpouvanté d'un Plat s'etoist enfui au Ciel.

[8] Avant que de vous racconter la lettre que j'escrivis à mon Directeur de Conscience il est bon de vous avertir que quoyque je ne crusse rien, cespendant dans les lieux ou je rencontrois des Juifs je resentois un certain je ne scaj quoy en moy qui ne pouvoit trouver son fondament dans mon immagination, et que le Dieu d'Israel me soit tesmoin si ce que je vous vais dire n'est la verité. Quand je lisois la Bible quoyque je n'en crusse rien pour lors neantmoins je fremissois, j'entrois dans les passions qui concernoient l'Histoire d'une maniere que si je n'eusse pas été si pervenú j'aurois si parfaictement bien recounú ce que les tems suivans m'ont fait connoistre, mais avoué que la prevention est un crime si flateur qu'il est fort dificile de s'en defaire quoyqu' il cause quantité d'injustice. Je reviens à ma Lettre.

[9] Lettre escritte aú Precepteur
    Après les Complimens ordinaires, je commencois en ces termes

[10] Je vous avoue Mr. qui si les Jesuites du Japon et de la Chine ne faisoient pas plus de progrés que vous en avez fait en moy par vos remontrances, je conseillerois à ces Peres de demeurer au coin de leur feu leur vie plutost que d'abreger leurs Jours soit par leurs pretendús martires que par la longúeur du voyage.

[11] Je vous diray Mr. que j'ay enfin secoué le joug de votre imper-
tinente doctrine. Je ne suis plus petit enfant pour que vous me faisez
peur des Loups—je suis revenú de cette erreur mais vous croyez
m'épouventer par vos diables. Je crois l'Escritture pour un moment,
prouvez moy par elle leur creation. En verité je ne puis comprendre comment les hommes qui sont parvenû a'láge de discretion et
ayant acquis une raison capable de discerner les choses probables
d'avec les Fables demeurent encore dans l'erreure de l'enfance. Il
est naturel aux Enfans de croire par crainte ce que leurs enseignent
leurs parents, mais lors quils sont en âge ils reforment leur enten-
dement qui s'etoit trompé, et se rendent raisonables en tout si ce
n'est en ce qui regarde la religion en cecy ils sont toujours enfans,
toujours attachés aux Fables sacrées de leurs Prestres, et obstinés à
les soutenir mesme quelque fois despens de leur vie. J'ay de la peine
à decourir la cause d'un efect si bizarre, les hommes par tout ailleurs
jugent sagement, et meurement ils font parroistre dans les autres
choses une penetration extraordinaire, mais sur le faict de la religion ils sont des Estourdis, et des Extravagants que croyent des choses
incompatibles avec le sens commun, et la raison.

[12] Je ne croirois jamais les Histoires des anciens Payens, qui nous
parlent de l'adoration qu'ils rendoient à des ouvrages de peintures
et de sculture, si je ne voyois que les Chrêtiens font aujourd-huy la
mesme chose.

[13] Je ne croirois jamais non plus que les sages de l'antiquité eussent
estez capables de gouléer ce que leurs Prestres ont inventé au sujet
de leurs divinitées si je n'êstoit tesmoins occulaire de la superstitieuse
croyance en la vie et miracles de vos pretendús SSts. et SStes con-
tenûes dans vos Legendes.

[14] Pour moy je ne puis comprendre comment des gens versés dans
toutes sorte de Sciences puissent soutenir des contradictions mani-
festes en matiere de Theologie, aimant mieux en user de la sorte,
que de s'opposer aux traditions de leurs peres ou seulement de les
examiner.

[15] Puis-je bien me persuader qu' il y-a une religion quand je vois
que chacun travaille vigoureusement à la propagation de la sienne et
qu'il y employe ou l'artifice ou la violence; et que cespendant il y-a
si-peu des gens, pour ne pas dire personne qui fassent connoitre

par leur pratique qu'ils croyent ce qu'ils professent avec tant d'ardeur.
Au contraire je conclurois plûtot que tant de Cultes differens ont
êsté d'abord inventé par les Politiques chacun s'accommodant aux
inclinations des Peuples qu'il avoit envie de tromper. Je finirai donc
Mr. en vous asseurant que j'ay, et j'auray moins peur de vos Diables
immaginaires, que des coups dont vous me menaciez dans mon
jeune âge.

[16] Ma lettre etoit plus longue, et plus energique êtant dans ce
tems la persuadé de ce que j'escrivois au lieu que presentement je
suis convaincú du contraire par la grace de Dieu de nos Peres
Abraham Isaac, et Jaacob; da disgretion m'a ecarté de mon sujet.
J'y retourne.

[17] Vous pouvez juger par ma lettre l'Etat dans lequel j'êtoit, pour
lors nul au Monde ne m'eut peut persuader qu'il y-avoit une Religion,
niant le Royaume il estoit facile de nier le Roy, je veut dire Dieu.
Je courois par tout ou je scavois trouver des personnes qui estoient
d'humeur à flater mes sentimens, mais je ne trouvois pas deux compagnies qui s'accordassent. Les uns que l'on appelloit Theologiens
desinteressés soustenoient que l'Ame estoit immortelle, d'autres que
l'on nommoit Poétes parloient avec Anfuse des champs Elisées, Les
Chretiens Ecclesiastiques du Ciel, de l'Enfer et du Purgatoire, et
quelques autres de la Trasmigrations, mais de tout cela je ne sçavois
que choisir.

[18] Un jour que je sortois d'une de ces compagnies ou il avoit êté
agité de pareilles questions, revenú à mon logis je me couchais non
sens songer à la Bizarrerie du Genre humain sur pareille matiere.
Je faisois reflexion dis-je sur les questions agitées dans la compagnie, et je raisonnay ainsi. Je vois partout des gens faisant profession
de quelque religion rendant des honeurs Divins à quelqu' Être ou
Etres superieurs selon qu-ils-ont êté êllevéz cela me fait croire que
la religion n'est qu'un effect de l'êducation. Puis revenant tout à
coup au sisteme de Descartes je dis je pense donc je suis, mais cela
ne m'apprend rien, je suis cela est incontestable, mais qui-suis-je?
Comme il m'arive en dormant quelque fois de penser être Monarque
je m'immagine que toutes mes pensées ne sont que songes, et mesme
que je ne suis qu'une Idée que les hommes s'immaginent exister
réelement, enfin que tout ce que nous voyons n'est qu'une grande

Chimere ou un rien masqué. Je me laisserois facilement persuader à ces vaines immaginations, si après ces pensées feroces mes sens ne se reveilloient pas par le sentiment d'un couleur ou d'un plaisir present qui existent mes desirs assoupis par example quand je eús la faim la soif, le froid, ou le chaud. je trouves alors par experience que je suis quelque chose de plus qu'une simple pensée, ou on songe mais un composé qui a besoin de viande, de boisson, d'habits, et rafraichissement—alors sens m'embarasser dans des recherches vaines, et sens fins je conclus humblement que je suis ce que l'on appelle un homme. Je met le Pirrhonismes à l'ecart; et sens doubter d'avantage, je bois, je mange, et prend les autres commoditez que la nature exige.

[19] Mais après m'avoir ainsi rafraichi je ne tombe insensiblement dans d'autres reflexions, quoy est-il possible dis-je que moy je ne me puisse pas passer de ces bêttes ou de ces herbes pour vivre cela me fait conclurre qu'estant redevable aux autres creatures du bonheur que je sens, je le suis aussi de mon Étre à quel qu'autre chose qu'à moy mesme. J'examine mon origine et je trouve que ceux qui m'ont mis au Monde êstoient hommes semblables à moy sujets à pareilles reflexions qui sont nés d'hommes aussi, et ainsi à l'infiny. L'infiny passé ne m'embarasseroit pas beaucoup, mais le future j'avoue m'embarasse un peu, que puis-je donc resoudre dans un si present besoin, me disois-je à moy mesme, croire donc est au dessus de la raison, mais ne croire rien est au dessous. Je veux prendre un juste millieux, et deriger ma foy par ma raison.

[20] Cette faculté me dit que si j'avois du penchant à adorer les Astres par leurs beauté je pourrois par la mesme raison adorer mes yeux sens le secours des quels je ne pourrois pas voir ces objets de tentation.

[21] Qu'adorerai-je donc, ou à qui rendrai-je grace des biens dont je jouis (car de cette vie j'ay quelque goût de la Divinité) à quel Étre dis-je adresserai-je mes voeux, et mes suplications? sera-ce à une Image taillé par un homme? j'aimerois mieux adorer le Soleil ou les autres Astres, mais cespendant ils sont definis, et il faut qu'ils ayent ce un commencement, et il faut que quelqu'un plus ancien, et plus parfaict l'ait commencé. Qui est donc digne de mes adorations? Ce ne peut éstre que Cet Estre qui n'a point de ressemblance,

qui n'est ny divisé, ny borné, dont le centre est par tout, et la cir-
conference nul part, un seul tout puissant d'ou êmanent toutes choses
et au quel elles retournent. 'A cet Étre dis-je je suis redevable de
tout ce que j'ay, et je veux luy rendre tout ce que je puis.

[22] Comme si Dieu eut voulú me recompencer d'une si juste resolution il se presentoit tous les jours dans mon immagination la
grandeur de son Étre, et m'accostumant à l'aimer dans mes pensées, alors j'ay resolu de luy rendre des honneurs, et des voeux qui
n'estoient deues qu' à luy seul.

[23] Mais comment luy rendre ces voeux et ces obbeissances me
disois-je? sera-ce dans la compagnie des Chretiens? il faut examiner
d'ou ils tirent leur origine, ils la tirent des Hebreux, peuple que toús
les Sectateurs de la Terre confesse avoir tant esté cheri de Dieu,
qu'il daigna descendre du Trone de sa Gloire pour leurs parler, les
adopter, et leur donner une loy, Peuple pour qui il a tant de fois
manifesté sa Gloire. Voulant donc me ranger sous quelques Estendard
j'ay voulú sens prevention ayant comme vous avez vú cy-devant
rejeté les prejuges de ma naissance.

[24] Je examine toute chose en l'origine de leurs race qui est aussi
ancienne que le Monde contenu dans le Genese la protection de
Dieu envers eux, si memorable, et si miraculeuse, contentu dans l'ex-
ode. La mesme j'y adore sa bonté tout misericordieuse qui donne à
un Peuple qu'il s'estoit elú sa sacré Loy, qui n'a besoin pour son
apologie (contre les Impies qui la croyent inventée par Moyse) que
son sacré stil. Dans le Levitique l'on y voit ces loix politiques aux
quelles tous les Peuples du Monde se sont soumis. Dans les Nombres
l'on-y admire l'effect de la promesse de Dieu fait à Abraham, que
sa posterité ne se pourroit pas un jour nombrer. Mais le Deuteronome
le Sceau de ce sacre, et Divin Livre, qu'on peut apeller un extrait
de la Loy de Dieu promet aux devots observateurs les Benedictions
du Ciel et aux Empies prevaricateurs de si terribles maledictions
jusque la de les priver de la presence de Dieu, qu'il faudroit mieux
être mort que d'en resentir les Effects ensuitte dans les livres suiv-
ants on y lit en diferentes fois le chatiment, et la protection de Dieu
sur son Peuple selon leurs bonnes ou mauvaises actions. Qui seroit
insensible aux promesses de Dieu par ses Prophetes l'on voit par
suitte des tems l'acomplissement de leurs propheties tout le mal qui

leur est predict pour leurs pechés, s'accomplit et est connú de tous
les Nations de la terre. Qui ne perdroit courage à des sanglants
effects de la Justice d'un Dieu irrité, s'il ne les consolait luy mesme
par cette tant attendue promesse d'un Liberateur; alors recconnois-
sant disent ces hommes Divinement inspirés de Dieu que ces maleurs
ne leurs sont arrivés que par l'ingratitude qu'ils ont envers le bonté
de Dieu. Se corrigeant sur les fautes passées ils se donneront bien
de garde de y retomber derechef. Pendant que je lisois ces sacres
Caracthères j'enviois le bonheur de ce Peuple, et je conclu de la
que Dieu estant immuable ne peut pas ne vouloir, ce qu'il a une
fois voulú. Il a aimé Israel, donc il l'aimera toujours. Estoit il me
disois je moins leur Dieu dans le tems qu'il le chatioit, que dans celluy qu'il les combloit de mil et mil Benedictions? Non, sens doute,
car si nous accoutons les Proverbes de Salomon (Chap. 3. ver. 11.
12.): Mon fils ne rebute point l'instruction de l'Eternel et ne t'en-
nuie point de ce qu'il te reprend. Car l'Eternel reprend celluy qu'il
aime même comme un Pere l'Enfant etc. à le François qui nous dis
Qui aime bien chatie il nous sera facile de voir que Plus Dieu les
chatie plus il les aime. Mais comme après que le Maistre a chatie
les Enfans il jette les verges au feu, il est à craindre pour ceux à
qui le chatiment des Enfans d'Israel est confié.

[25] Mais pour ne pas juger en dernier resort en faveur de la Religion
Judaique j'ay voulú bien examiner, quoyque je fusse pour lors pre-
venú en sa faveur la religion Chrestienne.

[26] Son fondement est que le Messie promis aux Juifs est venú.
Qu'il est venú pour sauver tout le genre humain en perdonnant le
peché originel, non pour detruire la loy donnée de la boûche de
Dieu, mais pour l'accomplir, pour enseigner la Divinité trinitaire et
unitaire. Je ne parle pas de l'invocation des SSts., et de leurs pre-
tendus merites, choses inventés par ces Feneans de Moines, Sansues
des Royaumes, pour atirer l'argent de ceux qui donnent dans leurs
fables. Comme c'est un point qui a estez si souventes fois disputé,
mal attaqué, mal defendú, de la part des Juifs par leur timidité, et
de celle des Chestiens par l'attachement pour les richesses, Je m'es-
tendraj plus emplenent. Les Juifs et les Chretiens sont d'accord qu'il
est promis un Messie, et ils conviennent entre eux qu'il sera de la
Tribu de Juda de la maison de David &c. Mais moy qui n'estois
pour lors ny Juif ny Chretien j'ay resolú absolument de ne regarder

aucune de leurs disputes scachant bien que l'homme, et principale-
ment un Jeune Écolier se laisse aisement prevenir en faveur du premier, mais revennant au second, et oubliant toutes les raisons du
premier il se range du parti des reflexions dernieres qui par leur
emprainte n'ont laissé aucune trace des premieres.

[27] Ecoutéz je vous prie mon raisonnement et pardonnez s'il n'est
pas selon les regles de la Philosophie, d'autant que ce n'estoit pas
un Philosophe qui raisonnoit, mais un Jeune-homme inspiré de Dieu
pour connoitre la verité.

[28] Je commence par chercher tous les passages qui parloient de
ce messie, et j'ay remarqué que nul verset dans l'Ecritture ne parle
de luy qu'aprez que Dieu menace Israel de le chatier, ou pour le
consoler aprez l'avoir chatié, ce qui me fist prendre l'envie pour ne
me point brouiller dans cette recherche de me restraindre en trois
points, sçavoir, Que viendra faire le Messie, Quelles serront ses marques, de peur de nous y tromper, Et pour qui ou à qui il viendra?
J'ay crú qu'il estoit plus à propos, quoique contre l'ordre de la
Rhetorique de sçavoir ce qu'il viendra faire, avant que de sçavoir
qui il est davant que nous ne desirons sa personne que par l'oeuvre qu'il doit faire. Pour bien sçavoir ce que viendra faire le Messie
il faut sçavoir le chatiment que Dieu a envoyé à son Peuple. Il leurs
a envoyé la Peste, la Famine, la Guerre intestine et estrangere, ils
ne sont pas corrigé, ils provoquoient Dieu en se confiant en la presence du Temple de Dieu au milieu d'eux. Dieu pour leur faire voir
que le sacre Temple n'êtoit respectable que par sa presence, l'ab-
bandonna alors il fut detruit, brule la ville rase, les habitans une
partie tuez, et l'autre mené Captifs et cela pour n'avoir pas observez
la saincte Loy donné sur le Mont Sinai en Horeb.

[29] Qui ne croiroit que Dieu a abbandonné son Peuple les marques en sont presque evidentes, c'est pour cela qu'il est dit (Psalm.
79. ver. 10). Quare dicent gentes ubi est Deus eorum? mais toutes
ces apparences se renversent lorqu'il est dit dans le Deuteronome
lorsque vous vous convertirez à moy alors je me resouviendray de
vous, et si vous etiez dispersez jusqu'au Ciel ou au fond des Abismes
je vous-en retireray par ma main forte, et alors vous repossederez
la terre que j'ay jurez à vos Peres. C'est ce qui confirme Jaacob lors
qu'avant sa mort il bênit tous ces Enfans en particulier, mais à Juda

qui fut êlu Roy sur Israel au prejudice de ses aimés Rhuben, Simeon et Levy cellui la pour avoir souillê la Couche de son Pere, et ceux cy pour s'être laissé emporté à la colere, et avoir fausé la parole qu'ils avoient donné aux Enfans de Sichem, il luy en donna deux sçavoir une particulier qui fut le Royaume, mais l'autre qu'on prend pour une Benediction, et qui n'est qu'une prophetie qui regarde tout Israêl en la personne de Juda comme Roy marque assez la grandeur, et la gloire d'Israel à sa venüe, car plusieurs Peuples se joindront à Israel, et non pas Israel à d'autres Peuples, il explique assez claire-ment l'abbondance dont jouira le Royaume puisqu'un chacun sera si riche que le plus paure pourra lier son propre Cheval à sa pro-pre vigne. Il est vray que les Hebreux, et les Latins discordent sur le mot de Schebet, les premiers se defendent mal sur l'objection de la part des derniers qui soutiennent que Schebet signifie sceptre; J'aprofondiray en trois mots le fait, Scebet ainsi que conviennent les Latins signifie trois choses Tribú, Sceptre, et Verge de chatiment. Sens prevention estudions la verité la plus vraysemblable. Le pas-sage dit Shebet ne sortira point de Juda &c. Le mot de 'sortira' est un future qui marque la presence du mot Shebet, examinons si le sceptre estoit pour lors en Juda (Car si je-dis Isaak ne sortira pas de cette ville que Jaacob ne vienne mon commandement ou ma promesse (comme il vous plaira d'apeller) marque indubitablement qu' Isaac est dans la ville si non mon commandement est nul). Un chacun scait que Jaacob estoit pour lors le Pere, et par consequent le maitre, et que c'estoit luy qui avoit le Sceptre. Estoit-il de la mai-son de Juda? vous me direz peut être Monsieur, qu'il s'en dépouil-loit entre les mains de Juda. Je vous demande à mon tour, si aprez la mort de Jacob quelqu'un eut êtez assez hardi pour la disputer à Joseph qui n'êtandoit pas son pouvoir seulement sur ses freres mais sur tout le Royaume d'Egypte, ce qui se verifie par la priere qu'ils luy firent prosternes à ses pieds après les funerailles de son Pere de leur accorder sa protection. Allons plus loin. Moise qui sortit les Israelites d'Egypte jusqu'au tems de sa mort estoit de la Tribu de Levi. Josué sous la conduitte du quel ils conquirent la Terre saincte estoit de la Tribú d' Ephraim. Cespendant on ne peut pas nier qu'ils n'eussent le gouvenement General, ou le *Sceptre*. Il faudroit un vol-ume pour nommer l'un après l'autre. Les Juges qui gouvernerent après qui furent de toutes les Tribus. Mais ce qui doit clore la bouche aux Chrestiens est que Saul premier Roy d'Israel fut de la Tribu de Benjamin. Enfin le mot de *sortira* qui est un future, et qui marque la presence de *Schebet* denote que *Schebet* ne veut poin dire *Sceptre* puis qu'il n'êtoit pas present, et mesme qu'on ne peut pas dire y avoir êtez.

[30] Voyons presentement si *Schebet* signifie chatiment, ou verge. Je finis en trois mots. Nous estions en exil en Egypte, *Schebet* ou chatiment estoit present, et nous n'avons estez en paix que de tems de Salomon, estant toujours tourmenté pas les Guerres intestines ou êtrangeres. La division du Royaume, Tributaires des Rois voisins, Nos villes pillées, et brulées, Nostre Temple saccagé et prophané.

[31] Nous soumes vagabonds, et errants, par tout le Monde, *Schebet* est present, et c'est l'ouvrage du Messie que Jaacob apelle *Schilo* que signifie pacifice. Contraire à ce qu'a faict celluy que les Chrestiens croyent être le Messie puis qu'il dit: Je ne suis point (pas) venú pour aporter la Paix mais la Guerre. Ma conclusion est donc que la Messie ressemblera les tristes restes des Enfans de Jaacob, et les reconduira dans la Terre que Dieu a juré à leurs Peres ou il cultiveront en paix, et en recuilleront le fruict, dont ils se nourirront en servant Dieu en Esprit et en verité. Ce qui est denoté par la suitte de la Prophetie de Jaacob. Je diray un mot en passant de *Mechoquek* qui signifie un Escrivain, cela ce confirme par la Prophetie de Jeremie, et des autres Prophetes lors qu'ils disent que Dieu frapera une nouvelle Alliance avec son Peuple, et qu'il luy escira la Loy dans le Coeur, si nous avions la Loy dans le Coeur, nous n'aurions pas besoin d'Escrivain pour nous la mettre devant les yeux, et qu'un chascun ne dira plus à son prochain vennez connoissez Dieu, puisque toute la Terre sera remplie de sa Gloire.

[32] Quelles serront les marques du Messie tous conviennent qu'il doit être fils de David, ne d'homme, et de femme, c'est que nous virifiont par les paroles de Moise au Deuteronome: Il s'êlevera un d'entre vos freres semblable à moy, Moise êtoit fil d'Amran, et de Jocabeth que l'Ecriture ne qualifie point du titre de Divinité, donc l'autre Messie qui luy sera semblable ne sera non plus que le fil d'un homme, et d'une femme. Il sera doué de l'Esprit de Dieu, et revetu de sa puissance, et cheri de luy. Il retirera Israel de captivité, Prechera par son exemple non seulement l'unité d'un Dieu, mais pour couper toute racine d'Idolatrie il publiera l'unité de son nom. Il n'y aura plus de Guerre, Chascun sera content de son Heritage, et comme

dit Idaie La Terre sera pleine de la Gloire de Dieu, tous connoistrons (ou connoitroit) cet Être qui n'a ny commencement ny fin brief. Il n'y aura qu'une seule Religion dedié à un seul Seigneur.

[33] Voila quelles seront les marques du Messie.

[34] Pouqui il viendra? Ou à qui il viendra? à cela je repons à qui il a estez promis, c'est aux Juifs, donc il viendra pour eux.

[35] Aprez que j'eut donc examiné ces trois points j'ay consideré, si votre Legislateur est conforme au Portrait que je vien de faire du vray Messie. Vous dites qu'il est fils de Dieu et d'une vierge? ce n'est point la sa marque. Qu'il est venu pour sauver le genre humain en effaçant le peché originel? Il estoit bien impuissant de ne pouvoir pas faire ce qu'il a voulu, et pourquoy il a tant soufert puisque nous voyons que la Chrestienneté n'est qu'un doigt du Corps de l'Univers.

[36] Quant au peché originel, Messieurs les Docteurs Chrestiens n'ont pas lu le Genese? car si votre Legislateur est venú pour effacer le peché originel, n'estant plus coûpables, nous ne soumes plus sujet à la peine, la peine qui fut imputé à Adam pour sa desobbeissance. Fut qu'il gagneroit son Pain à la Sueur de son Corps. Et qu'aprez tant de peine il mourroit et ce fut son peché que luy fist appercevoir qu'il estoit nud; Que sa femme enfanteroit avec douleur; Et que le Serpent perderoit l'usage de la voix, Et qu'il remperoit sur sa Poictrine. Si donc votre Legislateur a effacé ce peché nous devons rentrer dans notre ancien éstat d'Innocence et jouir des Privileges dont jouissoient nos Peres avant leurs peches; scavoir Que nous n'avons plus besoin d'habit ignorans que nous soumes nuds. La Terre doit produire d'elle mesme et brief; Nous ne devons point mourir; Nos femmes doiuent enfanter sens douleur; Le serpent doit recouvrer l'usage de la parole, et ne plus ramper; Mais comme cela n'arive pas, j'ay lieu de doubter d'une pareille doctrine. Il n'est pas venú dit il pour abolir la Loy, mais pour l'accomplir. J'avoue que je ne scait que repondre à cela, car comme dit le François: A sotte demande ne faut point repondre. Qu'il a enseigné la Divinité trinitaire unitaire? Voila des termes un peu embrouillés. Mais examinons pour y respondre. Vous dites que c'est un seul Dieu en trois Personnes: Pere, Fils, et S. Esprit ([in Hebrew:] God forbid!) qui ne sont qu'un seul Dieu? fort bien. Mais

Pere Fils et S. Esprit sont trois noms, ce que ne s'accorde pas avec l'unité de Dieu et l'unité de son Nom qui est une des marques du vray Messie.

[37] Vous pouvez bien juger, Mr. par ces reflexions que je n'ay pas embrasse la Loy des Juifs sans fondement. Mais je revien à la suitte de mon Histoire. Convaincu donc de la verité de la Religion Judaique, et consequemment de la fausseté de la Chrestienne souvent il me prennoit envie de me faire Juif, mais la peur de manquer me retint pendant 3 ans mais ce ne fut pas sans agitation de conscience que je les ay passés. En fin estant tombé malade, qu'on croyoit que je mourrois je fis voeux d'abbandonner tout pour suivre la loy des Juifs; ne desirant autre chose que ce Jacob exigea de Dieu lors qu'il fuy-oit de devant son frere pour se retirer au pres de Laban. Je ne vous raccontrai point les visions que j'ay eut pendant ma maladie ny comment j-ay recouvrez la santé. c'est tout vous dire que 3 Mois après être rellevé j'ay pris la Poste, et fus à Amsterdam. Ce fut la que j'ay scele de mon sang l'alliance de Dieu avec nos Peres Abraham Isaac, et Jaacob.

[38] Pardonne à la confusion de mon stil mais je repareraj cette faute par un Livre que je composeray sur le sujet de ma miraculeuse conversion, dans le quel je traiteray plus amplement des matieres du different entre nos Religions.

[39] Je prie le Dieu des Armées de vous faire connoistre la verité de la saincte Loy et de vous combler de biens dans ce monde pour que vous puissiez jouir dans l'autre de la celeste compagnie des Anges, et bienheureux.

[40] Je salue Mr. le Baron De Staff, et suis avec un profond respect

Monsieur
Votre humble et tres
obbeissant serviteur
Aáron Dántan

[II.]

'A Mons.r De la Croze Bibliothequier du Roy de Prusse à Berlin
  [1] Puoique vous glissiez dans vos belles, et agreables, mais dificiles

questions quelque sujet au regard de la Religion, je vous declare Mr. que vous devez être persuadé que je ne quiteray point la foy de mes Peres pour la vôtre, et pour ne point consummer le tems en choses inutiles, je ne vous fairay aucune reponce aprez Mr. m'avoir contenté sur la teneur de ma precedente. aussi elloquement que clairement, vous me demandez pour payement ce que c'est que l'áme, et pour cela vous me dittes, que c'est dommage qu'une aussi belle ame que la mienne (je me sert de votre expression) soit damnée, en meme vous m'exortez de y bien penser et de prendre garde de ne y tromper le reste de ma vie; car si l'homme despuis sa Creation n'a encor peut comprendre si la Terre que nous voyons, et touchons tourne, ou si elle est ferme, comment moy Jeune, et comme vous scavez, peu expert dans le sublime, n'ayant jamais eut l'education dont les Chrestiens ornent l'Esprit de leurs Enfans pourrai-je decouvrir ce que tants d'habiles Theologiens de votre Religion n'ont encore peut faire, voila je vous l'aduoue Mr. de quoy m'occuper au moins un an, et je m'estimerois fort heureux si encor j'y peus reussir mais comme jusqu' à present je n'ay pas vecu comme une Bêtte qui boit et mange, et s'embarasse peu de l'avenir. Je vous diray pour reponce seulement à votre lettre, mais non pas à la question ce que j'ay pensé jusqu' alors, et que je penseray jusqu' à ce que je scache plus parfaictement mais je pense qui n'arivera pas si tot estant une question dificile à repondre. Tout le Monde convient (ou peu s'enfaut) d'un premier principe, mais on differe presque tous de ses atributs, les uns luy concedent le premier rang entre les autres Etres dont il a estez disent ils le principe, et mesme le gouvernement general de toutes choses, mais nient le gouvernement particulier, on le nomme Naturaliste ou Atheistes. Les autres soûtiennent que rien sens luy ne peut subsister, tant le General que le particulier, mesme jusqu'à nos moindres actions, et pensées ce sont le Religionaires. Mais entre ces religionaires il se trouve encor quelque sentiment particulier. Les Hebreux admettent Un Dieu Createur de tout ce que nous voyons et mesme de ce que nous ne voyons pas, le croyent êstre seul, et c'est pour cela qu'il est dit: Deus unicus et nomen illius unicum, si donc Dieu eut pretendû que les hommes reconnussent trois Personnes en luy, il est vray que pour marquer son unité, sens nier cespendant ([in Hebrew:] *God forbid! This is of course only a hypothetical assumption*) sa pluralité des Personnes il eut-peut-dire Deus unicus, mais nomen illius unicum renverse entierement, disons nous, la pluralité des Personnes. Car Pere, et Fils, et S. Esprit sont ([in Hebrew:] *God forbid! This is of course only a hypothetical assumption*) un seul Dieu, il est vray, Deus unus; mais ce sont trois Noms ce qui ne s'accorde pas avec Nomen illius unicum. Quoiqu'il semble que je me soit egaré du sujet pour parler de la Religion contre ce que j'ay dit dans mon Exorde, cela n'est cependant pas à mon avis, mais je n'ay faict qu'expliquer votre creance ensemble avec la mienne, au bien que l'eusse dû faire après, mais vous pardonnez à ma Jeunesse. Ad scopum redeo.

[2] L'Ame ne fait rien au sujet de la Religion davant que l'ame a precedé la Religion, ainsi rejettant tous les prejugez de la religion, et ne raisonnant que sur le premier principe, Je diray que le premier Éstre qui a estez capable de créer tants belles choses, doit Étre au dessus de toutes ces belles choses, il faut qu'il soit par tout pour gouverner et entretenir toute son Oeuvre sens le quel rien ne pourroit subsister. Si donc rien ne pourroit subsister sens cest ètre, il est facile de conclurre que cet èstre est l'ame de toutes choses; et que de la mesme maniere qu'un seul feu dans l'univers brule et entretient tous les Feux du Monde tant que la matierre corporelle soit consommée, de mesme l'ame universelle entretient, et vivifie tous les Corps capables de contenir une partie, sens être separée de son tout de cette Ame universelle qui est l'Éstre supreme et le Dieu des Hebreux.

[3] Alte, Alte, me direz vous, Monsieur, et pour quoy prennez vous donc tant de peine dans votre Religion, car selon votre Sisteme l'ame de la Bêtte est autant que la notre; et alors si vous croyez de necessité devoir suivre votre Religion en quelle veue le faites vous?

[4] Je vous expliqueray tout mon sentiment et puis je respondrai à toutes les objections que vous pourriez me faire. L'Esprit de l'homme qui ne peut rien comprendre sens quelque comparaison qui luy puisse faciliter l'intelligence humaine est une marque d'un èstre au dessus de luy sens cela l'orgueil de l'homme qui n'a pour ainsi dire que cette borne se seroit laissé emporter aux doux plaisir de croire que nul au Monde, ou pour mieux dire dans la Nature ne l'eut êgalé et par consequent qu'il estoit; O aveuglement humain! et le Createur, et le Creature. La comparison donc que j'ay trouvez la plus convenable à l'Éstre des Estres est le Soleil. Comme le Soleil est le principale Planette, et nos Corps comme celluy des bettes est la Terre,

ou les autres objects eclairés par le Soleil Divin qui est le Divin Estre, ainsi quand le Soleil eclaire sur un Diament en est il plus pur, que quand il eclaire sur de la boue! Ce Soleil, dis-je, elaire t-il moins sur cest object vil et bas que sur l'autre objet brillant et eclatant? non, sens doubte, mais la deffectuosité de la matiere faict que le Soleil est plus eclatant sur l'une que sur l'autre ou plustost qu'il le parroist. Ainsi le Soleil comme je lesuppose est cest Estre qui est si peu parfaictement connû de l'homme. Les hommes sont les Diamants, et les bestes sont le Cuivre et les Arbres sont comme la Pierne brutte, ou plus tost pour me servir d'une comparaison plus digne l'homme est le feu de ce feu, La Beste l'Eau, et l'Arbre la Terre qui sont les trois Elements de la Nature, niant l'Aire pour Element comme vous scavez. Il est dificil de m'ôter de l'Esprit que tout cest qui arive dans le Monde y arrive en vain. Ces Religions passées qui on fleuries avec tant d'eclat, et des quelles nous n'avons nul vestige, si ce n'est ce qui nous en est raconté par les Historiens marquent à mon avis que rien dans ce monde n'est stable, et que tout perit hors cet Estre Premier.

[5] Ma Religion, parlant sens prevention, qui entre toutes paroit la plus probable, me prouve qu'il doit y-en avoir une, et la votre qui s'est ellevé, pour ainsi dire, sur les debris de la nostre sens pourtant l'avoir êbranlée pourroit signifier que les hommes comme je pense avoir dit cy devant, par leur orgueil insuportable se sont eforcés, s'enforcent et s'enforceront de detruire la Divinité, comme nos Peres ont veu, comme nous voyons, et comme nos Neveux verrons. Quant à ce que je dis je ne veut pas le faire passer pour ma croyance, mais pour mon sentiment present. Je ne veut pas mesme dire qu'il n'y-ait quelque chose de bon, c'est à dire à êtudier, Car Dieu qui a voulu cela ne l'a pas faict pour rien, car si Dieu n'eut eû dessein que d'exterminer les Cannanéens certainement il ne les eut pas fait naistre, ainsi si nous considerons ce que vous trouvez de bon dans votre Religion, je ne void pour faire une comparaison parmis la turbe de ses Articles, que le Batême et la Trinité. Le Batême, en ce que nous ne pouvons acquerir le Ciel, je m'expliquerai cy après, sans la purification ce que rappresente le Batême, et la Trinité en ce que Dieu Étre des Étres sort trois choses qui ont êstéz jusques alors ignorées par les hommes, ainsi que je vous dit cy devant, sçavoir, trois Ames, L'Ame de l'homme, L'ame de la Bêste, et celle de l'Arbre qui sont trois, et cespendant qui n'est qu'un egard à l'Ame

universelle, mais qui est trois et distingue par raport aux trois Ames.
Soyez persuadez Monsieur, que j'estime plus votre Religion que
vous ne pensez, si vous en exeptez ce que l'avarice des Moines y-a
adjouté.

[6] Faites voir cette Lettre à Mr. Le Baron De Staff, et il sera autant
surpris de voir un Juif Trinitaire que je le serois de voir un Chretien
unitaire. Ne divulguez point, Mr., mon sentiment à nos Juifs, car ils
ne manqueroient pas d'être confirmés que je suis en notre langue
un [here is an empty space for the Hebrew word, but the word is
missing. Perhaps: *Goy*?].

[7] Il ne reste plus qu' à vous expliquer mon sentiment sur le fait
de la religion vous sçavez, Mons., ce que j'ay eut l'honneur de vous
dire dans le Jardin de votre Roy et dans sa Bibliotheque au sujet
de votre disertation sur les Athées; sçavoir qu'il êtoit toujours beaucoup plus seur de suivre une Religion que de n'en point avoir et
ensuitte j'eut l'honneur de vous faire avouer que la religion Judaique
etoit la plus seure pour un homme qui n'admettoit point l'Ecritture.
Mais aujourdhuy Mr. je vous parleray tout autrement c'est à dire
naturellement, sens avoir recours aux Escitures. Philosophiquement
parlant toute chose doit retourner à son centre comme le Feu en
haut, la Pierre en bas &c. C'est une verité qui n'est contestée de
personne, ainsi j'argumente l'Ame selon mon Sisteme est une emanation sens méme étre separée de son tout, si nous pouvons dire
que le Feu d'une Chandelle soit encore joint à son tout, de l'Etre
Supreme. Or est il que chasque chose dans la nature doit retourner
à son centre, donc l'ame doit retourner à son centre qui est l'Être
Supreme de qui elle avoit estez emanée. Mais comme rien ne retourne
à son centre avant que d'estre parvenu à un degré de perfection,
ainsi l'ame avant que d'être purifiée ne peut se rejoindre à son centre qui est Dieu la Pureté mesme. Mais comme se faict cette
purification, me direz vous? pour la bien comprendre il ne faut que
sçavoir que l'ame êtant spirituelle elle est impossible si elle n'a un
moien corporel pour la faire soufrir, si cela se peut dire, ainsi la
punition arive par la Metempsicose, car pourquoi verrions nous des
Pauvres qui ont autant pour les moins d'Esprit qu'un grand Roy, et
des Roys plus stupides que des Bergers? D'autre part ne croyez pas
que la recompence soit comme se l'immaginent les Chrestiens, d'estre
eternellement tout transporté en Dieu dans un Paradis immaginaires,

car si j'ay detruit le cruel suplice que les Chrétiens font apprehen-
dre, Je ne suis pas cependant pas plus flateur qu'indulgent. La recompence selon mon avis aussi bien que la Punition n'est que la
matiere qui rencontre un autre fois ce rayon qui eclaire ce Corp ou
plus tost qui l'anime, est plus ou moins pure, selon la vie que nous
avons menez dans ces jours. Je n'admetterai pourtant point que l'ame
raisonable sorte de son Centre comme l'ont crú certain Philosophes
anciens, car comme les Montagnes, et les Abismes sont toujours
Montagnes et Abismes de mesme l'ame de l'homme anime toujours
un homme, Et ainsi de l'ame sensitive, et de la vegetative. Il me
resteroit encore à parler si les ames des animaux se purifient aussi
semblablement à celles des hommes, mais le Papier me manquant,
et ne voulant rien adjouter au nombre des feuilles dont nous soumes
convenú je diray en passant ce que j'expliqueray, et prouveray plus
amplement dans ma premiere, que l'ame des Bestes n'a point besoin
de purification n'estant à mon avis que l'ombre de nous autres qui
sommes la Lumiere animé par l'ame universelle, ainsi que vous pour-
rez l'examiner si vous considerez les Effects du Soleil ou d'un
Flambeau.

[8] Je vous salue Mons.r, excusez l'obscurité de mes expressions,
mais les visites dont je suis accablez jointes à mon peu d'exprience
dans l'Art d'Escrire me serviront d'excuses aupres de vous.

[9] Je salûe Mons.r Le Baron de Staff et suis sincerement
Monsieur

Votre affectionné Servit.r
signez Aaron D'Antan

LORD GEORGE GORDON AND CABALISTIC FREEMASONRY: BEATING JACOBITE SWORDS INTO JACOBIN PLOUGHSHARES

Marsha Keith Schuchard

> The first Christian Prince that expelled the Jews out
> of his territories, was that heroick King, our Edward
> the First, who was such a scourge also to the Scots;
> and it is thought diverse families of these banished
> Jews fled then to Scotland, where they have prop-
> agated since in great numbers; witness the aversion
> that nation hath above all others to hogs-flesh.
>
> —James Howell (1652)

> To make the wrong appear the right,
> And keep our rulers in;
> In Walpole's time 'twas Jacobite,
> In Pitt's, 'tis Jacobin.
>
> —Edward Coxe (1805)

My interest in the quixotic figure of Lord George Gordon grew out of a research project on the Cabalistic-Masonic milieu of four equally *outré* eighteenth-century characters—Emanuel Swedenborg, Dr. Samuel Jacob Falk, Count Cagliostro, and William Blake. In the process of tracing the transformation of Jacobite Freemasonry into Jacobin Freemasonry—in Sweden, Poland, France, and Britain—the strange career of Gordon emerged as a palimpsest of the more extreme factors in that transformation. Moreover, it became clear that his sensational conversion to Judaism was not the irrational act of an eccentric fanatic but the rational conclusion to an ancient Scottish tradition of philo-Semitism, in which radical patriots proudly identified themselves with the embattled Jews.

Though most historians continue to portray "Rabbi" Gordon as "obviously insane," a more flattering portrait is given by the biographer Percy Colson: "Lord George was the first aristocratic Socialist in England, the first pacifist in the modern sense, and one of the first to make a protest against the extreme brutality of the penal

laws."[1] He was also the firebrand demagogue who brought England
to the brink of violent revolution, when much of London went up
in flames in the Gordon Riots of 1780. Seven years later he was
revered by thousands of Jews as a reborn Moses who would lead
them back to the Promised Land. It is testimony to the eclecticism
and complexity of Freemasonry in the eighteenth century that Gordon
found a Masonic niche for his idealistic and antinomian personality.

George Gordon was born in 1751 in the family townhouse in
London, the sixth and posthumous child of Cosmo, Third Duke of
Gordon. The Gordons were proud—even haughty—about their
ancient Scottish lineage, and the family still possessed enormous
wealth and property in the North. They also possessed notions of
European grandeur, which colored Lord George's grandiose sense
of his own destiny. His father was named for Cosimo III de Medici,
Duke of Tuscany, who had been a close friend of George's grandfather. The Gordons also boasted of their blood-ties to many Polish
aristocrats—all of whom were active in Polish-French versions of
Scottish Masonry (which were generically called *Écossais* rites).[2] As
Gordon learned later, several of these Polish families had Jewish
blood and were fascinated by Sabbatian forms of Jewish Cabalism.[3]
Three years after his father's death, Gordon's mother Catherine set
her sights on Stanislaus Poniatowski, King of Poland, who claimed
not only Gordon but Stuart and Jewish blood.[4] She dressed her
young sons up as cupids and had them shower the visiting King

---

[1] Percy Colson, *The Strange History of Lord George Gordon* (London, 1937), xvii. A
recent important exception to the "insanity" verdict is given in Iain McCalman's
articles, "Mad Lord George and Madame La Motte: Riot and Sexuality in the
Genesis of Burke's *Reflections on the Revolution in France*," *Journal of British Studies*, 35
(1996), 358, and "New Jerusalems: Prophecy, Dissent and Radical Culture in England,
1786–1830," *Enlightenment and Religion: Radical Dissent in Eighteenth-century Britain*, ed.
Knud Haakonssen (Cambridge, 1996), 319.

[2] *The Gay Gordons* (London, 1908), 53; Ernst Friedrichs, *Freemasonry in Russia and
Poland* (Berne, 1908), 57–62; Lusqif Haas, *Sekta farmazoni warszawskiy* (Warszawa,
1980), 85–87, 96, 177.

[3] Abraham Duker, "Polish Frankism's Duration," *Jewish Social Studies*, 25 (1963;
Kraus rpt. 1972), 303.

[4] Poniatowski was the great-grandson of Lady Catherine Gordon; see J.M. Bulloch,
Bibliography of the Gordons (Aberdeen, 1924), 175–76. For Poniatowski's Stuart, Jewish,
and Masonic relations, see Claude Nordmann, *La Crise du Nord au Début du XVIIIe
siècle* (Paris, 1962), 152–53; Stanislas Mnemon, *La Conspiration du Cardinal Alberoni et
Stanislas Poniatowski: la Franc-Maçonnerie et Stanislas Poniatowski* (Cracovie Universite,
1909), 60–67.

with silver darts, as she reclined seductively on the sofa.[5] Failing to win Stanislaus, she took the children off to Scotland, where they played happily on the vast Gordon estates.

Gordon frequently alluded to his close family and historical relationship to the royal Stuart family, who portrayed themselves as the Solomonic architects of the royalist Temple of Wisdom.[6] However, the Jacobite rebellion of 1745, in which supporters of the Stuart Pretender James "III" rose against the Hanoverian King George II, triggered a traumatic split in the Gordon clans. George Gordon's uncle Lord Lewis Gordon enthusiastically joined Prince Charles Edward Stuart, the "Young Pretender," and became a dashing commander of the Scottish forces.[7] Despite appeals from Lord Lewis, his brother Cosmo followed the advice of their grandfather (who had fought in the failed 1715 rising) to avoid involvement in politics.[8] In the decade after the Jacobite defeat of 1746, while Lewis languished in exile in France, Cosmo's widow persuaded King George that her husband's passive loyalty deserved royal recognition. Thus, George II agreed to stand as godfather to Cosmo's posthumous son—an act the king's grandson George III would later regret. Though the Gordons were traditionally Catholic, the Duchess now raised her sons as strict Presbyterians. For George Gordon, his parents' break with their Jacobite and Catholic traditions was an intensely serious step that would color his political and religious thinking for years. To justify it, the Protestant government of the "Elector of Hanover" (as he always called George III) must continuously prove its moral superiority—or it did not deserve to replace the legitimate Stuart heirs.

The political split within the Gordon clans was mirrored in a Masonic split as well. Since 1717 Jacobites and Hanoverians had struggled for dominance within Freemasonry, and rival systems of lodges emerged in Britain and abroad. The Gordon name appeared

[5] Christopher Hibbert, *King Mob: The Story of Lord George Gordon and the Gordon Riots* (London, 1958), 2.

[6] For the Solomonic-Masonic notions of the seventeenth-century Stuart kings, see my *Restoring the Temple of Vision: Cabalistic Freemasonry and Stuart Culture* (Leiden, 2002).

[7] Henrietta Tayler, *The Jacobite Epilogue* (London, 1941), 170–72; Frank McLynn, *Charles Edward Stuart* (1988; rpt. Oxford, 1991), 161, 175, 202, 581 n. 65.

[8] Christopher Sinclair-Stephenson, *Inglorious Rebellion: The Jacobite Risings of 1708, 1715, and 1719* (New York, 1972), 136.

frequently in Masonic annals, on both sides, throughout the century.[9] George's older brother William later married Jean Maxwell, whose great-uncle Robert Maxwell joined the Jacobite rebels, was arrested, sentenced to death, but then reprieved and shipped to India. When the Stuart Prince arrived in Scotland, Robert Maxwell was working on a compilation of the historical records of the Masonic lodge of Holyrood House, of which he was an activist member. Unfortunately, there is a gap in the records from September 1745 to 7 April 1746, so there is no documentation for the alleged initiation of Prince Charles into the Masonic chapter of Knights Templar at Holyrood.[10] Rumors about this ceremony circulated in the high-degree lodges of *Écossais* Masonry, reaching the far-flung corners of Sweden, Russia, Poland, Germany, France, and Italy.

According to shadowy Scottish traditions, not only the Templars but the Jews expelled from medieval England found refuge in Scotland, where they assimilated into the local population and infused their traditions into the Scottish lifestyle.[11] In the later seventeenth-century, when the Stuart kings protected the Jews, there was an infusion of Jewish mystical lore into Masonic rituals.[12] The radical pantheist John Toland, who had participated in Rosicrucian-Masonic societies in Scotland in 1689–90, later claimed that a considerable "part of

---

[9] Robert S. Lindsay, *A History of the Mason Lodge of Holyrood House (St. Luke's), Number 44* (Edinburgh, 1935), I, 63–73, 225.

[10] See my article, "The Young Pretender and Jacobite Freemasonry: New Light from Sweden on His Role as Hidden Grand Master," in *Consortium on Revolutionary Europe 1750–1850: Selected Papers*, ed. Donald Horward (Florida State University, 1994), 363–72; also, C.C.F. Nettlebladt, *Geschichte Freimaurerische Systeme in England, Frankreich, und Deutschland* (Berlin, 1879; facs. rpt. Wiesbaden: Dr. M. Sandig, 1972), 128–30, 249; J.E.S. Tuckett, "Dr. Begemann and the Alleged Templar Chapter at Edinburgh in 1745," *Ars Quatuor Coronatorum*, 33 (1920), 40–62.

[11] On the Templars in Scotland, see Michael Baigent and Richard Leigh, *The Temple and the Lodge* (1989; rpt. London: Corgi, 1993), 102–15, 127–57. On the Jewish ancestry of Scots, see Arthur Williamson, "A Pil for Pork-Eaters'": Ethnic Identity, Apocalyptic Promises, and the Strange Creation of the Judeo-Scots," in *The Expulsion of the Jews: 1492 and After*, eds. Raymond Waddington and Arthur Williamson (New York, 1994), 237–58.

[12] For a Masonic manuscript dated 1665 which featured Hebrew lettering, Jewish symbolism, and Stuart loyalism, see John Thorpe, "Old Masonic Manuscript. A Fragment," *Lodge of Research, No. 2429 Leicester. Transactions for the Year 1926–27*, 40–48; for the 1675 contribution of Rabbi Leon "Templo" to restored Stuart Freemasonry, see A.L. Shane, "Jacob Judah Leon of Amsterdam (1602–1675) and his Models of the Temple of Solomon and the Tabernacle," *Ars Quatuor Coronatorum*, 196 (1983), 146–69.

the British inhabitants are the undoubted offspring of the Jews," for "a great number of 'em [Jews] fled to Scotland, which is the reason so many in that part of the Island, have such a remarkable aversion to pork and black-puddings to this day, not to insist on some other resemblances easily observable."[13] During the 1715 and 1745 Jacobite rebellions, many royalist Jews on the Continent continued to support the Stuart cause.[14]

As exiled Jacobite Masons developed increasingly Cabalistic higher degrees, the Hanoverian government in London counter-attacked. In 1747 Henry Fielding utilized his government-subsidized journal to link the Jacobites with occultist (Templar) Freemasonry, claiming that they enacted secret rituals for political subversion and sexual perversion.[15] In 1748 Fielding argued that the Jacobites were not only Masons but Jews:

> . . . it is the unhappy Fate of both these People, who have been alike deprived of their own divinely constituted Kings, to live under Governments which they hold to be damnable and diabolical, and no Allegiance nor Submission due to them: But, on the contrary, are daily hoping and looking for their Destruction . . .

> . . . the Jacobites, when they set this surprizing Mark on themselves, had a View to imitate the Jews . . . I mean in the Humour of Circumcision, which at present so universally prevails upon the Jacobites equally with the Jews. The Original of the Practice was set on Foot, as I am told, soon after the Battle of Culloden, and was performed in memory of that Victory, or as they call it Massacre . . . From that

---

[13] John Toland, *Reasons for Naturalizing the Jews in Great Britain and Ireland* (London, 1714), 37. For his association with occult societies in Scotland, see F.H. Heinemann, "John Toland and the Age of Enlightenment," *Review of English Studies*, 20 (1944), 127–28, and "John Toland, France, Holland, and Dr. Williams," *Review of English Studies*, 25 (1949), 347. Heinemann, who discussed Toland's Rosicrucian activities, was unaware of the long association of Rosicrucianism with Scottish Freemasonry. For Toland's role in a Masonic-style secret society in Holland in 1710, see Margaret Jacob, *The Radical Enlightenment: Pantheists, Freemasons, and Republicans* (London, 1981).

[14] For the attraction of many Jews to 17th–18th century Stuart Freemasonry, see my article "Dr. Samuel Jacob Falk: a Sabbatian Adventurer in the Masonic Underground," in *Jewish Messianism in the Early Modern Period*, eds. Matt Goldish and Richard Popkin (Dordrecht, 2001), 203–26. Further information on Jewish Masons is given in Marcus Lipton, "Francis Francia—the Jacobite Jew," *Transactions of Jewish Historical Society of England*, 11 (1928), 190–205, and in John Shaftesley, "Jews in English Regular Freemasonry, 1717–1860," *Transactions of Jewish Historical Society of England*, 25 (1977), 150–209.

[15] Henry Fielding, *The Jacobite's Journal and Related Writings*, ed. W.B. Colby (Middletown, 1975), 95–98, 103, 109.

day the Custom hath been universal; and I am credibly informed there
is not a *Jacobite* now in England who is uncircumcised.[16]

For Prince Charles, who became the "hidden" Grand Master of the
Masonic Knights Templar, the Franco-Scottish tradition that linked
the "Judaized" Templars with nationalist hostility to the Papacy
would prove attractive, as he struggled to remove the taint of autocratic "Papism" from his campaign in Britain. Despite Hanoverian
propaganda that painted the Stuarts as bigoted Catholic tyrants, the
Prince was known as a free-thinker, whose call for complete religious toleration in Britain was supported by Voltaire, his great
admirer.[17] After the Jacobite defeat at Culloden, Freemasonry in
Scotland underwent a dark period, from which few records survive—
particularly those of Jacobite sympathizers. In 1756 the despised
Edward Wyvil, who had supplied a list of known rebels to the authorities, joined the famous Jacobite lodge of Canongate-Kilwinning and
led it towards Hanoverian submission.[18]

In that same year, however, a Scots-Irish Mason named Laurence
Dermott published *Ahiman Rezon* (London, 1756), which promoted
the "Ancient" system of lodges as rooted in the superior Masonry
of the Cabalistic Jews and the Scottish kings.[19] In 1764 Dermott
went further in stressing the Jewish traditions of "Ancient" Masonry,
noting that the coat of arms for the restored Stuart fraternity was
designed in 1675 by "Brother" Jacob Judah Leon, Jewish architect
of a famous model of the Jerusalem Temple. The "Ancients" insisted
on esoteric ceremonies which the "Moderns" rejected, especially the
Cabalistic higher degrees of Knights Templar, *Rose-Croix*, and Royal
Arch.[20] Under Dermott's energetic leadership, the "Ancients" seceded
from the "Modern" Grand Lodge and soon attracted many recruits
from the disaffected artisan classes in London.

The government increased its pressure on the former Jacobite
lodges in Scotland, and after the French-Jacobite invasion scare of
1759, the lodge at Holyrood cautiously moved from Jacobitism to

---

[16] Ibid., 281–85.
[17] Laurence Bongie, "Voltaire's English, High Treason, and a Manifesto for Prince
Charles," *Studies on Voltaire and the Eighteenth Century*, 171 (1977), 7–29.
[18] R.S. Lindsay, *Holyrood*, 71–79.
[19] Shane, "Jacob Judah Leon," 146–69; Robert F. Gould, *The History of Freemasonry*
(New York, 1885), III, 186–217.
[20] Bernard Jones, *Freemasons' Guide and Compendium*, rev. ed. (1950; London, 1956),
199–202, 495, 511.

Whiggism in the 1760's—a shift that did not imply admiration for King George III. During the same period, the "Ancients" recruited aggressively in the American colonies, where they emerged as the dominant system of Masonry and significant contributors to the independence movement. Among the "Ancient" recruits were many Jews, who shared the resentment against English encroachments on American rights. As the Jewish-American Freemason Dr. Isaac Wise affirmed in *The Israelite* (1855), "Masonry is a Jewish institution whose history, degrees, charges, passwords, and explanations are Jewish from beginning to end, with the exception of only one by degree and a few words in the obligation."[21] Moreover, he added, Jews in the American colonies in the mid-eighteenth century were most attracted to the Ancient or "Scottish Rite," in which they became not only Knights of the Temple but Scottish Masters.

Meanwhile, against a background of polarization and confusion in Scotland, Lord George's widowed mother was determined that her family would emerge from the Jacobite defeat in sound financial shape. She married a 21 year-old American officer, raised a regiment of Gordon Highlanders for George II's service, and sent her sons off to Eton to become properly Anglicized (a move that failed signally with her youngest son). George, when barely adolescent, was given a naval commission and shipped out to America. Despite his officer status, he identified and sympathized with the common sailors, whose appalling conditions he protested to his superiors. Gaining the lifelong epithet of "the sailor's friend," he also gained the lifelong resentment of the officer class.

During a six-month stay in Jamaica, Gordon became incensed at the brutal treatment of the slaves. "What sort of world is it," he declaimed, "that allowed such inequality and such injustice, that viewed without concern the sugar planters growing rich at the expense of the whipped, hungry, bleeding bodies of their slaves?"[22] Protesting to the governor and writing outraged letters to Parliament, Gordon vowed to devote himself to ending the slave trade. When his ship spent long periods in American ports, Gordon saw in the sturdy and independent colonists a new breed of men and a new type of society.

---

[21] Samuel Oppenheim, "The Jews and Masonry in the United States Before 1810," *Publications of the American Jewish Historical Society*, 19 (1910), 1–2, 41, 76–87.
[22] Hibbert, *King Mob*, 5.

As Dr. Robert Watson (his later secretary and biographer) remembered, Gordon observed that "the sacred flame of Freedom—with a large F—aided by reason was making rapid progress every day."[23] When the Americans began agitating against British rule, Gordon resigned his naval commission in 1773, "partly from a resolution never to imbrue his hands in the blood of men struggling for freedom."

Returning to Scotland, he determined to pursue a Rousseauian ideal of the simple life by spending long periods in the remote Hebrides. Like Diderot, Helvetius, and the French *philosophes* after the 1745 rebellion, Gordon believed that the Highlanders preserved the instinctive virtues of man in a natural, simple society.[24] Wearing Highland dress, speaking Gaelic, playing the bagpipes, and dancing reels, Gordon emerged as a local Celtic hero.[25] However, as news of the increasing grievances of the Americans reached the North, Gordon decided to enter Parliament as an advocate for the "Sons of Liberty." Burning with reformist zeal, he sensed a prophetic significance to his political activities from his earliest days in Westminster.

Years later, a disciple of Richard Brothers (self-proclaimed "Prince of the Hebrews" and advocate of "illuminist" Freemasonry) recalled that in 1774 he was visited by Gordon.[26] The new M.P. "actually read over the prophecies of Martha Fry and with great attention," which can be vouched for "by Dr. Hugh Mayson and Gordon's friends in London." Fry quoted scraps from the Hebrew prophets who proved that a great liberator would come "from the North" to save the people of Israel, and Gordon especially identified with one prophecy, which he continued to proclaim over the next decades:

> Behold the days come, saith the Lord, that I will raise unto David a righteous branch, and they shall no more say, the Lord liveth, which brought up the children of Israel out of the land of Egypt; but the Lord liveth, which brought up, and which led the seed of the house of Israel out of the *North Country*, and from all countries whither I had driven them; and they shall dwell in their own land.[27]

---

[23] Robert Watson, M.D., *The Life of Lord George Gordon, with a Philosophical Review of His Political Conduct* (London, 1795), 6–7.

[24] Frank McLynn, *Charles Edward Stuart* (1988; Oxford, 1991), 290, 310.

[25] Colson, *Gordon*, 32–33.

[26] [Anon.], *Wonderful Prophecies, Being a Dissertation on the Existence, Nature, and Extent of the Prophetic Powers in the Human Mind*, 4th rev. ed. (London, 1795), 77.

[27] Watson, *Gordon*, 79.

Gordon soon became famous as "the Third Party" in Parliament. Acting as a "minority of one," he challenged Whigs and Tories in cosntant debate. Gordon's colorful personality and daring speeches made him popular with the same artisans and shopkeepers who earlier took to the streets in support of John Wilkes, who opposed the government's military and imperial policies. Initially, Gordon was encouraged by his intimate friends Charles James Fox and Edmund Burke, though he later claimed to suspect even then that "they were no real friends to the people."[28] Like Fox, Burke, and his own brothers, Gordon was almost certainly a Freemason.[29] It was probably members of Burke's lodge, "Jerusalem, #4," who in 1769 initiated Wilkes, while he was confined in King's Bench Prison.[30]

In June 1776 Gordon accompanied William Hickey, a member of Wilkes's lodge, and several partisans of the American revolution on a rollicking visit to Paris, where they cheered the rebels with like-minded Frenchmen. When the American Declaration of Independence was issued in July, sympathetic Masons in Paris formed the lodge of "Neuf Soeurs," in an act of revolutionary solidarity with their American brothers.[31] After his return from France, Gordon became the Americans' most vociferous champion in Parliament. Claiming to represent the "party of the people," he soon identified the "voice of the people" with the "voice of God." To the disaffected citizens of London, who sullenly opposed the war against the colonists, Gordon's harangues were tonic. As Hibbert observes, "Sometimes their grotesque sarcasm, their unashamed rudeness or their splendid splenetic fury, seemed to raise them to a sort of grandeur."[32]

In summer 1778 his Isaiah-like denunciations found a welcoming audience among the new Protestant Associations formed to protest the passing of the Savile Act, which relieved Catholics of some of the disabilities imposed by William III in 1700. Though many of the Protestant protesters were motivated purely by anti-Catholic bigotry,

---

[28] Ibid., 8.

[29] F.W. Levander, "The Jerusalem Sols and Other London Societies of the Eighteenth Century," *Ars Quatuor Coronatorum*, 25 (1912), 29.

[30] W.R. Denslow, *Ten Thousand Famous Freemasons* (Transactions of Missouri Lodge of Research, 1959), I, 155; John Brewer, *Party Ideology and Popular Politics at the Accession of George III* (Cambridge, 1976), 194–97, 312.

[31] C.N. Batham, "A Famous French Lodge (*Les Neuf Soeurs*)," *Ars Quatuor Coronatorum*, 86 (1973), 312–17.

[32] Hibbert, *King Mob*, 8.

Gordon viewed the Act as a surreptitious trick to recruit poverty-stricken Catholic Highlanders into regiments who would fight the American revolutionaries. As his biographer Watson explained, in 1778 the war against the colonists was going badly, because the American "Sons of Liberty were an overmatch" for George III's "mercenary soldiers":

> ... [thus] the government, not from liberality of sentiment or a tolerating spirit ... proposed to the leaders of the Catholics to repeal the statutes enacted against them; provided they would contribute to support the American War by entering into the fleets or armies ... The Army and Navy found new supplies, and the Cabinet new vigour for prosecuting an unhappy civil war.[33]

In his protests, Gordon accurately pointed out that most Catholics were not in favor of the bill, fearing it would cause more problems than benefits.

The Savile Act also made clear that George III was still terrified of a Jacobite rebellion, especially after rumors circulated in 1775 that the "Young Pretender," now calling himself Charles III, was approached by Boston patriots who wanted him to serve as the figurehead of a provisional American government (a thrust *pour épater les Anglais*).[34] In 1778 there were more reports that the Stuart claimant, who greatly admired the American rebels, was preparing to sail to the new country. With France now fighting for the revolutionaries, the vision of a Jacobite descent on Scotland and French invasion of southern England loomed with paranoid *déjà vu*. While echoing the popular cries of "No Popery!" Gordon argued cogently that the only "relief" for the Catholics was the privilege of being dragooned into George III's troops bound for America. Moreover, they must renounce their long-cherished traditions of loyalty to the Stuarts, as demanded by the new oath:

> I *A.B.* do sincerely promise and swear, that I will be faithful and bear true allegiance to his Majesty King *George the Third*, and him will defend, to the utmost of my power, against all conspiracies and attempts whatever that shall be made against his person, crown, or dignity; and I will do my utmost endeavour to disclose and make known to his Majesty, his heirs, and successors, all treasons and traitorous conspiracies

---

[33] Watson, *Gordon*, 9–10.
[34] McLynn, *Charles Edward Stuart*, 519.

which may be formed against him or them . . . hereby utterly renouncing and abjuring any obedience or allegiance unto the person taking
upon himself the stile and title of *Prince of Wales*, in the lifetime of his
father, and who, since his death, is said to have assumed the stile and
title of *King of Great Britain*, by the name of *Charles the Third* . . .[35]

Encouraged by Gordon's harangues in Parliament, the Protestant
Association in Edinburgh presented petitions for redress and, when
they were ignored, provoked riots all over Scotland in early 1779.
An alarmed government then agreed that Catholic Relief would not
be extended north of the Tweed. One politically-astute observer of
these developments was the Highland-born Robert Watson, who had
recently returned to his native country.[36] Watson had served in the
revolutionary army in America, where he rose to the rank of Colonel
and became intimate with General George Washington. Watson was
probably aware that Washington played a leading role in "Ancient"
Freemasonry and that he used Masonic initiations as a way of ensur-
ing loyalty and bolstering morale among his troops.[37] Made lame by
a war wound, Watson returned to Edinburgh, where he joined the
circle of radical Whig antiquarians led by the eccentric David Stewart
Erskine, eleventh Earl of Buchan, who was a cousin of Gordon and
leader of local "Ancient" lodges.[38]

Buchan collected the papers of Fletcher of Saltoun, a Scottish
nationalist and radical republican, who had organized resistance to
James II and William III in the late seventeenth century. Under
Buchan's tutelage, Watson became fascinated by Fletcher's ideals and
methods, which he viewed in quasi-Masonic terms. In Watson's biography of Fletcher, written in 1798 when he participated in a secret
political society affiliated with the United Irishmen, he hinted at the

---

[35] Colson, *Gordon*, 79.
[36] See "Robert Watson, M.D. and F.S.A." *Dictionary of National Biography*; Graham
Bain, *The Thunderbolt of Reason, being the Story of Mr. Robert Watson of Elgin* (Elgin,
1996). Though the date of Watson's return is unclear, I believe it was in 1779,
shortly before he became Gordon's secretary. Though Iain McCalman doubts that
Watson worked for Gordon in 1780, I see know reason to doubt Watson's claim,
which was not questioned by contemporaries who knew both men. See McCalman's
interesting article, "Controlling the Riots: Dickens, *Barnaby Rudge* and Romantic
Revolution," *History*, 84 (1999), 458–76.
[37] Bernard Fay, *Revolution and Freemasonry* (Boston, 1935), 242–51.
[38] Lindsay, *Holyrood*, I, 237; II, 611; Richard Sher, *Church and University in the
Scottish Enlightenment* (Princeton, 1985), 304–05.

similarities between the Scottish Covenanters, Protestant Associations, and United Brotherhoods:

> ... the people took an oath, called the solemn league and covenant, not unlike the oath of the united irishmen, by which they bound themselves to support one another, and persevere until they obtained a redress of grievances.[39]

Watson cautiously did not refer to Freemasonry, which was under government surveillance in 1798, but he was undoubtedly aware that Masons had been involved in the seventeenth-century Covenanting movement, which was influenced by the fraternity's methods of secret communication, bonding, and organization.[40]

In 1779 Watson also visited France, where he evidently contacted his old friend Benjamin Franklin, Master of the "Neuf Soeurs" lodge, who was organizing French support for the Americans.[41] According to his own claim, Watson subsequently became secretary to Gordon. As his later career revealed, Watson was a hard-core revolutionary, who excelled in radical propaganda and clandestine organizing.[42] Though he called himself "secretary" to Gordon, it is clear that he attempted to manipulate his volatile employer to serve his political agenda. As a free-thinking deist, Watson did not share Gordon's ardent religiosity, and he was unaware of the impact that his advocacy of the Covenanting movement would have on his protégé.

---

[39] Robert Watson, M.D. and F.S.A., *The Political Works of Fletcher of Salton* (London, 1798), 39. "It is worth remarking, that the Scots, in the neighborhood of Glasgow, were the first people who took a secret oath to counteract the encroachments of despotism; and so lasting has been the impression, that their descendants in Ireland and America have copied their example. This mode of opposing tyranny, after making the tour of America and Europe, seems to be revived with increased enthusiasm, in the very country which gave it birth." On the Masonic origins of the United Irishmen, see A.T.Q. Stewart, *A Deeper Silence: The Hidden Roots of the United Irish Movement* (London, 1993).

[40] See David Stevenson, *The First Freemasons: Scotland's Early Lodges and Their Members* (Aberdeen, 1988), 28, 69–73; Allan Macinnes, *Charles I and the Making of the Covenanting Movement* (East Linton:, 1996), 168. On the Masonic-Templar association with the oaths of the United Irishmen and United Englishmen, see Albert Goodwin, *The Friends of Liberty* (Cambridge, 1979), 436–39.

[41] Nicholas Hans, "UNESCO of the Eighteenth Century: La Loge des Neuf Soeurs and its Venerable Master, Benjamin Franklin," *Proceedings of the American Philosophical Society*, XCVII (1953), 512–24.

[42] For Watson's later revolutionary career, see G. Bain, *Thunderbolt*, 9–28; also Andrew Lang, "A Wild Career," *Illustrated London News* (12 March 1892), 331; Marianne Elliott, *Partners in Revolution: The United Irishmen and France* (New Haven,

As Williamson reveals, since 1581 Scottish Protestants viewed their nation as contracted to the God of Israel, for their anti-Papist "Covenant" replicated Moses's engagement on Mount Sinai, and by 1638 the Covenanters vowed to rebuild the Jerusalem Temple in the North: "Judaized identities, Judaized politics, and enduring fascination with contemporary Jewry all deeply informed Scottish political culture in the seventeenth century."[43] Stevenson stresses the "awe-inspiring belief" that "the Scots were the successors to the Jews as a chosen people of God," which motivated them to fight against all odds to carry out the earthly mission of the God of Israel.[44] Opponents of the Covenanters often charged that they were "ethnically related" to the Jews, who allegedly intermarried after their escape to Scotland in medieval times.[45]

On 12 November 1779 the Protestant Association in England was so emboldened by the Scots' successful rejection of the Savile Act that they asked Gordon to serve as their president. In his acceptance letter, Gordon made clear that he was not interested in religious persecution:

> I trust that coolness and temper in the proceedings of the Association will soon demonstrate to the Roman Catholics that we are far from being possessed of a persecuting disposition; and I hope the attention of Parliament to the petitions of Englishmen will be so very respected and prudent, so as not to raise the apprehensions of the lower classes of people. Had the addresses of the provincial Synods in Scotland been duly respected, and attended to, the houses and chapels of the Scotch Papists would never have suffered by the resentment of an enraged populace.—The Roman Catholics must know as well as we do, that Popery when encouraged by the Government has always been dangerous to the liberties of the people.[46]

However, Gordon also made clear in this letter that his real concern was the military recruitment, for it alarmed him exceedingly "to see with what eagerness and joy the Papists were willing to contribute

---

1982), 141–47, 178, 186; Mary Thale, *Selections from the Papers of the London Corresponding Society, 1792–1799* (Cambridge, 1983), 20–24, 397.

[43] Williamson, "'A Pil for Pork-Eaters,'" 237–58.

[44] David Stevenson, *Union, Revolution and Religion in 17th-Century Scotland* (Aldershot, 1997), 46.

[45] James Howell, *The Wonderful and Most Deplorable History of the Latter Times of the Jews* (London, 1652), sig.A5v. Though Howell was initially a royalist, he had gone over to Cromwell by the time he published this edition of the chronicle *Jossipon*.

[46] Watson, *Gordon*, 16.

their mite in support of an unhappy civil war, against the Protectorate in America."[47]

Elated with his new power, Gordon delivered a strangely threatening harangue in the House of Commons on 25 November:

> Mr. Speaker: I should not have troubled the House were it not for the absurdities with which the speech from the Throne is replete. It is totally destitute of common sense. His Majesty tells us that in consequence of our addresses he has ordered certain papers, relative to Ireland, to be laid before us. Why was not that order made in consequence of the addresses from Ireland? Was the Irish Parliament unworthy of his majesty's notice? The truth is His Majesty's ministers are no less odious in Ireland than they are in England. In Scotland the people are ready to break with the Ministry as in Ireland . . . I do not deliver my own sentiments only; government will find 120,000 men at my back who will avow and support them! . . .
>
> The coast of Scotland, Sir, is left naked and defenceless; the people of Dumfriesshire had therefore petitioned for arms to defend themselves. That country is in such a position that Paul Jones might with utmost facility have destroyed Glasgow . . . and Edinburgh in one expedition . . . Could it have occurred to any one that the Administration would have denied so reasonable a requisition? . . . And yet the Secretary of the Elector of Hanover has had that presumption! The Royal Family of Stuart have been banished from their kingdom for not attending to the voice of the People, and an Elector of Hanover is not afraid to disregard it! . . . The Scots . . . are convinced in their own mind that the King is a Papist.[48]

Gordon probably knew that the privateer John Paul Jones had been initiated into Freemasonry in Scotland in 1770, was currently affiliated with the radical lodge "Neuf Soeurs" in Paris, and collaborated with its Master Ben Franklin.[49]

Despite—or possibly because of—the threatening tone of this speech, the King granted Gordon a personal interview on 29 January 1780. According to Gordon, he delivered into the King's "own hand the English appeal against the Popery Bill drawn up by . . . the Protestant Association."[50] Complaining that Lord North had refused to deliver it, Gordon asked if he might report to the Association that the King had received the appeal "very graciously." However, Horace

[47] Ibid., 15.
[48] Ibid., 17–18.
[49] Hans, "UNESC0," 512–24.
[50] Hibbert, *King Mob*, 27.

Walpole reported that Gordon also pulled out an Irish pamphlet and read it for an hour, to the distress of the cornered King.[51] The author Francis Dobbs was an ardent Irish nationalist, who later boasted that he "was the first man in Ireland, who exerted himself openly, and called loudly for the liberties of this country."[52] In the pamphlet, Dobbs boldly attacked Lord North and his Ministry for violating Constitutional law in his domineering policies over Ireland:

> If, whilst poor, you claim absolute power over us, by what chain of reasoning are we to suppose you will relinguish it, should we become rich? It makes no difference that this power is vested in the legislature of Great Britain, and not in a single hand. Absolute power in one or in many is the same. Its effect is equally destructive to the happiness of a state or individual.[53]

Following Gordon's lead in demanding arms for Scottish "self-defense," Dobbs called for armed Protestant militias in Ireland on the basis of the Crown's increasing encroachments on Irish rights:

> The Law and Constitution gives a positive right to every Protestant in Ireland to carry arms ... Should it ever happen that a King of great Britain and Ireland becomes jealous of his People, it will be high Time for the People to be jealous of him; and to take care that they have a Power superior to any he can command.[54]

Dobbs's pamphlet expressed cogently the growing assault by Celtic radicals and nationalists on the illegitimacy of the autocratic government of the "Elector of Hanover."

The struggle of the Americans, bolstered by the "Ancient" and Scottish-rite Masonic lodges, gave a new twist to formerly Jacobite disaffection. As Lenman observes, the demise of effective Jacobite opposition in the 1760's led the Welsh nationalists to look to the American rebels for inspiration—"The future lay with the radicals in America."[55] According to Jenkins, the formerly Jacobite Masonic lodges in Wales "helped to carry the old alliance between Jacobitism

---

[51] Horace Walpole, *Correspondence*, ed. W.S. Lewis (New Haven, 1971), XXV, ix, 11.

[52] [Francis Dobbs], *Memoirs of Francis Dobbs ... and His Prediction of the Second Coming*, 2nd. rev. ed. (Dublin, 1800), 7.

[53] Francis Dobbs, *A Letter to the Right Honourable Lord North, on his Propositions in Favour of Ireland* (Dublin, 1780), 15.

[54] Francis Dobbs, *Thoughts on Volunteers* (Dublin, 1781), 9–10.

[55] Bruce Lenman, *The Jacobite Risings in Britain, 1689–1746* (London, 1980), 291.

and radicalism into the last quarter of the century."[56] What was true
for Wales was even more true among the supporters of Dobbs in
Ireland and Gordon in Scotland, for the American Revolution was
essentially "Celtic radicalism made flesh." Curiously, Dobbs—like
Gordon—would later become a philo-Semitic Zionist and an initiate of Cabalistic Freemasonry.[57]

Gordon's reading of Dobbs's pamphlet convinced the King that
"the mad Scotchman" might prove dangerous. Thus, he instructed
Lord North to attempt to bribe him with money and a naval command as rewards for resigning from the Protestant Association.[58]
Gordon indignantly refused, much to the delight of his admirers who
resented the greed and venality of most members of Parliament (on
both sides). It was perhaps the King or Edmund Burke who sent
Lord Petre to visit Gordon in spring 1780. Petre was not only a
leader of the Catholics and an advocate of toleration, but he had
recently served as Grand Master of "Modern" or Hanoverian Freemasonry (1772–77).[59] He was still a Masonic power and he expected
to have some influence with Gordon, who was an old family friend.
Petre flattered Gordon and warned him that the Protestant Association
was "a mean set of people," which only goaded Gordon's proud
egalitarianism. When Petre asked him to postpone presenting the
petition for repeal, Gordon answered with his peculiar mixture of
Jacobite threat and Protestant defiance:

> I replied that if the Popery Bill stood as it was, and any one Papist
> should use half the honest pains to restore the ancient and hereditary
> royal family of Stuart to the throne than I took to promote the glory
> of the God of Israel, and of the people, the present illustrious Sovereign,
> and all the rest of the House of Hanover might find themselves in
> exile in a fifth of the time his lordship required . . . If I was a Papist,
> or could tolerate Popery, I would not take any oath of allegiance to
> the House of Hanover (being Protestants) as long as there was an
> hereditary Popish Prince, of the antient and royal family of Stuart (my
> own near, dear, and lawful relations) to be found on the face of the

[56] J.P. Jenkins, "Jacobites and Freemasons in Eighteenth-century Wales," *Welsh History Review*, 9 (1978–79), 392.

[57] Francis Dobbs, *A Concise View from History and Prophecy* (London, 1800), 65, 159, 241–52; Clarke Garrett, *Respectable Folly: Millenarians and the French Revolution* (Johns Hopkins University, 1975), 118–19.

[58] Colson, *Gordon*, 67.

[59] Gould, *History*, III, 227–30; Hibbert, *King Mob*, 25–26.

earth, and in just and necessary banishment from the throne of these kingdoms, merely for his idolatry in being reconciled to Popery.[60]

As Gordon observed, Lord Petre seemed puzzled by this outburst, with its peculiar combination of claims for Stuart legitimacy, Protestant superiority, and Hebrew religiosity. Gordon later remarked that he could easily have refuted Petre, "from the Word of God and those arguments deducible from the commandments binding upon the Jews and Christians."[61] This linking of Jewish law with the Protestant cause and the "Sons of Liberty" provides an early clue to Gordon's subsequent conversion to Judaism.

When Gordon told Edmund Burke about his rejection of Petre's proposals, Burke broke off their once intimate friendship. He would later become an inveterate enemy of Gordon.[62] While the government repeated their offers of bribes and positions to Gordon and members of his family, he continued to seek redress personally from the King, frequently reminding George III that his own grandfather had been the petitioner's godfather. In a fourth interview on 19 May 1780, Gordon revealed "the dark secret" to the King that the English Popery Bill was passed "for the diabolical purpose of arming the Papists against the Protestant Colonies in America,—and not from any mild, benevolent, enlightened views of the legislature," which deliberately hid "the real design from the deluded people of England."[63] He recounted secret conversations between the war-making Ministers and the Catholic Bishop Hay, who himself asserted that "the Roman Catholics had enlisted in great numbers into the last regiments raised in Scotland, to go out to the war against the American colonists."[64]

As the King evaded his probing questions—claiming he knew of no secret correspondence—Gordon again threatened him with a Protestant re-run of the Jacobite rebellions. "I told him that the encouragement given to Popery by King James the Second, was the chief reason for our antient and hereditary royal family of the House of Stuart being forced and banished from the Throne of these

---

[60] Lord George Gordon, *Innocence Vindicated and the Intrigues of Popery and its Abettors Displayed*, 2nd ed. (London, 1783), I, 7–8.
[61] Ibid., I, 9.
[62] See McCalman, "Mad Lord George," 343–67.
[63] Ibid., II, 20.
[64] Ibid., I, 8.

kingdoms."⁶⁵ You Hanoverians were brought over only "to defend and promote the Protestant interest"; therefore, you should not be countenancing "the same dangerous system" as the exiled Stuarts. "For his Majesty's honour and security in the present distracted state of these kingdoms and colonies," he should clear away "all the suspicions of Popery from his government." Oddly, Gordon seemed to cling to the hope that his parents' desertion of the Jacobite cause would be justified by the "right action" of the Hanoverian protectors of British Protestantism. However, he had already quarreled with his brothers for their toadying before the war-making Ministry. The stubbornness of George III—and his personal determination to crush the rebellion in America—eventually led to Gordon's disgust with all kings. If Britain could not have its legitimate Stuart heir and his Protestant replacement proved to be absolutist and "Papist," then Britain should have no king.

In the meantime, the Protestant Association had amassed over 120,000 signatures to their petition for repeal of the Catholic Bill. Encouraged by the Lord Mayor and Aldermen of the City of London, who despised the Ministry, Gordon advertised in the papers for tens of thousands of sympathizers to gather at St. George's Field in Lambeth to prepare for a mass march to Parliament. The Association "would consider the most prudent and respectful manner" of presenting their petition, would organize the people into four divisions "for the sake of good order and regularity," and would request the attendance of City magistrates so "that their presence may overawe and control any riotous or evil-minded persons who may wish to disturb the legal and peaceable deportment of His Majesty's Protestant subjects."⁶⁶ These cautionary words, published in the *Public Advertiser*, would eventually help save Gordon from execution.

On 2 June 1780, a great sea of people—wearing blue cockades on their hats—marched in orderly fashion across the Thames bridges towards the seat of government. Led by Gordon, dressed defiantly in Scottish plaid, and by Scottish drummers and bagpipers, the crowd seemed to embody Gordon's threatened re-run of the Jacobite rebellions—this time in purely Protestant form. When the House refused to consider the petition, Gordon informed the crowds, whose ranks

⁶⁵ Ibid., II, 15–16.
⁶⁶ J. Paul DeCastro, *The Gordon Riots* (Oxford, 1926), 25–26.

were being swelled by ruffians, criminals, and drunks. On the morning of 6 June, an inflammatory handbill entitled "England in Blood"
was circulated, which urged the populace to unite "as One Man"
to defend their religious and civil libertie.[67] As Erdman argues, the
young artist William Blake united "as One Man" with the crowd
that burned Newgate Prison and later paid tribute to the Gordon
rioters in his sketch, "Albion rose from where he laboured at the
Mill with Slaves."[68]

By 7 June, reports reached the king that *agents provocateurs* from
France and America were directing the mobs and that the next targets were the National Bank, Stock Exchange, and Arsenal at
Woolwich. Thus, thousands of troops were ordered into the city and
a virtual state of martial law was imposed. According to Thomas
Holcroft, an officer in the service of the American Congress revealed
the revolutionary design of the riots:

> ... the Congress had much difficulty to persuade the Americans to
> continue the war another year, and that they were at last only pre-
> vailed upon, in consequence of being assured that the Cities of London
> and Westminster would be burnt and destroyed this summer ... Gov-
> ernment is of the opinion that something besides Religion has been the
> occasion of the Disturbances.[69]

Adding to the government's alarm was the fact that most of the
troops fraternised with the protestors and shared their abhorrence
of "Papist" moves against the American rebels. Infuriated, George
III ordered severe measures and at least some of the troops obeyed
orders to fire into the mobs, shooting over 700 and hanging a few
more from lampposts.

On 9 June 1780 Gordon was arrested and, guarded by the largest
military force ever accorded a state prisoner, he was taken to the
Tower. Huge crowds cheered their hero in route. Horace Walpole
reported that "it was much apprehended that there would be a rising in Scotland," especially as a handbill circulated charging that
George III was a Roman Catholic and should therefore lose his
head: "Down with them that is! Lord George Gordon for ever. Tho'

---

[67] Hibbert, *King Mob*, 195.
[68] David Erdman, *Blake: Prophet Against Empire*, 3rd. rev. ed. (Princeton, 1977), 10.
[69] William Vincent [Thomas Holcroft], *A Plain and Succinct Narrative of the Late Riots*, 3rd. rev. ed. (London, 1780), "Appendix," 59.

he is in the Tower he will make them Rue for a Army of Scottish is coming 100,000 men in Arms, for George will lose his Crown."[70] Samuel Johnson, still a Jacobite at heart, sympathized with Gordon and recognized the government's fears of a Jacobite-style rebellion. As Johnson wrote Mrs. Thrale, "We frighten one another with 70,000 Scots to come hither with the Dukes of Gordon and Argyll, and eat us, and hang us or drown us."[71]

Provocatively, Gordon's secretary Dr. Watson wished Gordon had gone even further into outright treason, for he regarded the "terrible June 7 as a disappointingly abortive Day of Judgment."[72] In fact, it is possible that Watson was indeed an agent of the American revolutionaries who vowed to send London up in flames. Given his later career as a clandestine organizer of armed revolutionary action and naval mutinies, it seems likely that Watson deliberately exploited Gordon's popularity to plan a much more serious assault on the government than Gordon himself envisioned. As Watson remembered,

> For many days a dreadful vengeance threatened the guilty city . . . and a certain *Great Personage* [George III] is said to have prepared for quitting England. Lord George was carried in triumph by the multitude, and nothing presented itself to the astounded spectator but devouring flames. It is certain that *he* [Gordon], who afterwards dragged a painful existence, in a loathesome jail, might have then overturned the government, and founded a constitution agreeable to the wills and true interest of the people—100,000 men were ready to execute his orders, and ministers trembled for their personal safety. The unprincipled lawless *banditti* who commenced the riots, were miscreants set on foot by French agents, for at that time, France was governed by a perfidious *king*. Lord George was an enemy to plunder and devastation, he was shocked with the violence of their proceedings; and those excesses which government afterwards laid to his charge, undoubtedly saved them from destruction; for the timorous and those unaccustomed to revolutionary movements withdrew, whilst administration had time to recover from their panic, and to rally their desponding forces.[73]

In fact, Gordon was so distressed at the violence—especially the attacks on Irish workingmen—that he sought an audience with the King to offer his help in calming the rioters. But George III refused, citing his doubts about Gordon's "loyalty."

---

[70] Hibbert, *King Mob*, 195.
[71] Ibid., 195.
[72] Colson, *Gordon*, 107.
[73] Watson, *Gordon*, 22.

Interestingly, the government suspected that American agents then in London—such as William Bailston, who helped organize the Boston Tea Party—had cooperated with Benjamin Franklin in Paris to manipulate the rioters. And, in fact, Bailston would frequently visit Gordon in the Tower.[74] Watson himself probably knew of the lead role that the St. Andrews Lodge, an outgrowth of Jacobite Masonry, played in the Tea Party, and that Franklin utilized Masonic networks to further his diplomatic agenda.[75] Though some of the rioters had targeted the house of Lord Petre, still a leader of "Modern" Masonry, and Freemasons Hall itself, the Masons in general were suspected of complicity in the disorders. Certainly, many of the "Ancients" were involved—just as they had been in the anti-war Wilkes Riots of 1774.[76] The mob violence of 1780 intensified the political polarization within Freemasonry; over the next two decades, supporters of the government labored to control the "Moderns" and suppress the "Ancients." Frome Wilkinson claimed that this repressive policy put a severe check on "these benevolent combinations": "Records were destroyed, and the most vigilant secresy obtained."[77]

While Gordon was imprisoned in the Tower for eight months, he expanded his campaign against "Papist" autocracy to foreign rulers. Probably aware that a disaffected Russian nobleman had participated in the London riots, Gordon wrote on 29 August 1780 to Baron Grimm, agent of Catherine the Great, to lambaste the Empress (head of the Greek Orthodox Church) for committing the "abomination" of attending a Latin mass.[78] The Empress responded by exiling the nobleman to Siberia, for she considered him a violent revolutionary in contact with radical Masonic groups.[79] Watson would later proclaim that the Empress "little knew that a grand fraternal union is

---

[74] Hibbert, *King Mob*, 132.

[75] Fay, *Revolution*, 239–40.

[76] For charges and counter-charges about Masonic complicity, see Jacob Bronowski, *William Blake and the Age of Revolution*, rev. ed. (London, 1972), 23; J. Frome Wilkinson, *Mutual Thrift* (London, 1891), 12–16; George Smith, *The Use and Abuse of Freemasonry* (London, 1783), 249.

[77] Wilkinson, *Mutual*, 25.

[78] Jacques Grot, ed., *Lettres de Grimm à l'Imperatrice Catherine II*. Sbornik Imperatorskago Russago Istoricheskago Obschestva. 2nd rev. ed., 44 (1885), 87.

[79] The Empress had just driven out of Russia the Masonic leader Cagliostro, who would later collaborate with Gordon. See Constantin Photiades, *Les Vies du Comte de Cagliostro* (Paris, 1932), 176–81.

already formed, which will eventually hurl her from her throne, and emancipate the world from bondage."[80]

From the Tower, Gordon continued to issue his inverted "Jacobite" threats to the British royal family. On 8 September he published a letter in the *General Evening Post*, revealing that he had urged the Hanoverian Prince of Wales and Lord Southampton to support the Protestant Association. Southampton had treated Gordon with great civilities in Paris and London; moreover, they both shared Stuart blood:

> We NOBLEMEN, whose ancient families have been so closely related, allied, and attached to the Royal House of *Stuart* in former times of dangerous politicks, have the discerning eyes of the true Protestant people throughout Europe, and America, most steadily fixed upon US at this present moment: Therefore, OUR advice and conduct (as faithful friends to the House of Hanover, being Protestants) ought to be exemplarily decided in support of Reformation and Revolution principles.

As the trial approached, Gordon was lucky to get the counsel of Thomas Erskine, a young lawyer who was not only his cousin but a member of a distinguished Masonic family.[81] Thomas's brother Henry Erskine was serving as Master of the Lodge Canongate-Kilwinning at Edinburgh in 1780. His other brother David, Earl of Buchan, was Watson's mentor; he would serve as Scottish Grand Master ("Ancients") in 1782–84.

In Thomas Erskine's brilliant defense of Gordon, he did not hesitate to use the inverted Jacobite ploy, as he reminded the Court that George III owed his crown to the "wise" acts that restricted Catholic rights.[82] By implication, the Catholic Relief Bill denied George III his legitimacy. Huge crowds waited outside the courtroom, waiting for the verdict. As Watson boasted, "The politics of both hemispheres depended on his acquittal."[83] When the jury brought in the verdict of "Not Guilty," the exhausted Erskine fainted; the

---

[80] Watson, *Gordon*, 129.

[81] Like his brothers, Thomas Erskine was probably already a Mason; his name appears with those of George Gordon and Robert Watson in the "Grand Master's Lodge Record" for 1788 (in Grand Lodge Library, London). See also Denslow, *Ten Thousand*, II, 25; Lindsay, *Holyrood*, I, 237; II, 611.

[82] *Mr. Erskine's Speech, at the Trial of Lord George Gordon, in the Court of King's Bench, on Monday, February 5, 1781* (London, 1781), 84.

[83] Watson, *Gordon*, 24.

crowds carried Gordon in triumph and celebrations erupted all over Britain. The government, though disappointed, considered Gordon a broken man, just as "that Devil Wilkes" had become "an exhausted volcano" after the Wilkes Riots. Moreover, the subdued Gordon seemed ready to withdraw from public life and to devote himself to his voluminous international correspondence and to religious study.

Gordon now abandoned his bold plaid trousers and dressed in Puritanical black, while he invited groups of Quakers to hold meetings in his house. Like Gordon, many Quakers had moved into political radicalism from their earlier involvement in Jacobite and Masonic affairs.[84] However, though Gordon admired the Quakers' simple lifestyle and opposition to the slave trade, he could not accept their passivity in the face of arbitrary power. Gordon seemed to need stronger religious meat—and a religion that was not contrary to his radical political opinions. Though he agreed to run for Parliament in summer 1781—and had 4,000 voters ready to work for him— Gordon withdrew from the race. From this point on, Gordon's life became so shrouded in mystery that it still baffles scholars.

Percy Colson and Cecil Roth, his most thorough biographers, claim that after his acquittal Gordon became involved with Dr. Samuel Jacob Falk, a Sabbatian Cabalist and radical Freemason, who influenced his conversion to Judaism.[85] As we shall see, Gordon's increasing interest in Judaism was already evident when he was in the Tower, but his daring decision to convert was probably stimulated by the charismatic Dr. Falk. In order to comprehend the appeal of the Jewish magician to a Scottish radical like Gordon, it will be necessary to briefly trace Falk's strange career.

A native of Poland, Falk moved to London circa 1740, where he acted as a *Baal Shem*, master of the Cabalistic names of God, and expert in the transmutation of metals.[86] Falk was associated with an extremely secretively French-Jacobite lodge in London, where he

---

[84] See David Stevenson, *The Origins of Freemasonry: Scotland's Century, 1590–1710* (Cambridge, 1988), 203–04; Vincent Buranelli, *The King and the Quaker: a Study of William Penn and James II* (University of Pennsylvania Press, 1962).

[85] Colson, *Gordon*, 169–72. Professor Roth was an anonymous co-author with Colson and wrote the section on Falk and Cagliostro. Roth's widow Irene claims to be the great great grand-daughter of Dr. Falk, and the Roths collected many documents about Falk and Gordon. I am grateful to Irene Roth for her assistance in my research.

[86] According to the Count of Rantzow, Falk arrived in London circa 1740 (not

infused Cabalistic theosophy into their rituals. As a secret disciple of
Sabbatai Zevi, the seventeenth-century "false messiah," Falk was willing to pose as a Christian sympathizer in order to recruit Christian
occultists to his instruction. I have described elsewhere Falk's relationship with Emanuel Swedenborg, Theodore von Neuhof, Simon
van Geldern, and various Freemasons who would later move in
Blake's circle.[87]

Supported by wealthy Jewish banking families—the Boases in
Holland and the Goldsmids in England, who were also Masons—
Falk sought political as well as magical influence in the affairs of
Europe.[88] He maintained contact with occultist Masons in Poland,
who included families related to Gordon (especially the Czartoriskys
and Lubomirskis).[89] In 1773 Prince Adam Czartorisky, leader of
Polish Masonry, sought Falk's assistance in his campaign to reclaim
the Polish throne from Stanislaus Poniatowski, who was now dom-
inated by the Russian Empress.[90] Czartorisky was intrigued by the
role that Cabalism and Masonry could play in Judaeo-Christian col-
laboration, which was crucial to the Polish nationalist struggle. It is
unknown whether Czartorisky also called on Gordon, who was kinned
to him and always interested in Polish affairs. After his London mission to Falk, Czartorisky visited the *Écossais* lodge of the Duke of
Chartres in Paris.[91]

It was probably Czartorisky who informed Chartres, Grand Master
of the Grand Orient system of Freemasonry, about Falk's magical
and political powers. In late 1776 or early 1777, Chartres travelled

1742 as usually claimed); see his *Mémoires de Comte de Rantzow* (Amsterdam, 1741),
I, 201–17.

[87] Marsha Keith Schuchard, "Yeats and the Unknown Superiors: Swedenborg,
Falk, and Cagliostro," in *Secret Texts: The Literature of Secret Societies*, ed. Marie Roberts
and Hugh Ormsby-Lennon (New York, 1995), 114–68, and "Dr. Samuel Jacob
Falk," 203–26.

[88] Several Boases appear in registers at Grand Lodge Library, The Hague. In
Register of the Grand Lodge, London, "New Castle Lodge of Harmony #26,"
appear the names of Abraham and Benjamin Goldsmid of Leman St., Goodman's
Fields, initiated in January 1777.

[89] Jacob Schatsky, *The History of the Jews in Warsaw* [Yiddish] (New York: Yiddish
Scientific Institute, 1947–53), 88–89; *Gay Gordons*, 53.

[90] Solomon Schecter, "The 'Baalshem'—Dr. Falk," *Jewish Chronicle* (9 March 1888),
15–16; M. Kukiel, *Czartorisky and European Unity (1770–1861)* (Princeton, 1955).

[91] Amedée Britsch, *La maison d'Orleans à la fin de la Ancien Régime* (Paris, 1926),
239.

to London to solicit Falk's support for his political agenda.[92] The *Baal Shem* consecrated a talismanic ring of lapis lazuli, whose Cabalistic inscription guaranteed that the Duke would mount the French throne. In 1777 Falk also instructed a Sicilian adventurer, Joseph Balsamo, who came to London to learn the secret rituals of the "Egyptian Rite," an amalgam of Swedenborgian theosophy and Cabalistic magic.[93] Balsamo was allegedly a Marrano, a crypto-Jew, who was attracted to Falk's antinomian Sabbatianism.

Balsamo drew on Falk's contacts in the schismatic "Antiquity" lodge, established by the Scottish Mason William Preston, a former Jacobite.[94] When Falk visited the lodge, he listed himself as a member of the lodge "Observance of Heredom, Scotland."

One member of the lodge, General Charles Rainsford, later explained that the Mount of Heredom featured in the *Écossais* degrees, was not an actual mountain in Scotland but a Cabalistic symbol for the *Mons Domini* or *Malchuth*:

> The word "Heridon" is famous in several degrees of Masonry, that is to say in some invented degrees . . . Apparently, the enlightened brethren who have judged it proper to make the law, that Jews should be admitted to the Society have received the word with the secrets (*mystères*) which have been entrusted to them.[95]

Rainsford would later be considered an expert on the contributions made by Swedenborg and Falk to Cabalistic Freemasonry.[96]

In 1777 Balsamo assumed the name "Count Cagliostro" and the role of "Emissary of the Grand Cophta," whose identity as Falk would be revealed only to elite adepts. He left London and carried the "Egyptian Rite" to *Écossais* lodges in Holland, Germany, Russia,

---

[92] Herman Adler, "The Baal Shem of London," *Transactions of the Jewish Historical Society of England* (1908), 155; Elkan Adler, ed., *Jewish Travellers* (London, 1930), 357–59.

[93] On Cagliostro's career, see Constantin Photiades, *Count Cagliostro*, trans. K. Shelvankar (London: Rider, 1932). The original French edition contains more thorough documentation.

[94] William Wonnacott, "The Rite of Seven Degrees in London," *Ars Quatuor Coronatorum*, 39 (1926), 63–98. Also documents in London Grand Lodge, Wonnacott Files: "Falck, John Christian" (marginalia identifies him as the *Baal Shem*); MS. Minute Book of Lodge St. George de l'Observance, 1777–79.

[95] Gordon P. Hills, "Notes on Some Contemporary References to Dr. Falk, the Baal-Shem of London, in the Rainsford Papers in the British Museum," *Transactions of the Jewish Historical Society of England* (1918), 98.

[96] Gordon P. Hills, "Notes on the Rainsford Papers in the British Museum," *Ars Quatuor Coronatorum*, 26 (1913), 93–129.

and Poland. In Russia, the Empress Catherine became alarmed at Cagliostro's Masonic intrigues and expelled him in March 1780. In response to Baron Grimm's report on Cagliostro's subsequent Cabalistic exploits, Catherine wrote a revealing letter on 9 July 1781:

> M. Cagliostro ... est arrivé dans un moment tres favorable pour lui, dans un moment ou plusieurs loges de francs-maçons, engouées des principes de Swedenborg, voulaient a toute force voir des esprits; ils ont donc couru a Cagliostro, qui se disait en possession de tous les secrets du docteur Falk.[97]

As part of her campaign to crush "illuminist" Freemasonry, she later lampooned Falk and Cagliostro in the character of "Kalifalkerston" in her satirical comedy *The Deceiver* (1786).[98] Cagliostro was initially more successful with her puppet in Poland, King Stanislaus Poniatowski, who viewed his Cabalistic demonstrations, but the Empress soon brought Poniatowski to heel as she paid agents to infiltrate Polish Masonry.[99] The Czartorisky family, earlier seekers of Falk's magical powers, continued to lead the nationalist Polish Masons in their struggle for independence from Russian domination.

After contacting members of the politicallly radical "Illuminati" in Germany and Austria, Cagliostro settled in Strasbourg, where he was patronized by Cardinal Rohan and many wealthy Masons. In November 1780 Cagliostro boasted to Rodolphe Saltzmann of his previous Masonic connection in London with Swedenborg and Falk. As Saltzmann reported to a fellow Mason:

> Il [Cagliostro] dit beaucoup de bien de Svedenborg et le plaint d'avoir été persecuté. En vain les Suèdois veulent à present quasi resusciter sa cendre, ils ne découvriront rien. Le plus grand homme en Europe, c'est la célèbre Falke à Londres. C'est dans cette capitale qu'il y à 5 ou 6 maçons qui ont des connaissances, mais la clef leur manque. Il me dit encore qu'en operant il faut des cercles des mots—quatre circles—et des hieroglyphes. Il m'a paru pencher vers le Judaisme; ce n'est cependant qu'une hypothèse que je ne donne pas pour vraie.[100]

---

[97] Grot, *Lettres de Grimm*, 212–13.

[98] Wilfrid-René Chettoui, *Cagliostro et Catherine II: la satire impériale contre le Mage* (Paris, 1947), 51–54.

[99] B. Ivanoff, "Cagliostro in Eastern Europe," *Ars Quatuor Coronatorum*, 11 (1927), 66–70.

[100] London, Wellcome Institute: MS. 1047. Dr. E. Lalande's transcript of letter from Saltzmann to Willermoz (7 November 1780).

Saltzmann also revealed that Cagliostro planned to journey to Paris to initiate the Duke of Chartres into the Egyptian Rite.

In late 1781, Savalette de Langes—royal treasurer in Paris and head of the *Philaléthes* lodge of occult research—described Dr. Falk to his Masonic agent:

> Dr. Falc, in England. This Dr. Falc is known to many Germans. From every point of view he is a most extraordinary man. Some believe him to be the chief of all the Jews, and attribute all that is marvelous and strange in his conduct and in his life to schemes which are entirely political . . . He is practically inaccessible. In all the sects of Adepts in the Occult Sciences, he passes as a man of higher attainments. He is at present in England.[101]

The *Philaléthes* expected to learn more about Falk from General Charles Rainsford, who collaborated with him in Masonic affairs.

At this time, Falk was working in an intensely secretive effort to develop a Jewish-Christian Masonic order, which became known as the "Asiatic Brethren."[102] Drawing on the antinomian rationale of the Sabbatians, Falk and his Jewish disciples pretended a sympathy for Christianity while carrying out an essentially Zionist political agenda.[103] As Scholem observes, the radical Sabbatians called for a reversal of religious and political norms that led some daring adepts into revolutionary action.[104] While trying to maintain a difficult balance between liberal Christianity and Cabalistic Judaism, the "Asiatic Brethren" increasingly occupied a "no man's land" between two extreme tendencies of rationalism and mysticism.[105]

Given this context of clandestine Masonic and political intrigue in 1778–82, it becomes possible to place Gordon in situations where he may have met Falk. First of all, during the petition drive for the Protestant Association, Gordon spent much time in Whitechapel, center of London's Jewish community.

James Fisher, the secretary of the Protestant Association who invited Gordon to serve as president, lived in Whitechapel, in close

---

[101] J.E.S. Tuckett, "Savalette de Langes, Les Philaletes, and the Council of Wilhelmsbad, 1782," *Ars Quatuor Coronatorum*, 30 (1917), 153–54.

[102] Gershom Scholem, *Du Frankisme au Jacobinisme* (Paris, 1981), 39.

[103] Michal Oron, "Dr. Samuel Falk and the Eibeschuetz-Emden Controversy," in *Mysticism, Magic, and Kabbalah in Ashkenazi Judaism*, ed. Karl Grözinger and Joseph Dan (Berlin, 1995), 243–56.

[104] Gershom Scholem, *Kabbalah* (New York, 1974), 277–309.

[105] Scholem, *Du Frankisme*, 27–28.

proximity to Falk's house in Wellclose Square. Gordon often attended meetings at Fisher's house, and many of the signatures were collected in the area.[106] At least one Jew, Samuel Solomons, joined the Gordon protesters, and he would later display a dignified courage before his execution.[107]

As a sign of his growing wealth and prestige, Falk had built a tabernacle in the center of Wellclose Square and maintained a synagogue in his mansion. By 1780 he was an internationally famous figure, whose long white robes, elaborate turban, and flowing white beard were almost a tourist attraction. Falk's portrait reveals his charismatic appearance and his Masonic role, as he holds a Masonic compass over a Cabalistic amulet.[108] Archenholz, a German Mason who visited London in 1780–81, described Falk as "a noble and interesting figure," who was an able chemist; he lived soberly and gave generously to the poor.[109] It was an image that would have appealed to Gordon.

While in the Tower, Gordon demonstrated his increasing interest in Jewish traditions. When the Methodist leader John Wesley visited him, he found Gordon studying the Hebrew scriptures and preoccupied with religious questions.[110] The blue-stocking Hannah More also reported Gordon's preoccupation with the Hebrew prophets: "I heard from a person who attended the trial of Lord George Gordon, that the noble prisoner (as the papers call him) had a quarto Bible open before him all the time, and was very angry because he was not permitted to read four chapters of Zecharia."[111] More then repeated the rumors that Gordon was a sensualist who unashamedly consorted with whores. For a time, Gordon attended the sermons of the Methodist "revivalist" Martin Madan, who advocated the legalization of polygamy and concubinage as a solution to problems of

---

[106] De Castro, *Gordon Riots*, 16.

[107] Colson, *Gordon*, 103–04.

[108] Cecil Roth attributed the portrait to John Singleton Copley, but the art historian Stephen Lloyd (Scottish National Portrait Gallery), who examined it with Mrs. Roth's permission, suggests that it was painted by Phillipe Jacques de Loutherbourg.

[109] J.W. de Archenholz, *A Picture of England*, new trans. (London, 1797), 177–78.

[110] John Wesley, *The Works of John Wesley* (Grand Rapids, 1958), IV, 194–95.

[111] Hannah More, *Memoirs of the Life and Correspondence of Mrs. Hannah More*, ed. William Roberts (New York, 1837), I, 118.

adultery, prostitution, and abortion.[112] Arguing that the Hebrew scriptures and Mosaic law provided the basis of all truth, Madan referred to conversations with Jewish friends who convinced him that the Jews were more compassionate and wise about sexual desires and problems than were the Christians.

Charges also circulated that Gordon indulged himself in the "Celestial Bed," designed by his Scottish friend Dr. James Graham, which infused the body with electric and magnetic currents in order to increase potency and fertility.[113] A radical Freemason, Dr. Graham believed that "scientifically" increased sexual vigor would serve the revolutionary cause. The fact that the Jewish religion—especially in its Cabalistic and Sabbatian form—did not separate sexuality from spirituality may have strengthened its appeal to Gordon. Like Watson, he admired the writing of the radical Covenanter Samuel Rutherford who portrayed Scotland's marriage to the God of Israel in "startlingly sexual imagery"—the Jewish church will join the Protestant church in Jesus's bed of love and suck each other's breasts.[114] From Dr. Falk's diary and reports on his Sabbatian brethren, it seems that rituals of sexual magic were practised by some members of the sect.[115]

While he was in the Tower, Gordon was guarded by Colonel Rainsford, a kinsman of General Charles Rainsford, the Masonic colleague of Falk. According to Watson, "A gentleman in the tower, whom it is not safe to name, offered him his service, and was the faithful bearer of his correspondence."[116] Thus, it is possible that Gordon made contact with Falk through the Rainsfords. At this time, according to Archenholz, Gordon had supporters in the Jewish

---

[112] McCalman, "Mad Lord George," 358–59; Martin Madan, *Thelyphthora* (London, 1780–81), II, 335–36; III, 279, 352, 273–78.

[113] J.S. Barwell, "The Ingenious Dr. Graham," *The Saturday Book*, ed. John Hadfield, XVI (1956), 174.

[114] Arthur Williamson, "The Jewish Dimension of the Scottish Apocalypse," in *Menasseh ben Israel and His World*, eds. Y. Kaplan, H. Méchoulan, and R. Popkin (Leiden, 1989), 159–60.

[115] Michal Oron, *Samuel Jacob Falk, the Baal Shem of London* [Hebrew] (Jerusalem, 2002). For Falk's dream description of a phallic ritual, see her article "Dr. Samuel Jacob Falk," 243–56. For the masturbation rituals practiced by some radical Sabbatians, see Elijah J. Schochet, *The Hasidic Movement and the Gaon of Vilna* (London, 1994), 44–48.

[116] Watson, *Gordon*, 23.

community. After visiting Masonic lodges and the Jewish neighbor-hood around Wellclose Square, Archenholz attended the trial of Gordon, where he was "a witness of a very singular scene between him [Gordon] and a German Jew who appeared at his bar in rags."[117] With "great effrontery," the Jew offered himself as a security for £300 pounds. Archenholz guessed that "some rich Jews present prob-ably slipped the bills to him," for the German Jew actually had the cash. It is certainly possible that Falk sent some of his banking friends to offer bail for Gordon, who would later call upon those bankers to support his scheme for financial pacifism. Among Gordon's loyal Quaker friends was Dr. John Coakley Lettsom, who was also inti-mate with the Goldsmid brothers, the powerful bankers who were patrons of Dr. Falk.[118]

Some months after Gordon's release from the Tower, a strange pamphlet appeared, entitled *The Fourth Book of the Chronicles, or the Second Book of Gordon, to which are added the Chapters of Donellan, etc., originally written in Arabic by an Oriental Sage in the Time of the Jewish Captivity* (London: printed for the translator by J. Wade, 1781). The book related in Scriptural style the trial of Gordon and included his portrait by J. Lodge.[119] The peculiar reference to an Oriental sage who wrote in Arabic may have applied to Dr. Falk and/or his emis-sary Cagliostro, who was currently uttering pseudo-Arabic conjura-tions in the Egyptian lodges in France.[120] In fact, Gordon's unexplained reason for traveling to Paris in late 1782 may have been linked to the Masonic endeavours of Falk and Cagliostro.[121] According to Moses Margoliouth, a nineteenth-century historian of Anglo-Judaica and Freemasonry, Gordon secretly converted to Judaism *before* leaving for Paris.[122]

Margoliouth possessed a Hebrew manuscript letter written by Meyer Joseph, who claimed that as a young man he acted as Gordon's preceptor in Judaism—before the 1782 visit to Paris. Meyer or Michael Joseph was the Anglicized name of Meyer Königsberger

---

[117] Archenholz, *Picture*, 271–72.
[118] J.J. Abraham, *Lettsom: His Life, Times, Friends, and Descendants* (London, 1933), 251, 445.
[119] Ibid., 423.
[120] Ivanoff, "Cagliostro," 45–80.
[121] Colson, *Gordon*, 171–72, 184.
[122] Moses Margoliouth, *The History of the Jews of Great Britain* (London, 1851), II, 122–24.

a Hebrew poet who came to London from Germany in 1780.[123] It
is possible that Joseph was sent to London by Cagliostro, who had
visited the Masonic lodges in Königsberg in February 1779.[124] The
new immigrant evidently met Dr. Falk, whom he later praised as a
"pious and benevolent" benefactor of the Great Synagogue.[125] Thus,
Joseph may have been the German Jew, in rags, who offered himself as security for Gordon's bond. According to Joseph, Gordon visited and read publicly in the synagogue; he was "pretty well tutored
in Jewish rites and customs, and was able to read Hebrew with some
degree of fluency."[126] If Gordon studied under Falk, the secresy of
his conversion would have been in keeping with Sabbatian beliefs.[127]
In a correspondence that is now lost, Gordon applied to Rabbi
Tevele Schiff, of Duke's Place Synagogue, and asked to be received
into the Jewish fold. Schiff received his appointment through Falk's
assistance and remained his patron and protector.[128] Unfortunately,
the date of Gordon's overture is unknown, as are Schiff's reasons
for rejecting his request.

During the months before he went to Paris, Gordon demonstrated
unusual knowledge and concern about Jewish political affairs on the
Continent. On 14 March 1782 he wrote to Joseph II, "Emperor of
Germany and King of the Romans," to condemn his "ordinance
against the Jews" and to recommend changes in it.[129] Though Gordon's
letter is lost, he apparently pointed out the shortcomings in Joseph
II's "Edict of Toleration" which, as Venturi points out, "rather more

---

[123] Israel Solomons, "Lord George Gordon's Conversion to Judaism," *Transactions
of the Jewish Historical Society of England*, Sessions 1911–1914 (London, 1715), 238.

[124] Constantin Photiades, *Count Cagliostro*, trans. K.S. Shelvankar (London, 1932),
101–02. The original French edition contains more thorough documentation.

[125] [Michael Joseph], *Laws of the Congregation of the Great Synagogue, Duke's Place,
London* (London, 1827), viii.

[126] Margoliouth, *History*, II, 122.

[127] According to the late Gedalia Yogev, the Prager Papers in the Public Record
Office shed light on Gordon's conversion. Because the Jewish bankers featured in
the papers include Falk's friends, Yogev's statement is intriguing. Unfortunately,
when I attempted to examine the collection in the P.R.O., they began to crumble
and were removed for conservation, which will allegedly take many years. For
Yogev's reference, see his *Diamonds and Coral: Anglo-Dutch Jews and Eighteenth-Century
Trade* (Leicester, 1978), 186.

[128] Solomons, "Gordon's Conversion," 241; Cecil Roth, "Lord George Gordon's
Conversion to Judaism," *Essays and Portraits in Anglo-Jewish History* (Philadelphia, 1962),
187–210.

[129] Solomons, "Gordon's Conversion," 229–30.

posed than resolved the Jewish question in his empire."[130] Gordon, who was accurate in recognizing the Edict's deficiencies, may have been prompted by Falk, whose fellow Masons in the "Asiatic Brethren" were struggling to find their way in Austria.[131] The Emperor Joseph was a rationalist Mason, and he was sympathetic to the messianic Cabalist Jacob Frank, who with his disciples had converted to Catholicism. However, Joseph was not aware that the Frankists secretly maintained their Sabbatian beliefs and maintained contacts with Dr. Falk and other clandestine members of the sect. As Falk may have informed Gordon, the Emperor did not approve of "les confréries esoteriques du type de la Stricte Observance ou des Fréres Asiatiques."[132]

Whatever projects Gordon may have undertaken with Falk were aborted one month later, for on 17 April 1782 the "Grand Cophta" unexpectedly died. General Rainsford, who shared in Falk's ambitions for the "Asiatic Brethren," wrote to a *frère* in Paris about their Masonic project:

> As to the Kabbala, all is upset by the unexpected death of Dr. Falk . . . up to now I have found nothing certain relating to that famous Rabbi, whether he is genuine or a knave . . . Believe me, I have found news about that Jew, among the Jews of Algiers and they have told me some extraordinary stories about him, even so far as to attribute their success against the Spaniards to him—*voila*! I don't know his real origin . . . I have found some rather curious MSS. at Algiers in Hebrew relating to the Society of *Rosicrucians*, which exists at present under another name with the same forms. I hope, moreover, to be admitted to their true knowledge . . .[133]

Gordon may have learned of Falk's claims to revolutionary powers—whether in the Jewish resistance to Spanish aggression in Algiers

---

[130] Franco Venturi, *The End of the Old Regime in Europe, 1776–1789*, trans. R.B. Litchfield (Princeton University Press, 1991), 646.

[131] Jacob Katz, *Jews and Freemasons in Europe, 1723–1939*, trans. L. Oschry (Harvard University Press, 1970), 26–53; Arthur Mandel, *The Militant Messiah* (Atlantic Highlands: Humanities Press, 1979), 94–95; Denyse Dalbian, *Le Comte de Cagliostro* (Paris, 1983), 162.

[132] Scholem, *Du frankisme*, 27, 37. The "Strict Observance" had developed out of Jacobite Masonic rites, and many members still considered the Young Pretender to be their Grand Master.

[133] Hills, "Notes on Some Contemporary References to Dr. Falk," 125.

or in the Polish nationalists' resistance to Russian aggression. After all, Prince Adam Czartorisky, who sought Falk's Cabalistic assistance and who was called a "half-Sabbatian," and Prince Marius Lubomirsky, who converted to Judaism and married a Sabbatian, were also kinned to Gordon. As members of French-affiliated *Écossais* lodges, these Polish Freemasons had benefited from the infusion of Cabalistic mysticism into the higher Scottish degrees.

On 13 May 1782 Gordon revealed his immersion in Jewish and Covenanting fantasies, when he crashed a secret meeting of Scottish noblemen and gentlemen at St. Albans Tavern, London.[134] Of the 100 attendees, nearly all can be identified as Masons, whom the government was wooing with places and pensions. Gordon repeated his boasts of Stuart ancestry and aristocratic foreign kinsmen (i.e., Polish). He then argued that any militia raised in Scotland must be limited to Presbyterians. He harangued the shocked assembly with quotes from the Hebrew scriptures and National Covenant, which declared Scotland's uniquely Jewish relation to God. As Williamson observes, in the inflamed minds of the Covenanters, "Scots and Jews had indeed become brethren in the world created within the revolutionary northern realm."[135] When Gordon demanded that the attendees defend "the true Church of Jehovah" in order to receive the "countenance and blessings of the God of Israel," a "great uproar arose in the Assembly . . . and the Cry was, Order! Order! Order!."[136]

Having alarmed his more conservative countrymen with his allusions to "these rebellious times," Gordon hoped to find support in France. He must have kept his plans secret, for almost nothing is known of Gordon's visit to Paris in late 1782. He claimed that he was presented to Marie-Antoinette and many aristocrats, who probably included the Duke of Chartres. Gordon would later greet Chartres as an old friend when the Duke visited London. In 1782 Chartres shared Gordon's interest in the welfare of Protestants and he hoped to brink back the Edict of Nantes, which once granted rights to

---

[134] *A Speech of Lord George Gordon's, Containing a Spirited Defense of the Antient Constitution of the Church and State of Scotland* (n.p., n.d.). This rare, 8-page pamphlet is in the National Library of Scotland.

[135] Arthur Williamson, "British Israel and Roman Britain: The Jews and Scottish Models of Polity from George Buchanan to Samuel Rutherford," in *Jewish Christians and Christian Jews*, eds. Richard Popkin and Gordon Weiner (Dordrecht: Kluwer Academic, 1994), 111.

[136] Gordon, *Speech*, 8.

French Protestants.[137] Gordon was appalled by the abuses of power
carried out by the Queen and her Court—a view shared (not so
disinterestedly) by Chartres. Perhaps Falk had advised Gordon to
contact Chartres, who not only wore the *Baal Shem*'s magical talis-
man but was now the most powerful Grand Master in Europe.
Colson and Roth believe that Gordon also met Cagliostro, for he
and the *magus* would demonstrate "an immediate and close intimacy"
in 1786 in London.[138] Provocatively, Chartres subsequently joined
Cagliostro's Egyptian Rite.

Gordon may have learned of Cagliostro's strategy of gaining the
support of powerful bankers when he began a Masonic campaign in
a town. As Cagliostro later boasted:

> As soon as I set foot in any country, I there find a banker who sup-
> plies me with everything I want; thus in France, Sarrasin of Basle or
> Mons. Sancolaz [Sancotar] at Lyons, would give me their whole for-
> tunes, were I to ask for it.[139]

According to Watson, Gordon returned from Paris "more firmly
resolved than ever to prosecute the plan of general reform."[140] Perhaps
inspired by Gordon, Cagliostro planned to re-visit London in 1783,
but he was delayed in Bordeaux by the importunities of Freemasons
who begged him to establish an Egyptian lodge.[141]

Unfortunately for the historian, in 1783 Watson entered the
University of Aberdeen, where he completed a Master of Arts degree
in March 1787.[142] He was thus unable to shed much light on Gordon's
increasing immersion in Judaism during those years. From other wit-
nesses, we learn that Gordon continued his study of Hebrew and
visited synagogues, where he discussed Jewish traditions and beliefs
with the members. In a second edition of his pamphlet *Innocence
Vindicated and the Intrigues of Popery and its Abettors Displayed*, published
in summer 1783, Gordon defended not only his actions in the Gordon
Riots but added a eulogy to the "plain, natural unaffected manners
and phrases of the Hebrews."[143] The language and morals of the

[137] Hubert La Marle, *Phillipe Égalité. "Grand Maître" de la Revolution* (Paris, 1989), 52.
[138] Colson, *Gordon*, 184.
[139] "Memoirs of Count Cagliostro," *European Magazine*, 9 (May 1787), 328.
[140] Watson, *Gordon*, 36.
[141] Dalbian, *Cagliostro*, 95.
[142] G. Bain, *Thunderbolt*, 4.
[143] Lord George Gordon, *Innocence Vindicated*, 2nd.ed. (London, 1783), II, 18.

ancient Jews are "the surest and quickest ways of moving the hearts" of those who are not perverted and hardened "through the ensnaring corruptions of deceitful Courts." Indentifying himself with Moses, he pointed out that Moses "was as high-bred a courtier as Pharaoh" and that Moses mastered the occult knowledge of the Egyptians in order to turn it against them: "He easily detected and exposed the paltry tricks and Egyptian devices of the different coalitions of sorcerers and magicians in the royal cabinet." That Falk and Cagliostro claimed to teach the true Jewish origins of the Egyptian Cabala was probably relevant to Gordon's odd statements. Gordon went on to praise the Jews' "great and religious pattern of opposition to tyranny," and he looked forward to the happy time when the Lord "shall cause them that come of Jacob to take root; Israel will blossom and bud, and fill the face of the world with fruit."

On 26 August 1783, Gordon sent a letter to Elias Lindo, Nathan Salomon, and other Jewish financiers, urging them to oppose the government's commercial negotiations with France. Larding his proposal with Hebrew phrases ("*Shemah Israel! Shemah Koli!*"), Gordon assured them that "The eyes of all Israel are upon you . . . Believe me, Israel! I am your friend."[144] He then warned them not to believe George III's "present servants" and to stand firm with the Protestants in their rightful demands in Europe and America. Elias Lindo, a wealthy merchant, was definitely a Freemason, and Nathan Salomon, lay head of the synagogue, was probably one.[145] An intimate friend of the Goldsmid brothers, Nathan Salomon greatly admired Gordon and introduced him to important Jews in the City. It was at this time that Gordon launched his remarkable scheme to convince Jewish bankers world-wide to refuse to grant credits to governments for the purpose of making war.[146] As Watson recalled,

> . . . Lord George . . . wrote a variety of papers upon finance, and distributed them amongst the Jews in England and Holland—he knew that as long as Ministers could borrow with facility, the war system would never cease; what they cannot accomplish by valour, they will attempt to achieve by gold, and his design was to shew the incapacity

---

[144] *Copy of a Letter from the Right Honourable Lord George Gordon to Elias Lindo, Esq., and the Portuguese, and Nathan Salomon, Esq., and the German Jews* (London, 1783).

[145] John Shaftesley, "Jews in English Regular Freemasonry, 1717–1860," *Transactions of the Jewish Historical Society of England*, 25 (1977), 183.

[146] Cecil Roth, *Anglo-Jewish Letters, 1158–1917* (London, 1938), 185.

of them all to pay; every government in Europe (in his opinion) being on the eve of bankruptcy.[147]

In another letter to Emperor Joseph II, Gordon claimed that by 18 September 1783, the "reproaches, insults, and injuries" inflicted on him by anti-Semitic Austrian agents in London convinced him of the insincerity of Joseph's Edict of Toleration.[148] Gordon then threw himself into the campaign of the "Patriots" in the Netherlands, who resisted the attempt of the Emperor to extend Austrian control. In November 1784, in a bizarre display of his strategy of Scottish threat and radical subversion, he marched to St James dressed in a Dutch naval uniform and carrying an immense Highland broadsword.[149] He laid the sword at the feet of the Dutch ambassador and persuaded the Dutch Guard to "rest their forelocks" and signify "their attachment to the Protestant cause."

Appealing to the discontented, unemployed sailors and soldiers who thronged to London, Gordon vowed that the Atholl Highlanders and thousands of sailors were ready to fight against Popery in Holland. It may be relevant that the Third and Fourth Dukes of Atholl had served as Grand Masters of Scotland and of the British "Ancients" system (in 1771–72 and 1775–81, respectively).[150] Moreover, the Fourth Duke had persuaded the Grand Lodge of Scotland to break off relations with the "Moderns." Thus, the appearance of the name George Gordon on the register of an "Ancients-Atholl" lodge (#225) in 1784 suggests some kind of political-Masonic maneuvering.[151]

By September 1785, rumors circulated that Gordon had secretly converted to Judaism. The lurid tabloid *Rambler's Magazine* broke the story in a wicked article entitled "The Loss of the Prepuce, or Lord George Riot Suffering a Clipping in Order to Become a Jew."[152] The journalist portrayed Gordon conversing with Mordecai, who speaks a burlesque-version of Frenchified English. When Gordon declaims, "I love the Jews, and the Emperor knows I do . . . but he seems to pay very little attention to the hints I have repeatedly given him," Mordecai replies:

---

[147] Watson, *Gordon*, 75.
[148] Solomons, "Gordon's Conversion," 229.
[149] Hibbert, *King Mob*, 157.
[150] Lindsay, *Holyrood*, 193–94; Gould, *History*, III, 196–99.
[151] Grand Lodge, London: Atholl Register F, vol. VI, f.383.
[152] *Rambler's Magazine* (September 1785), 342–43.

Vat you say be very true—he no love *les Juifs*: he be one dam bad prince. I wish your lordship was emperor—you would sett all de world to rights dans un instant. *Vous ave un tete*—you have got a head—you knows things well. I wish you was gran sovereign of *tout le Monde*, of all de vorld.

After a comical negotiation on ways of disguising pork as mutton, Gordon agrees to be circumcized. Mordecai assures him that if he "vent vidout *breeches*, as dey do in Scotland, you not have de trouble to unbutton." Then his daughter Suzannah emerges with a pair of scissors and proceeds to clip Gordon's prepuce. It was probably from this date that Gordon became known as "Lord Crop." In the accompanying engraved print, a small boy points to an open Hebrew book, while a bearded Jew dressed in slouch hat and robes, reads on the sidelines. Gordon himself would later dress in the same garb of a Polish or Hasidic rabbi—a costume that would eventually make a startling appearance in William Blake's *Jerusalem*.[153]

A few months before *Rambler's* broke the story, Gordon was in friendly relations with the Prince of Wales and his intimate friend the Duke of Chartres, now Duke of Orleans, who visited London in 1785. According to a rare Masonic pamphlet, the rebellious Prince of Wales—who despised his father George III—was secretly initiated into Freemasonry that year, probably under the aegis of the visiting Grand Master of France.[154] In summer 1785, while Orleans was at Brighton with the Prince, the latter asked Gordon to entertain Madame de Genlis, an initiate of Cagliostro's female lodge ("Isis") and collaborator in Orleans's Masonic schemes.[155] Gordon subsequently visited Scotland in winter 1785–1786, where he evoked cries of "Gordon and Liberty!" from the crowds that watched his political campaign against his family's conservative candidate.[156] Though the name George Gordon is listed as Senior Grand-Warden in the Scottish Grand Lodge in November 1785, it is not clear if he is our man.[157] Worried by these radical outbursts in Scotland, a conservative English

---

[153] See articles on "Lord George Gordon" and "William Blake," *Encyclopaedia Judaica* (Jerusalem, 1972).
[154] A.E. Hubert, *The Phoenix Lodge, #173 (1785–1909)* (London: private circulation, 1910), 1.
[155] Britsch, *Jeunesse de Orleans*, 414; Dalbian, *Cagliostro*, 134.
[156] Colson, *Gordon*, 142–43.
[157] Alexander Lawrie, *The History of Freemasonry* (Edinburgh, 1804), 235.

publisher re-issued (in 1786) James Howell's seventeenth-century claim that the Scots are descendants of the Jews and Nathaniel Crouch's sensational account of the arrival of a shipload of Sabbatian Jews in Aberdeen in 1666.[158]

When Gordon returned to London in early 1786, he followed with passionate interest the bizarre trial of the Diamond Necklace, a scandal that rocked the throne of France. Cagliostro and Cardinal Rohan, who had been arrested on orders of the French Queen, became the vehicles of the smouldering discontent throughout France. While Cagliostro was accused of being the "Wandering Jew and Anti-Christ," Rohan was accused of conspiring with the Orleanist-Masonic faction to take over the government. The case was watched nervously by the British government, for it reeked of earlier French-Jacobite-Masonic conspiracies. On 5 April 1786 the *Gentleman's Magazine* described an unholy trio who must have given George III and Prime Minister Pitt nightmares:

> The Duke de Fitz-James, grandson of the Pretender, accompanied the Duke of Orleans from Paris here ... On their arrival they went to Gray's jeweller in Bond Street, on business relative to the Cardinal Rohan, whose part they warmly espouse. His R.H. the Prince of Wales happening to be there ... invited them to dinner ... and the three Princes spent a most chearful afternoon and evening together at Carlton House.

Since Gray the jeweller had allegedly received the famous diamonds from Cagliostro's enemy Madame de La Motte, Orleans hoped to gather information from him to use against the Queen. Moreover, Orleans had recently participated in Cagliostro's Cabalistic rituals and still wore Falk's politically potent amulet. The former Jacobite Fitz-James was a devoted member of Orleans's system of *Écossais* Freemasonry.[159]

While reading of Cagliostro's bold and flamboyant protests against arbitary power, Gordon was amused to learn that he himself had been ex-communicated by the Archbishop of Canterbury on 7 April 1786. He laughingly replied, "To expel me from a society to which I never belonged is an absurdity worthy of an Archbishop."[160] On

---

[158] Howell's argument was included in R. Burton [Nathaniel Crouch], *Memorable Remarks Upon the Ancient and Modern State of the Jewish Nation* (Bolton, 1786), 48, 125–63.

[159] La Marle, *Philippe Égalité*, 20, 40, 95, 111, 508.

[160] Solomons, "Gordon's Conversion," 231.

17 May the *Public Advertiser*, which was always sympathetic to Gordon, explained the serious ramifications of the ex-communication, for Gordon could no longer serve on juries, be a witness in court, recover lands, or attend Christian services. As Gordon continued to ignore the Archbishop's summons, the newspaper reported on 13 May that he "is not yet committed to Newgate" but "imprisonment is looked for every hour."

While the *Public Advertiser* carried sympathetic accounts of Gordon and Cagliostro, it also reported on Masonic developments at home and abroad. On 29 May and 13 June 1786, the paper reported that Joseph II had suppressed all Masonic lodges in the Austrian Netherlands, while in England the flourishing lodges advertised their meetings in the free press. As journals all over Europe reported on Cagliostro's Egyptian Rite, the trial in Paris became a lurid showcase for conflicting images of Masonry. Cagliostro was acquitted by the rebellious *Parlement* in May, and huge crowds cheered him on his release from the Bastille. But the Court confiscated Cagliostro's property and then banished him from France. "Flying from slavery to freedom," Cagliostro arrived in London on 16 June. There he was taken up as a hero by the radical Freemasons in the Prince of Wales' circle, but his boldest champion was Gordon—with fateful results for both.[161] Gordon later claimed that Cagliostro sought his protection, which certainly suggests an earlier acquaintance or a mutual link through Dr. Falk.

Encouraged by Gordon, Cagliostro and his French lawyer composed an open *Lettre du peuple francais* (1786), which circulated widely despite the effort of the French government to confiscate copies.[162] Cagliostro described a Kafka-esque world in which innocent cititzens could be hauled from their beds and plunged into the dungeons of the Bastille, where they would rot for years, without even knowing the identity of their accuser or the nature of the charges against them. He warned the citizens of France that everything they cherished was vulnerable to the whimsical orders of arbitrary ministers:

---

[161] Sophie von la Roche, *Sophie in London, 1786, being the Diary of Sophie von la Roche*, trans. Claire Williams (London, 1933), 139. For the overtures of Cagliostro and Gordon to Blake's artistic and Swedenborgian colleagues, see my "William Blake and the Promiscuous Baboons: A Cagliostroan Séance Gone Awry," *British Journal for Eighteenth-Century Studies*, 18 (1995), 187–200.

[162] Louis Petit de Bachaumont, *Mémoires Secrets* (Londres: John Adamson, 1788–89), II, 253–54.

Am I coming back to France? Only when the site of the Bastille has become an open square . . . Let your parliaments work for this happy revolution. Then will reign over you a prince who will seek his glory in abolishing the royal warrants, and in convening your States-General. Realizing that abuse of power destroys, in the end, power itself, he will be the first among Frenchmen.[163]

Probably because of his association with Gordon, Cagliostro had a hard time finding a printer in London bold enough to publish it. Though he did not directly attack Louis XVI, allowing that the King had been misinformed, most of his readers knew that the reformist Prince of his utopian vision was the Duke of Orleans.

Cagliostro's letter so incensed the French government that his friends feared he would be kidnapped and returned to the Bastille. Thus, Gordon insisted on accompanying him when Cagliostro was summoned to the French embassy. Cagliostro peremptorily refused the ambassador's "invitation" to return to France, and Gordon subsequently published passionate defenses of his friend in the *Public Advertiser* (22 and 24 August 1736). He was fully aware of the risk he ran in attacking Marie-Antoinette and the French government, and he promised H.S Woodfall, the editor, that he would pay for any prosecution against him. Interestingly, Woodfall had earlier been prosecuted for publishing a radical attack on the Glorious Revolution, which charged the Hanoverians with "bribery, corruption, dissipation, gambling," and the debauchment of the morals of the British people." According to Monod, the author was probably the antiquarian Joseph Ritson, a Jacobite who became a radical republican.[164]

With Woodfall's paper backing Cagliostro and Gordon, the French government pushed its resident spy, Theveneau de Morande, to attack the flamboyant duo in the *Courier de l'Europe*. As the newspaper war raged, the Prince of Wales began to get cold feet about his dabbling in the Egyptian Rite, and he backed off from his public support of Cagliostro. Morande cleverly attacked Cagliostro's partisans in London who, though they included many illustrious persons, were deceived by his Masonic tricks. In an anonymous pamphlet, Morande revealed Cagliostro's earlier Jacobite pretenses when he allegedly assumed the name of "Count Balthymore" and claimed a confidential

---

[163] Harry Schnur, *Mystic Rebels* (New York, 1949), 282.
[164] Monod, *Jacobitism*, 41–42.

relationship with Cardinal York (Henry Stuart, brother of the Young Pretender).[165] After attacking the "mad" George Gordon, Morande tried to intimidate his brother "le lord Wm G . . ." and other Scottish nobles into supporting the government's campaign against the radical Masons.

A visitor from Germany, the novelist Sophie von la Roche, left an interesting account of Cagliostro and Gordon in September 1786.[166] Friendly with many of Cagliostro's Masonic disciples in Europe, she elicited frank remarks from the two embattled radicals. She noted that the Prince of Wales certainly welcomed Cagliostro, but that now the "Cophta" spends nearly all his time with Gordon. Cagliostro looks upon different religions as so many different systems of education, but he likes the Catholics least, because their clergy are too powerful and mistreat humanity and nature. Especially by maintaining monasteries and advocating celibacy, the Catholics act against nature's law. Gordon spoke highly of the principles of the Jewish religion and quizzed her about Moses Mendelssohn. He promised that he would never encourage violence, for the earlier riots still grieved him deeply.

That same month, Gordon caused a sensation when he led a huge crowd to the French Embassy and publicly burned a copy of the Treaty of Commerce signed between France and England. Watson charged that the treaty was an unholy alliance between two autocratic courts which aimed to crush the growing democratic spirit.[167] But "Lord George and burning" were enough to set the government machinery of repression into serious action, and Cagliostro's recruitment to the Egyptian Rite fell off precipitously. Perhaps pushed by his artistic supporters—Richard Cosway, Phillipe de Loutherbourg, and Francesco Bartolozzi—Cagliostro decided to approach members of the "Ancient" lodges and the Swedenborgians, many of whom were Masons, to bolster his position.

On 1 November Cagliostro, a party of French disciples, and presumably Gordon visited the Lodge of Antiquity, #2, which was meeting at Freemasons Tavern. Cagliostro was introduced to the lodge

---

[165] [Theveneau de Morande], *Ma Correspondance avec M. le Comte de Cagliostro* (à Hamburg [London], aux dépens de la société des Cagliostriens, 1786), 12–15, 21, 25, 62.

[166] La Roche, *Sophie*, 138–39, 148–49, 160.

[167] Watson, *Gordon*, 75.

by the Chevalier Bartholomew Ruspini, dental surgeon and Masonic mentor to the Prince of Wales.[168] Ruspini was a founding member of the "Nine Muses" lodge, which was a branch of the radical "Neuf Soeurs" in Paris. He had long laboured to link the "Ancient" lodges with sympathetic lodges on the Continent. He evidently hoped that Cagliostro would help heal the breach within the Antiquity Lodge, which had split the ranks of liberal and theosophical Masons. Among the French visitors to Antiquity #2 was the Marquis de Vichy, who reported to the Masonic convention of *Philaléthes* that he was very satisfied with the workings of the Egyptian Rite, as he observed them in London.[169] According to a later account by a lodge member, so were most of the attendees at the Antiquity lodge.[170]

On the next day, Caglistro placed an ad in the *Morning Herald* (2 November 1786), which appealed to "all true Masons" to join with the Swedenborgians in a common effort at "regeneration." Announcing that "the time is at hand when the building of the new Temple or New Jerusalem 3, 8, 20, 17, 8 [church] must begin," he told them to meet the next day at O'Reily's tavern on Great Queen Street. There they would "plan for laying the first stone of the foundation of the True 3, 8, 20, 17, 8 [church]." Though most British historians have assumed that Cagliostro got no response to this ad, Nicholas de Bonneville (who was attending meetings of the "Modern" Grand Lodge in London) testified that the ad "fit beaucoup de bruit."[171] Cagliostro's former disciple in Courland, Charlotte von der Recke, an initiate of his female rite, and his fascinated critic Johann Wolfgang Goethe, a *Rose-Croix* Mason, both heard that Cagliostro was welcomed by the Swedenborgians and Masons in London.[172]

Despite the improving fortunes of Gordon and Cagliostro in the first three weeks of November, Morande soon located new allies

---

[168] Rylands, *Records*, II, 29; J.P. Dawson, "The Chevalier Bartholomew Ruspini, 1728–1813," *Ars Quatuor Coronatorum*, 86 (1973), 87–99.

[169] Charles Porset, *Les Philaléthes et les Convents de Paris: Une politique de la folie* (Paris, 1996), 213, 488.

[170] Rylands, *Record*, II, 31–32; *General Advertiser* (2 December 1786).

[171] [Nicholas de Bonneville], *La Maçonnerie Ecossoise comparée avec les Trois Professions et le Secret des Templiers du 14ᵉ siècle* (Orient de Londres [Berlin], 1788), I, 28–29; II, 84–86.

[172] Charlotta von der Recke, *Nachricht von des Beruchtigten Cagliostro in Mitau* (Berlin and Stettin, 1787), 6; Johann Wolfgang Goethe, *Italian Journey (1786–1788)*, trans. W.H. Auden and E. Mayer (London, 1962), 245.

among the Freemasons, who added their satire to his vendetta. On 21 November the engraver James Gillray published a satiric print, entitled "A Masonic Anecdote, designed by a Brother Mason, a Witness of the Scene."[173] As Cagliostro stands before the lodge, he asks, "Are you shot through the heart? take a drop of my Balsamo." The English members, deep in their cups, drunkenly shout "Huzzas!" and insult the visiting French brothers, who mutter "Quelle insolence." Beneath the print, a doggerel "Abstract of the Arabian Count's memoirs" appears:

> Born God knows where, supported, God knows how. From whom descended ... difficult to know. LORD CROP [Gordon] adopts him as a bosom friend, And madly dares his character defend ... This self-dubb'd Count, some few years since became A Brother Mason in a borrowed name ...

Spurred on by the wide circulation of Gillray's print, Morande may have pressured another Mason, this time a Frenchman, to publish a critical article in the *General Advertiser* (29 November 1786). Breaking all Masonic rules of secresy, the Frenchman described the meeting at Antiquity and claimed that Cagliostro was insulted and exposed by "Brother Mash," a British member. On 2 December, Brother Cooper sent a rejoinder to the paper, claiming the previous article was a misrepresentation. On 6 December Brother Black showed Gillray's print to the lodge and dismissed it as a falsehood. Curiously, Bonneville saw in the increasing popularity of Cagliostro's Egyptian Rite a challenge to the secular, deistic aims of the Berlin Freemasons. Influenced by Morande's charges, he would soon publish a wild *exposé* that claimed that the Jesuits had infiltrated the *Écossais* lodges and were still hoping for a Stuart restoration![174]

In late November, Cagliostro and Gordon fought back by publishing the *Lettre du Comte de Cagliostro au peuple anglois* (1786). He revealed that a gang of criminals had long sought his precious Cabalistic manuscripts that enabled him to predict lottery winners. He also appealed to the sympathy and protection of British citizens who had long stood for freedom. Though the French court pressed the British government to get rid of Cagliostro, George III and Pitt were more concerned about Gordon. As he built popular support,

[173] James Gillray, *The Works of James Gillray* (London, 1968), plate 37.
[174] Bonneville, *Maçonnerie Ecossoise*, passim.

he became more reckless and defiant. When Gordon visited the prisoners at Newgate and then published a protest against the legal penalties imposed on them, the government decided to move. In a curious mélange of Biblical exhortation and political ranting, Gordon condemned the severity of the British legal system, especially in its transportation of minor offenders to isolated penal colonies. The prisoners cry aloud from their dungeons and prisons that "the true record of the Almighty is falsified and erased by the Lawyers and Judges (who sit with their backs to the words of the living God and the fear of men before their faces) till the streets of our city have run down with a stream of blood."[175]

George III and Pitt decided that Gordon had finally gone too far, and on 23 January 1787 he was summoned to court. Unable to obtain the services of his brilliant cousin Thomas Erskine, Gordon attempted to defend himself with a series of clever ploys and legal games that held the prosecution at bay. The opposition newspapers rallied to his case, which soon became a *cause célèbre*. The court proceedings dragged on from February to June, as the government mounted intense surveillance on Gordon's associates and "irregular" Freemasons in an effort to build a stronger case. In the meantime, Cagliostro's friends feared that he too would be arrested. Thus, in January he and his wife secretly moved to Hammersmith Terrace, where they hid in the home of the artist Phillipe de Loutherbourg, a member of the Egyptian Rite. While the Cagliostros quietly practiced alchemy and Cabalistic séances with their Swedenborgian and Masonic supporters, Gordon continued to defy the government.

Having received his university degree, Watson returned to London, where he evidently helped to build Masonic support for Gordon. On 23 April, a petition to Gordon was published in the *Morning Post*. Signed by Sir Watkins Lewes, a Welsh Freemason and former Jacobite Mayor of London, it identified Gordon as President of the "Society of Friends of Freedom," and begged him to name the day on which he would meet the Stewards of the Society to fix the day for their anniversary festival.[176] Gordon later wrote the Abbé Henri Gregoire,

---

[175] [Lord George Gordon], *The Prisoners' Petition to the right Honourable Lord George Gordon, to Preserve the Lives and Liberties and Prevent their Banishment to Botany Bay* (London, 1786); Hibbert, *King Mob*, 161.

[176] Levander, "Jerusalem Sols," 47.

a radical Mason and advocate of Jewish emancipation, about the "dinner meetings" of these "Friends of Freedom":

> You ask me, is true liberty near to begin her realm in the three realms? We have eating and drinking clubs, as Lord Fitzgibbon denominates them. A certain restless faction . . . are suspected to be the contrivers, promoters, and leaders of these eating and drinking societies, who are themselves ignorant of their master's design . . . A toast from the Chair to the immortal and glorious memory of King William . . . and the nine huzzas that accompany it, promote such a charge of glasses, that *all regeneration operations and reformation work* is soon after drowned and overwhelmed in bawdy songs, or evaporated in smoke and dullness . . .[177]

The bawdy cheers and heavy drinking of English lodge meetings were portrayed in Gillray's satire on Cagliostro and "Lord Crop." Though Gordon was writing cautiously from his prison cell (his letters were regularly inspected), Gregoire would certainly have interpreted the "master" as a lodge master and the "regeneration operations" as high-degree rituals. Moreover, Gordon's name—along with Robert Watson, Watkins Lewes, Thomas Erskine, Chevalier Ruspini, and many Jews—appears in records of the Grand Master's Lodge in 1787–1788.[178] The name of William Sharp, radical Swedenborgian and artistic colleague of William Blake, is a provocative addition.

As Gordon's trial approached, Cagliostro secretly left London and sought refuge with the Sarasins, his wealthy banking friends, in Switzerland. After Gordon's conviction on a series of trumped up charges—libel upon the administrators of British law and upon the characters of Marie-Antoinette and Catherine the Great (whose sexual mores he had lampooned), he managed to avoid arrest and slipped out of the country to Holland. There he took refuge with his Jewish friends (including, perhaps, the Boas brothers who were then involved in political intrigue).[179] According to Archenholz, who reported on Masonic and political developments in the Hamburg-based *British Mercury*, Gordon planned to join Cagliostro in Switzerland, where the Egyptian Rite was flourishing.[180] But the Dutch magistrates succumbed to pressure from the French court, and they shipped

---

[177] Watson, *Gordon*, 119. My italics.
[178] Grand Lodge Library, London: Grand Master's Lodge Record, 13, 17, 23–24, 83.
[179] Alfred Cobban, *Ambassadors and Secret Agents* (London: Jonathon Cape, 1954), 107.
[180] [Archenholz, ed.], *British Mercury*, II (July 1787), 37, 41.

Gordon—under full military guard—back to England on 22 July. Archenholz announced: "Poor Lord George!—cannot find a resting place for the soles of his feet—even his good friends the Dutch have behaved uncivily to him—the Jews have refused him circumcision."[181] Though reports appeared that Gordon had gone to Scotland to seek refuge at Gordon Castle, he disappeared for six months. When police agents located him in the Birmingham ghetto in December 1787, he appeared in the full beard and long robes of a Polish Jew. He would spend the rest of his life in prison, while the government tried to exterminate "the Gordoniad" from its Jacobite-Jacobin nightmare.

In the annual mock election for a comical M.P. for Garrett, a candidate declared himself for the cause of his "friend Gordon"; he would "discover the longitude among the Jews of Dukes Place and the secret of masonry."[182] The candidate also threatened to expose the "informing busy bookseller of Spitalfields," who was thrown out of the synagogue as a Christian spy, and who evidently supplied the government with information on Gordon's hiding place. Probably in reaction to the charges about Cagliostro, Gordon and revolutionary Freemasonry, as well as Gordon's reckless indiscretion about Mrs. Fitzherbert, the Prince of Wales opened his private, namesake lodge in August 1787, which consisted of members strictly loyal to his political agenda.[183] The Prince's brothers, all Freemasons, and apparently the Prince himself (incognito) visited Gordon in his Newgate cell and enjoyed his Biblical jeremiads against the policies of their despised father.[184] Their uncle, William Duke of Gloucester, corresponded with Masons in Lyons about Cagliostro, and he hoped to introduce certain Cabalistic rituals into his English lodge. Their younger brother, Edward Duke of Kent, would later meet Cagliostro in Switzerland, and though the meeting did not go well, Kent was initiated into the Swiss version of the Egyptian Rite.

---

[181] *British Mercury*, II (13 August 1787), 206.

[182] "Sir Jeffry Dunstan's Address to His Constituents," *Wonderful Magazine* (1793), I, 334.

[183] Thomas Fenn, *Prince of Wales's Lodge, #259: List of Members from the Time of Its Constitution* (London: private printing, 1890), 5.

[184] For the radical Masonic associations of the Prince of Wales, his uncles and brothers, see my article, "Blake's *Tiriel* and the Regency Crisis: Lifting the Veil on a Royal Masonic Scandal," in *Blake, Politics, and History*, eds. Anthony Rosso and Jackie Di Salvo (New York, 1998), 115–35.

For a halcyon period, Gordon may have believed that his imprisonment was no obstacle to his political and financial schemes. During
the Regency Crisis, provoked by George III's mental illness, the
Prince of Wales accepted a secret loan arranged by Abraham Goldsmid
through the Boas brothers in Holland.[185] The loan was a replacement for a previous one from the Duke of Orleans, which Pitt
scotched in December 1786, and an even more imprudent post-obit
bond that would be paid on the death of George III, which the
lenders backed away from in December 1788 when they realized its
"treasonous" implications. As cooler heads warned the Heir Apparent,
"the death of the King is anticipated, and therefore subjects the parties to all the penalties of petty treason." Did Gordon and Orleans
then advise the Prince to work through the Goldsmids and Boases,
who were Masons and former patrons of Dr. Falk? Orleans was in
London at the time, and the royal brothers frequently visited Gordon
in Newgate. Huish, an early nineteenth-century contemporary of the
Prince of Wales, is the only biographer to even mention the top
secret transactions.

Interestingly, Huish also pointed to the troubling role of Freemasonry
in the radical politics of the time: "There was scarcely a throne in
Europe, that was not shaken by the secret operations of that tremendous society [the Masonic *Illuminati*], which held its meetings *everywhere* and *nowhere*."[186] In France, rumors circulated that Orleans had
participated in a Masonic ritual in which he acted out the symbolic
murder of the French King.[187] La Marle suggests that Orleans transformed the old Jacobite-Templar degree of vengeance into a new
Jacobin-Templar allusion to revolutionary politics. As the Whig leader
Fox campaigned for the Prince of Wales during the Regency Crisis,
he resorted to the Jacobite language of the hereditary right of kings.
Like Orleans, Fox would soon be accused of complicity in an international conspiracy of the Masonic Knights Templar.[188] In the increasing transvaluation of political terms, the Prince of Wales and his

---

[185] On these secret Jewish loans, see Robert Huish, *Memoirs of George IV* (London,
1831), II, 136–42, 168.
[186] Robert Huish, *The History of the Life and Reign of William IV* (London, 1837),
IV, 221.
[187] La Marle, *Phillipe Égalité*, 97–98.
[188] Monod, *Jacobitism*, 305; see René Le Forestier, *La Franc-Maçonnerie Templière et
Occultiste au XVIII⁰ et XIX⁰ Siècles*, ed. Antoine Faivre (Paris, 1970), 853.

brothers were branded as rank Jacobites for their "Jacobin" role in
the Regency Crisis.

Though Gordon may have initially believed that his scheme of
utilizing Jewish Freemasons for "financial pacifism" and "regeneration operations" would liberate England from its autocratic Hanoverian
King, the recovery of George III and the Prince's steady loss of prestige subverted the dream. Moreover, the Boases went bankrupt as
the Prince avoided repayment on their loan, and the Goldsmid brothers eventually became the main financial lenders for the Government's
anti-Napoleonic military campaign.[189] Ironically, only Napoleon, who
still hoped to play a Jacobite card in the early 1800's, and Dr.
Watson, who brought the Stuart Papers from Rome to London, continued to link *Écossais* Freemasonry to revolutionary designs.[190]

Though Gordon was visited by streams of radicals from Britain
and France, and though his supporters played significant roles in the
London Coresponding Society and other reform organizations in the
1790's, his devotion to Judaism split his followers. Watson, who
claimed never to understand why Gordon converted, noted that the
rich Jews eventually abandoned Gordon while the poorer Jews looked
upon him as a mystical Messiah.[191] After Gordon's death from jail
fever in November 1793, Watson became increasingly militant and
rejected his mentor's aversion to violence. As a free-thinker, he
encouraged the deistic wings of the London Corresponding Society
to join with the anti-clerical Masonic societies on the Continent. He
would eventually be imprisoned on treason charges, escape to France,
and help Napoleon plan an invasion of Britain.

Watson's break from the religious apocalyptics that fueled Gordon
and his admirers in the early 1790's—such as the pious shoemaker
Thomas Hardy and the visionary artist William Blake—portended a
divisive crisis in the British radical movement. Gordon, with all his
eccentricity and recklessness, represented an authentic tradition of
Scottish philo-Semitism and British millenarianism that had deep religious roots. He was admired by artists and artisans with similar
beliefs, who found their world of millenarial reform taken over by

---

[189] Huish, *George IV*, II, 136–42; Paul Emden, "The Brothers Goldsmid and the
Financing of the Napoleonic Wars," *Transactions of the Jewish Historical Society of England*,
14 (1935–39), 225–46.
[190] Lang, "Wild Career," 331; Bain, *Thunderbolt*, 29–37.
[191] Watson, *Gordon*, 90.

the new radicals—skeptical "modern men" who no longer feared the God of Israel. But, when Blake—in his revolutionary prophecy *Jerusalem*—placed a figure who strikingly resembled Gordon on the frontispiece and issued a call to Cabalistic Jews to join illuminated Christians in the rebuilding of Jerusalem, one suspects that the Masonic dreams of Falk, Cagliostro, and Gordon were not completely forgotten.[192]

---

[192] William Blake, *Jerusalem: The Emanation of the Giant Albion*, ed. Morton Paley (Princeton, 1991), plates I and 27.

INDEX OF NAMES

BRILL'S STUDIES
IN
INTELLECTUAL HISTORY

82. McCALLA, A. *A Romantic Historiosophy.* The Philosophy of History of Pierre-Simon Ballanche. 1998. ISBN 90 04 10967 6

83. VEENSTRA, J.R. *Magic and Divination at the Courts of Burgundy and France.* Text and Context of Laurens Pignon's *Contre les devineurs* (1411). 1998. ISBN 90 04 10925 0

84. WESTERMAN, P.C. *The Disintegration of Natural Law Theory.* Aquinas to Finnis. 1998. ISBN 90 04 10999 4

85. GOUWENS, K. *Remembering the Renaissance.* Humanist Narratives of the Sack of Rome. 1998. ISBN 90 04 10969 2

86. SCHOTT, H. & J. ZINGUER (Hrsg.). *Paracelsus und seine internationale Rezeption in der frühen Neuzeit.* Beiträge zur Geschichte des Paracelsismus. 1998. ISBN 90 04 10974 9

87. ÅKERMAN, S. *Rose Cross over the Baltic.* The Spread of Rosicrucianism in Northern Europe. 1998. ISBN 90 04 11030 5

88. DICKSON, D.R. *The Tessera of Antilia.* Utopian Brotherhoods & Secret Societies in the Early Seventeenth Century. 1998. ISBN 90 04 11032 1

89. NOUHUYS, T. VAN. *The Two-Faced Janus.* The Comets of 1577 and 1618 and the Decline of the Aristotelian World View in the Netherlands. 1998. ISBN 90 04 11204 9

90. MUESSIG, C. (ed.). *Medieval Monastic Preaching.* 1998. ISBN 90 04 10883 1

91. FORCE, J.E. & D.S. KATZ (eds.). *"Everything Connects": In Conference with Richard H. Popkin.* Essays in His Honor. 1999. ISBN 90 04 110984

92. DEKKER, K. *The Origins of Old Germanic Studies in the Low Countries.* 1999. ISBN 90 04 11031 3

93. ROUHI, L. *Mediation and Love.* A Study of the Medieval Go-Between in Key Romance and Near-Eastern Texts. 1999. ISBN 90 04 11268 5

94. AKKERMAN, F., A. VANDERJAGT & A. VAN DER LAAN (eds.). *Northern Humanism between 1469 and 1625.* 1999. ISBN 90 04 11314 2

95. TRUMAN, R.W. *Spanish Treatises on Government, Society and Religion in the Time of Philip II.* The 'de regimine principum' and Associated Traditions. 1999. ISBN 90 04 11379 7

96. NAUTA, L. & A. VANDERJAGT (eds.) *Demonstration and Imagination.* Essays in the History of Science and Philosophy Presented to John D. North. 1999. ISBN 90 04 11468 8

97. BRYSON, D. *Queen Jeanne and the Promised Land.* Dynasty, Homeland, Religion and Violence in Sixteenth-Century France. 1999. ISBN 90 04 11378 9

98. GOUDRIAAN, A. *Philosophische Gotteserkenntnis bei Suárez und Descartes im Zusammenhang mit der niederländischen reformierten Theologie und Philosophie des 17. Jahrhunderts.* 1999. ISBN 90 04 11627 3

99. HEITSCH, D.B. *Practising Reform in Montaigne's Essais.* 2000. ISBN 90 04 11630 3

100. KARDAUN, M. & J. SPRUYT (eds.). *The Winged Chariot.* Collected Essays on Plato and Platonism in Honour of L.M. de Rijk. 2000. ISBN 90 04 11480 7

101. WHITMAN, J. (ed.), *Interpretation and Allegory:* Antiquity to the Modern Period. 2000. ISBN 90 04 11039 9

102. JACQUETTE, D., *David Hume's Critique of Infinity.* 2000. ISBN 90 04 11649 4

103. BUNGE, W. VAN. *From Stevin to Spinoza.* An Essay on Philosophy in the Seventeenth-Century Dutch Republic. 2001. ISBN 90 04 12217 6

104. GIANOTTI, T., *Al-Ghazālī's Unspeakable Doctrine of the Soul.* Unveiling the Esoteric Psychology and Eschatology of the Iḥyā. 2001. ISBN 90 04 12083 1

105. SAYGIN, S., *Humphrey, Duke of Gloucester (1390-1447) and the Italian Humanists.* 2002. ISBN 90 04 12015 7

106. BEJCZY, I., *Erasmus and the Middle Ages.* The Historical Consciousness of a Christian Humanist. 2001. ISBN 90 04 12218 4

107. BRANN, N.L. *The Debate over the Origin of Genius during the Italian Renaissance.* The Theories of Supernatural Frenzy and Natural Melancholy in Accord and in Conflict on the Threshold of the Scientific Revolution. 2002. ISBN 90 04 12362 8

108. ALLEN, M.J.B. & V. REES with M. DAVIES.(eds.), *Marsilio Ficino: His Theology, His Philosophy, His Legacy.* 2002. ISBN 90 04 11855 1

109. SANDY, G., *The Classical Heritage in France.* 2002. ISBN 90 04 11916 7

110. SCHUCHARD, M.K., *Restoring the Temple of Vision.* Cabalistic Freemasonry and Stuart Culture. 2002. ISBN 90 04 12489 6

111. EIJNATTEN, J. VAN. *Liberty and Concord in the United Provinces*. Religious Toleration and the Public in the Eighteenth-Century Netherlands. 2003. ISBN 90 04 12843 3

112. BOS, A.P. *The Soul and Its Instrumental Body*. A Reinterpretation of Aristotle's Philosophy of Living Nature. 2003. ISBN 90 04 13016 0

113. LAURSEN, J.C. & J. VAN DER ZANDE (eds.). *Early French and German Defenses of Liberty of the Press*. Elie Luzac's *Essay on Freedom of Expression* (1749) and Carl Friedrich Bahrdt's *On Liberty of the Press and its Limits* (1787) *in English Translation*. 2003. ISBN 90 04 13017 9

114. POTT, S., MULSOW, M. & DANNEBERG, L. (eds.). *The Berlin Refuge 1680-1780*. Learning and Science in European Context. 2003. ISBN 90 04 12561 2

115. GERSH, S. & ROEST, B. (eds.). *Medieval and Renaissance Humanism*. Rhetoric, Representation and Reform. 2003. ISBN 90 04 13274 0

116. LENNON, T.M. (ed.). *Cartesian Views*. Papers presented to Richard A. Watson. 2003. ISBN 90 04 13299 6

117. VON MARTELS, Z. & VANDERJAGT, A. (eds.). *Pius II – 'El Più Expeditivo Pontefice'*. Selected Studies on Aeneas Silvius Piccolomini (1405-1464). 2003. ISBN 90 04 13190 6

118. GOSMAN, M., MACDONALD, A. & VANDERJAGT, A. (eds.). *Princes and Princely Culture 1450–1650*. Volume One. 2003. ISBN 90 04 13572 3

119. LEHRICH, C.I. *The Language of Demons and Angels*. Cornelius Agrippa's Occult Philosophy. 2003. ISBN 90 04 13574 X

120. BUNGE, W. VAN (ed.). *The Early Enlightenment in the Dutch Republic, 1650–1750*. Selected Papers of a Conference held at the Herzog August Bibliothek, Wolfenbüttel 22–23 March 2001. 2003. ISBN 90 04 13587 1

121. ROMBURGH, S. VAN, *For My Worthy Freind Mr Franciscus Junius*. An Edition of the Correspondence of Francis Junius F.F. (1591-1677). 2004. ISBN 90 04 12880 8

122. MULSOW, M. & POPKIN, R.H. (eds.). *Secret Conversions to Judaism in Early Modern Europe*. 2004. ISBN 90 04 12883 2

123. GOUDRIAAN, K., J. VAN MOOLENBROEK & A. TERVOORT (eds.). *Education and Learning in the Netherlands, 1400-1600*. 2004. ISBN 90 04 13644 4

124. PETRINA, A. *Cultural Politics in Fifteenth-Century England: The Case of Humphrey, Duke of Gloucester*. 2004. ISBN 90 04 13713 0

125. SCHUURMAN, P. (ed.). *Ideas, Mental Faculties and Method*. The New Logic of Descartes and Locke and Its Reception in the Dutch Republic. 2004. ISBN 90 04 13716 5